SO-BZC-126

ACCLAIM FOR GREEN KINGDOM COME!

Stunning! I thought I knew the Jesus story. Here's a take that's fresh and thought provoking. It's a rollicking page turner.

Wayne Benenson, PhD
Argosy University, Seattle, WA

This book is a powerful resource to parents and grandparents who want to teach peacemaking and sustainable principles and practices to their children and grandchildren.

Deborah Gentry, EdD
Certified Family Life Educator

Great fun! Has light, humorous touch with serious intent. I enjoyed looking at the Aramaic meaning of the words of Jesus. Good job of linking biblical tradition with imaginative reconstruction for our day.

Vaughn Hoffmann
Senior Pastor of Wesley United Methodist Church

Professor Grabill's book is provocative and definitely worth reading. It challenges you to see Jesus and Mother Earth in completely new ways.

Ed Dodge, MD
Author of *Dan's Story: One Man's Discovery of His Inner Health Power*
and of *Tim's Story: A Spiritual Perspective of Health*

A refreshing look at Jesus! And, a compelling call to action to support the sustainability of our planet!

Rev. Alice Anderson
Senior Minister, Christ Church Unity,
Orlando, FL

This book is a wise, seasoned presentation on the meaning of Jesus for the coming ecological age. Joe Grabill's Jesus signals a sea-change — from theology to eco-theology. It leads us beyond "what would Jesus drive?" to ponder how Jesus would confront climate change.

Neil Douglas-Klotz, PhD
Author of *Blessings of the Cosmos: Wisdom from the Heart of the Aramaic Words of Jesus*, and co-author of *The Tent of Abraham*

This trend-setting book will hopefully provoke extensive discussion about the pressing need to partner with the living earth community once walked within by Jesus himself.

Mercy Davison
Organic farmer, Urban Planner, and former Chair of the Green Team, Town of Normal, IL

Dr. Grabill offers us a unique and inspirational "green" Jesus who cared deeply for all of creation. His partnership with Mary Magdalene and other women showed he was a "feminist."

Rev. Susan M. Ryder
Co-pastor, New Covenant Community

Fascinating! The author's treks through the native landscape of Jesus produce vivid insights. Shows wide reading and features stimulating ideas.

William Luther White, PhD
Former Chaplain at Illinois Wesleyan University and author of *The Image of Man in C. S. Lewis*

Dr. Grabill takes the reader on a fabulous journey — one that weaves his evangelical background with his teaching world religions. He constructs creative conversations with Jesus and with characters in biblical stories!

David Eaton, PhD
Founder of a retreat center, Agape Dome, for church communities in Texas

GREEN KINGDOM COME!

JESUS AND A SUSTAINABLE EARTH COMMUNITY

GREEN KINGDOM COME!

JESUS AND A SUSTAINABLE EARTH COMMUNITY

Joe Grabill, PhD

Kathy —
I value our
friendship. Blessings!

Joe

5/13/09

Green Kingdom Come!
Jesus and a Sustainable Earth Community

Copyright © 2009 Joe Grabill. All rights reserved. No part of this book may be reproduced or retransmitted in any form or by any means without the written permission of the publisher.

Published by Wheatmark®
610 East Delano Street, Suite 104, Tucson, Arizona 85705 U.S.A.
www.wheatmark.com

ISBN: 978-1-58736-090-9
LCCN: 2008938236

I dedicate this book to my grandchildren—
each one my favorite. Here are lyrics that I sing to them,
arranged in a form like the Tree of Life rooted in Earth.
Erik
Fireball hears
Earth's call;
Brianna Cocobana,
bright sunlight;
Calvin James plays sage games;
Chesran swirls and twirls live music;
Alexander, wise commander;
Nathaniel gallant, unique talent;
Lindsey Lee laughs
joyfully;
Celia bold
glows
heart
of gold;
Karl creates and integrates;
Andrew
lives
love..........true
!

This book is also dedicated to
those of us who value diversity and civil discourse
within our emerging, global public square.
We treasure the free exercise of conscience and
resist officially enforced ideologies from left to right.
Within our real differences,
we watch for steps, leverage points, and
hidden possibilities that can tip

little alliances
into an epidemic of commitment to
the common good.
The bonds of a unified Earth Community strengthen
as we stretch dialogues about diversity to include
all the peoples, species, and habitats
of our planetary
home.

Most of all,
I dedicate this book to green kingdom come.

Acknowledgments

Always and for everything giving thanks.
— *Ephesians 5:20*

Always and for everyone unnamed — mentors,
writers, students, friends, and relatives —
who contributed in ways deeper than words to this book,
I give bottomless thanks.

I particularly acknowledge my parents,
Clifford and Arveda Wulliman Grabill,
who initiated me into an unending
friendship and fascination with the Bible.
Brothers from different mothers
have boosted me incredibly.
Dave and Wib
have given unconditional cheerleading and insight.
Ron
has never tired in removing my blinders
and in improving clarity.
Fellow tree whisperer Jack and I
have shared zesty forest
meditations in all seasons.
He is my co-wanderer within the wonder
and surprise
of astounding Earth Community companions.

My courageous and creative wife,
Donella Hess-Grabill,
has flavored and spiced my journey
and the nuances of *Green Kingdom Come!*
Wife everlasting.
Our German Schnauzers, Lavani and Sassafras,
have bathed us with unreserved
dog (god spelled backwards) love.
Lord, help us to be the persons our dogs
think we are.
Deborah and Saadi
have meandered with me on foot throughout Galilee
and meandered within subtle meanings
throughout the Aramaic language.
Tamyala
has edited with the precision of a laser beam.
The team at Wheatmark
has provided grace and competence.
President Barack Hussein Obama,
in his Inaugural Address, has highlighted that "the ways
we use energy threaten our planet.
We will harness the sun and the winds," he stated,
"and roll back the specter of a warming planet.
We pledge to let clean waters flow" in
"a new era of responsibility."

Contents

PART THREE: Kind Community

Visuals

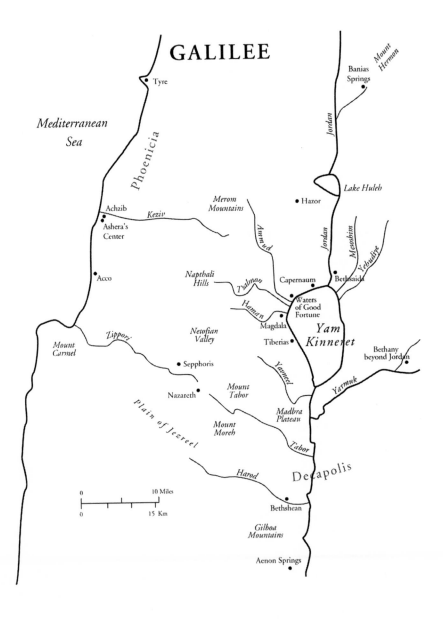

GALILEE IN THE TIME OF JESUS

J esus grew up and carried out most of his ministry in eco-diverse Galilee. This map shows the streams of Galilee, most of which Jesus forded. Nearly all of the place names on the map occur in the text. Off the map is the Jericho oasis, on the west bank of the Jordan River about seventy miles south of the Sea of Galilee. The Sea is labeled on the map by its Aramaic name, *Yam Kinneret*. Jerusalem is high in the hills fifteen miles west of Jericho.

PREFACE

BEFORE THE BEGINNING

We wave our pom-pom.
Mother Earth is our mom,
from deep green forests,
to snow-white ice caps,
from black sea trenches,
to fat orange full moon rises.
We wave our pom-pom
for our mom.

— My words to the song by Woody Guthrie,
"This Land is Your Land"

Right now as I begin writing the basic draft of this book in mid-December 2007, two feet from where I sit snowflakes float, spiral, and alight on the other side of the glass. Each snowflake is a wondrous, six-pointed, never-before-birthed, masterpiece of art. Nature outside my window is home, in the same way that for Jesus the hills of Nazareth, *Yam Kinneret* (Aramaic for the Sea of Galilee), and wilderness were home. *Yam* is the name of the Canaanite water deity, and *Kinneret* refers to the harp-like sounds of the water. As I type on my computer, fifty yards away and presiding over me are two giant white pines, their bundles of five needles swaddled with snow. Each of these magnificent, towering giants reminds me of the symbolic Tree of Life that represents the whole Earth Community. I sit writing on

Spirit Island, so named by the Ojibway Native Americans until European-Americans renamed it Madeline Island. Spirit Island is two miles off-shore from Bayfield, Wisconsin, in Lake Superior. In the western sky, I see the sliver of a new moon, named "Long Nights Moon" by the Ojibway.

TYPING AMIDST THE wintry environment of Mother Earth, I reflect on the central question addressed within this book:

What would Jesus do to spur today's green revolution?

I also reflect on the stunning earthiness of Jesus. Do you know what Jesus did that was green in his day? What would Jesus do that is green in our time? In seeking to answer these questions, I have decided that there are at least three reasons for writing a book about this search.

First, there is a scientific consensus that inaction about unsustainable living by our species will cause an ecological holocaust. The death and dislocation of millions in lowlands and flooded watersheds. Drought and starvation. Wildfires. The extinction of half the species on Earth. Waves of refugees. Wars over resources.

Second, there is an emerging green revolution to reduce the odds of such a holocaust and to revive the ancient human tradition of sustainability.

Third, there is the opportunity, for the first time in the history of Christianity, to recognize that Jesus is a mentor for a green insurgency. To my knowledge, no one has written a book linking Jesus to sustainability. It is past time for us, with a green heart, to examine an overlooked dimension of the Christian tradition.

People in the village of Nazareth, and those who joined the itinerant group led by Jesus, lived in a green way. These folks made incredibly fewer artifacts and products than Americans do today. Nazareth practiced mostly a barter economy with little use of money. Living close to the Earth, the people of Nazareth built their houses of fieldstones or lived in caves. Energy came from the sun, from human and animal muscle, and from olives that provided oil for lamps. Prior to and during his ministry, Jesus spent considerable time meditating in the eco-diverse wilderness areas of Galilee. He encouraged sharing food, clothing, and money. Rabbi Jesus emphasized traits that we would say today have a low carbon footprint. I frequently identify Jesus as Rabbi, meaning teacher, the most frequent form of address for him in the gospels.

The teaching and lifestyle of Jesus are compatible with the following ideas that summarize sustainability. To act sustainably we meet the needs of the present without compromising the ability of future members of Earth Community to meet their needs. We slow down and stop using Earth's resources faster than Earth can replenish them. We are made for Earth Community. Earth Community is not made for us.

My earliest training about Jesus did not call attention to him as a model for sustainability. In the 1930s and 1940s, my father was pastor first of an evangelical Missionary Church Association congregation in northeast Ohio and then of another congregation in the upper San Joaquin Valley of California where our family moved in 1938. Our focus upon the Bible and personal salvation was serious and paramount, but it did not exclude an occasional attempt at biblical whimsy.

"When is the first mention of baseball in the Bible?"

"Uh. I give up. When?"

"In the 'big' inning. Gen. 1:1."

The dramatic story of beginnings in Genesis, featuring God and Earth, caught my farm boy imagination. Earth appears in the story, I now know, over twenty times, often as an actor. "Let the earth bring forth grass and the fruit tree. Let the earth bring forth cattle" (Gen. 1:11, 24, KJV).

In retrospect, my youth, marked by no child left inside, had a strong green character. Dirt on every surface of my body signified normality. I read books in a top crook of a walnut tree, immersed in highly flavored whiffs. I explored miles around our house. I swam in an irrigation canal, roller-skated, and biked. I built tree house castles, constructed underground shelters, forked alfalfa, and somersaulted in leaps from a homemade diving board at the top of the barn loft into the sweet hay. My brother, Noel, and I, with hands on two teats on each side of our cow Bossie, pointed milk sprays underneath at each other.

Kid paradise was shoeless and exuberantly physical. Both my male and female friends played tackle football without gear in an empty lot and didn't let a concussion stop us from playing. I wrestled with Noel in poison oak, and broke out with blotched, itchy skin from my scalp to my feet. Would I need a body amputation?

During the Great Depression our family did not throw things away. My mother's mantra was "Darn it," until nothing existed in a sock except darn. My clothes were hand-me-downs from church families and relatives. We raised our own food, including rabbits. Regular church potlucks allowed more oatmeal cookies and pieces of rhubarb pie than in typical rations at home. Mother set up a card table and a meal for the homeless in the back yard. We didn't eat out in a restaurant. Daddy, at a low point, made three dollars a week.

In those childhood days, I unknowingly lived more sustainably than I have at any time since.

The family culture, focused as it was on the primacy of Christianity, led me in the 1950s to prepare for the Christian ministry at Fort Wayne Bible College (later Taylor University Fort Wayne). I determined, zealously, to know Jesus as well as he could be known. I had a strong animus against "modernists" in the mainline churches who used the Revised Standard Version (RSV) of the Bible rather than the King James Version. There was an anti-RSV saying, "If King James English was good enough for Jesus, it is good enough for me." I didn't examine carefully the contradiction of a King James fixation and a passion to take courses in Greek to know what Jesus really said. Only later did I learn that Jesus didn't speak Greek, but Aramaic, the everyday language of Semitic people throughout the eastern Mediterranean.

In the summers of 1955, 1956, and 1957, I was part of a team of college-age evangelists that participated in summer mission trips to forty-two countries in Asia and Latin America. Partnering with local missionaries in an evangelism program called Sports Ambassadors, we played basketball with local teams, preached and sung at halftime, and offered Bible correspondence courses in local languages. Hundreds came forward to receive Christ, including soldiers in Generalissimo Chiang Kai-shek's Army in Taiwan.

Travel abroad helped me to see my religious training about Jesus in an intercultural context. For example, in Japan, I walked in an underground, dark passage beneath a Buddhist temple that purportedly had the key to life hidden in a cranny. I felt high and low in the pitch-black tunnel. No key. The passage walk was like a Zen koan. What is the sound of one hand clapping? No sound. I saw in Buddhist terms that formlessness, or in Christian terms, Spirit is the key to form.

Some environmental impressions in Asia and Latin America were striking. I noticed that Japan retained 80 percent of its California-sized territory as forest, even with a high population density. Shinto temples were wooden and small—utterly unlike Gothic cathedrals—and located in nature preserves. An airplane flight into the rainforest in the state of Paraná in Brazil tutored me in spectacular diversity.

Graduate study in history at Indiana University in the late 1950s occurred before the sub-discipline of environmental history developed. I had classes in ancient history, which enabled me to put Hebrews and Jesus within a cross-cultural context. Also, I learned that the Aramaic language was the *lingua franca* of the Middle East from the time of the Assyrian Empire through the first century.

In 1968 I began to teach diplomatic and religious history at Illinois State University, and in 1975 our family moved near a lake surrounded by woods close to the Mackinaw (Painted Turtle) River. Today I have a painted turtle as a pet, and call her *Mikinak*, the Algonquian word translated Mackinaw. One day a friend, Anna, and I were strolling. Anna said, "Joe, you think you are superior to that bur oak tree, don't you?"

We stopped walking. She was pointing to a tree older than the United States of America. I marveled at the large leaves with lobes that widened toward the end. But I, in contrast, professed to know thousands of years of history.

I said, "Yes, I guess I do."

Anna said kindly, "You're not."

Strangely moved, I didn't feel accused.

After my encounter with Anna and the bur oak, I increasingly taught my courses from environmental and intercultural perspectives. In my American religious history course, I observed the role of an unspoiled continent protected by oceans. America's temperate, well-watered zone, with a relatively small human population, provided abundance and freedom of expression and religion. I also noted the proportionate growth of Buddhists, Hindus, Muslims, and Nones—those with no religious affiliation—in American society. In my world religions course, I compared nature religions like Shintoism with no formal scriptures, religions with formal scriptures like Hinduism which mixed nature and such transcendent deities as Brahman, and religions like Judaism, Christianity, and Islam, which elevated scriptures and a single deity above nature.

These comparative approaches helped develop the view that God, by any name or lack of a name, is present in every religion and culture. Put another way, the essence of the universe is present in every species, historical period, and location. At the same time, I did not give up my birthright as a Christian and nourished progressive spirituality. Eventually I joined a church called New Covenant Community—jointly sponsored by Presbyterian, Disciples of Christ, and United Church of Christ denominations—to which I still belong.

In the mid 1990s, I had an "a-ha" moment. I read in John Dominic Crossan's *Jesus: A Revolutionary Biography* the statement of Jesus that the presence of God is like a mustard seed (Matt. 13:31). For the first time I learned that in the time of Jesus mustard grew wild—untamed, undomesticated—in the Mediterranean world. Thus, God is green like the mustard plant. His presence is in the soil within which mustard grows, the rain that waters it, and the sun that stimulates chlorophyll. What else did Jesus say and do that showed this ecological aspect of God? I had to find out.

Stimulated by the story of the mustard seed, I systemically studied sources on the ecology, anthropology, archeology, zoology, economy, politics, and religion of first-century Palestine. In 1997 I took the first of seven trips to Israel and Palestine to probe the environmental dimensions of the life of Jesus. I walked everywhere I thought Jesus might have walked and experienced the ecosystems of Galilee as much like Jesus as I could. Included within these visits to the Holy Land were three eco-pilgrimages I helped lead.

I linked my ecological awareness of Jesus with sustainability strongly in 2005. I attended a workshop where an expert from Sweden talked about the eco-municipality movement there and the sustainability principles in the book by Karl-Henrik Robert, *The Natural Step Story*. Nordic countries lead the world in green goals and action plans. I learned of rooftop gardens, recycled water at car washes, and streets that absorb water rather than add to storm water runoff and erosion costs.

By early 2007, I realized that many evangelical Christians had adopted environmentalism. Bill Moyers did a documentary for PBS called *Is God Green?* The documentary featured interviews with a number of evangelicals who had turned to creation care, including a vice-president of the National Association of Evangelicals, Richard Cizik, and televangelist Pat Robertson. Moyers interviewed members of the Vineyard Church in Boise, Idaho, who were pro-Bush and creationist. The pastor, Tri Robertson, had become green after meditating on Genesis 9 in which God establishes a covenant with every living creature. The country's largest Protestant denomination and one of its most conservative, the Southern Baptist Convention, recently has issued a call to curb environmental degradation and to encourage preaching on the subject.

A piece by *New York Times* columnist Thomas Friedman entitled "The Power of Green" was a catalyst that prompted me to begin sketching out *Green Kingdom Come!* Friedman wrote that what our country needs is not the first woman or black president, but the first green president. America needs a Green New Deal that seeds research and sets standards, taxes, and incentives to clean up and green up. Friedman stated that green has hit Main Street as a hobby, but not yet as a way of life. Our kids, he said, will call us the *Greatest Generation* only if we become the Greenest Generation.

IN DECEMBER 2007, as I now sit at my computer on Spirit Island in Lake Superior, it's ten degrees outside. I have just walked down to Many Cedars Beach under a star-splattered sky. I pulled a cedar branch, with evergreen needle-like leaves, to my nose, and inhaled. Spruce, ash, red pine, and other species of trees stood securely around me. I marveled while watching as the new moon sliver of Long Nights Moon rose to the west. Waves at the beach kept giving new textures to ice sculptures that gleamed in the moonlight. It seemed as if the stars were singing together. I looked straight up and said to myself, "I'm a relative of the meteorite that just flashed right over my head. I'm a member of the gauzy circle of the Milky Way in an arc above me. I stand on my home, Mother Earth."

ON EARTH: AN INTRODUCTION

My nominee for 2007 Person of the Year
is a woman—Mother Earth.
—Brian Williams, anchor of *NBC News*

While writing I listen to a CD titled *American Wilds* by Delta Music. I hear eagles, loons, ravens, ducks, and songbirds in this recording. Elks rut and wolves howl. Rain splashes and thunder rumbles. Frogs, cicadas, and crickets sing their language. These sounds of wild citizens of Earth Community sometimes have me feeling that I, with them, am composing what I call "New Earth Symphony," a literary relative of Anton Dvorak's "New World Symphony." This composition is helping to recall and to remember in a new way the cultural norms that existed as recently as ten thousand years ago in every region and society of the world.

We are now reviving human traditions that existed throughout the globe ten thousand years ago, as marked by the epigraph above which honors Mother Earth as Person of the Year. Another part of the revival is the new Ecological Calendar. Unlike conventional calendars which have numbers marching like machine parts, the Ecological Calendar shows that Earth's annual revolution is about the whole Community of Life. This Calendar has four panels in different colors for the four seasons, bounded by solstices and equinoxes. Each panel has six bands from top down: sky, sun, moon, Earth, tide, and calendar. Within the bands we observe wonderful graphics portraying visible planet, star, and constellation configurations, ratio of daylight to darkness, solar phases, moon phases, activities of weather, minerals, plants and animals, and high and low tides. At the bottom, each of the 365 dates has a unique name selected from the names within flora, fauna, astronomy, meteorology, and geology all over the Northern Hemisphere. To view this calendar is to feel enveloped by amazing daily events that the universe and Earth Community provide. (See www.ecologicalcalendar.info)

WHAT FOLLOWS IN this introduction is a reminder of our current unsustainable habits, an analysis of sustainable practices and attitudes, an overview of experiences and sayings of Jesus that relate to sustainability, and the methods in my writing style that accentuate greenness. I use the words green and sustainable as roughly synonymous.

Profound unsustainable indicators within Earth Community

Our human species has been taking Earth's resources, since the start of the Agricultural Revolution ten thousand years ago, faster than the Earth can replenish them. In the Industrial Revolution, we increasingly have withdrawn more from the ecological bank than we have deposited. An industrial assumption is that we can be takers of anything we want, without regard to the health of Earth Community.

There are two basic stories and cultures within the human tradition, according to popular writer Daniel Quinn, labeled Taker and Leaver. The Taker story assumes that Earth Community exists for herders and farmers to use as they please. The Leaver story, a pre-agricultural tale, assumes that humans, just like salmon, sparrows, and gorillas, exist for Earth Community.

Takers assume they have the right to decide which species will eat and live and which will not eat and die, according to the needs and wants of protecting herds, clearing land for farming, and mining. Leavers leave it to the networks of animals, plants, and humans within Earth Community to decide synergistically and sustainably who gets to eat and who gets to die, as was the case in the Garden of Eden.

Today we consume more goods, waste more energy, and destroy more wilderness than other species. There is an average of approximately four acres of food-producing land per person on the Earth. Americans take, on average, twenty-four acres per person, the highest average in the world. This American Taker behavior leaves a fraction of an acre or no acreage for some people and species, with starvation of humans and extinction of species as a result.

A chief ramification of our consumption, waste, and destruction is the extinction of species. The prophecy of world-renowned biologist Edward O. Wilson astounds me. He set forth in *The Creation: An Appeal to Save Life on Earth* that the extinction of one million species is possible by 2050. In the last fifty years, 300,000 species have passed away, an average of one every two weeks. During the time that I write the basic draft of this book in half of a moon cycle, another species becomes extinct. More bird species, like the passenger pigeon, have disappeared in America than in any other country. The extinction capital of the United States is Hawaii. Our own human species, Wilson writes—including my great-grandchildren and yours—could die out by the end of this century. Why do so many of us debate about the origin of species and so few about the extinction of species?

Another ramification is climate change, of which global warming is one aspect. The cofounder of the Rocky Mountain Institute, Hunter Lovins, does not use the phrase global warming. She calls it Global Weirding, as reported by Thomas Freidman in the *New York Times*. Increasing craziness includes unpredictable spots of hotter heat, drier droughts, colder colds, more violent storm violence, more torrential flooding, and more fiery fires.

Columnist Ellen Goodman in *The Boston* Globe reported that Al Gore, when receiving the Nobel Peace Prize, spoke of this global craziness as humans waging war against the Earth with a possible MAD outcome: mutually assured destruction. He said that we dump tons of pollution into the ecosphere as if it were a sewer.

I do not see climate change as the most important variable involved with an unsustainable Earth. Global warming may continue, or a new cooling period, because of less energy coming from the sun, may occur. Regardless of global warming or cooling, our species is grasping far more than our share of Earth's resources and is putting ourselves and all other species in jeopardy. Our species, hypnotized by the Taker story, does not respect environmental limits, does not work for the common good, and acts violently. It is this Taker addiction that is at the root of unsustainability.

An analysis of sustainability

The incentive to go green is literally to save ourselves, our children, and our ecological neighbors. Salvation involves moving from human imperialism to creating Earth Community, ending the massive ecological and economic debt saddling governments and individuals because of our Taker compulsions, and re-learning (it's in our DNA) the creative joys of a sensory, rich and life-enhancing Leaver culture.

How do we do sustainability? I have developed new three Rs to help us answer the question. The old environmental three Rs — reduce, reuse, and recycle — deserve continued use, but the new three Rs of reduce, renew, and redouble are more comprehensive.

The first R, reduce, is in the original formula. Let's reduce the number of extractions from the Earth and the number of commercial products and services that are not supportive of renewable energy and of redoubled eco-diversity.

The second R, renew, includes the reusing of such things as ceramic cups, metal silverware, and cloth shopping bags, but concentrates on sources of energy. We need renewable energy sources like solar, wind, geothermal, algae, and other such forms of sustainable power to produce recyclable, biodegradable, and eco-degradable goods.

Reduce and renew lead to the third R, redouble, which is about reversing the decline of species. Let's redouble and multiply the range and variety of bio-diverse and eco-diverse areas throughout the world.

An overview of experiences and sayings of Jesus related to greenness

In my trips to the Holy Land I discovered a stunning earthiness about Jesus that had been there all the time but had gone unnoticed, like glasses forgotten on my forehead.

I invite you to enter three doors which give vivid pictures of the earthy life of Jesus in first-century Galilee. The first door opens into the childhood of Jesus in his village of Nazareth. Listen to him speak in an imagery conversation, part of an extended interview with him in the next part of this book. "My home village," he says, "was a farm town of about three hundred Jewish people belonging to three clans. It measured ten acres, 2,000 feet by 650 feet. No synagogue building. No scrolls or schools. Little or no literacy. No fortification. No palace. No bathhouse. One well. No paved streets. Limited use of coins. We lived in a dirt floor house made from fieldstones plastered with straw and dung and a flat roof made with reeds, branches, mud, and dung. We slept with our animals. My father had his workshop in a cave." Jesus grew up in a lifestyle with a low carbon footprint.

A sketch in the book pictures a curly-headed image of Jesus as a child, based on a carving on a Roman sarcophagus.

Another door opens into the public ministry of Jesus. Here in Galilee was, and still is today, a uniquely green place at the juncture of Africa, Asia, and Europe where thousands of species mix in extraordinary diversity. There were no deserts in Galilee then nor are there now. Watch him at his headquarters at Capernaum on the Sea of Galilee within a sunken bowl of hills seven hundred feet below sea level. Hot springs, with their odorous vapors, hugged the shore. The Sea is within the Jordan River watershed, extending from snow-covered Mount Hermon, ten thousand feet above the Mediterranean Sea, to the Dead Sea, the lowest spot on Earth, thirteen hundred feet below the Mediterranean. Around the Sea of Galilee over five hundred bird species warbled and flew either in migration or permanent residence. This number of bird species is about the same as in the entire United States today, but in an area over three hundred times smaller. In migrating season Jesus saw 100,000 to 300,000 storks and eagles (Uzi Paz, *Birds in the Land of the Bible*). The waters of the volcanic Sea of Galilee teemed with sardine and tilapia, food for both birds and humans.

A third door leads into the plain near Bethsaida on the north shore of the Sea of Galilee, where aromatic camel, lemon, and ginger grasses were green even in the dry season. Here Jesus and his associates on different occasions gathered crowds numbering as many as 4,000 and 5,000 folk. The strongest leader among his associates was the widow Mary Magdalene (there is an interview in the book with her as well) who lived on the shore in Magdala and ran a sardine business inherited from her husband. Children, women, beggars, and lepers were present in these crowds, which violated purity laws and which turned out to be communitarian potlucks. Rabbi Jesus demonstrated that everyone would have more than enough to eat if there was a fair distribution of food. A free translation of one of his Beatitudes is, "The hungry will pig out." Today if we want sustainability, including a reduction in the extinction of species, we will need equalitarian opportunities cooking on Earth' stove for all the insects, plants, animals, and humans.

Amid this lushness, Jesus developed an incredible sense of humor and a hilarious wit. A sketch after this introduction shows him laughing. A leader at Dallas Theological Seminary, Charles Swindoll, in his article "The Winsome Witness," assumes that Jesus enjoyed long side-splitting laughs. Best-selling author Anne Lammott writes of this laughter as carbonated holiness.

Green Kingdom Come! emphasizes laughing as an abdominal, respiratory, facial, and lively workout greatly beneficial to healthy green endeavor. Twenty seconds of guffawing equals a minute or more of cardiovascular exercise. Laughing is upper-body jogging that releases endorphins that numb pain like a drug but cannot cause a toxic overdose. The one who laughs lasts!

Concurrently with my trips to the Holy Land, I focused on the Aramaic language of Jesus, tutored among others by my friend Neil (Saadi) Douglas-Klotz, author of *The Hidden Gospel: Decoding the Spiritual Message of the Aramaic Jesus.* I came to understand that the Aramaic language has environmental overtones through its system of words belonging to a family with a root. Indo-European languages, such as Greek and English, have autonomous words that stand alone and don't have families of words with a root. For example, the English words "sun, hear, and heaven" do not immediately suggest linguistic or green connections to each other. But in Aramaic, these words are *shemesh* (sun), *shema* (hear), and *shemaya* (heaven), and are all related to the root *shem* (vibration or energy). The linguistic connection is obvious, and the green connection is that they all evoke the interdependent web of light and sound energy. *Shemaya* [she-MY-yuh], then, is not autonomously heaven and is not the opposite of Earth. Jesus spoke frequently about *Malkuta Shemaya,* the Presence of the Web of Energy, traditionally translated "the Kingdom of Heaven." For more on Aramaic, see at the end the section on the Aramaic Jesus, a glossary of Aramaic words, and a list of Aramaic phrases.

Jesus used interchangeably the names *Malkuta* [MAL-ku-ta] *Shemaya* (the Presence of the Web of Energy) and *Malkuta Al-laha* (the Presence of The One). *Malkuta Allaha* is traditionally translated "the Kingdom of God." He mentioned these phrases as his overarching themes over 120 times, more than any other subjects. The word *Allaha* (al-LAH-ha) combines two words, *al*, meaning the, and *laha*, meaning one. Thus, I capitalize both The and One. The Presence for him included human and non-human members of Earth Community, an inclusion that helped me to see Jesus as green and as having many traits compatible with what Daniel Quinn calls Leaver culture.

I agree with the evangelical leader Brian McLaren that today we need to release Jesus "into the wild of his native habitat" in Galilee. We also need to free a domesticated Jesus from being an "ornament on the guzzling Hummer of Western civilization" into his radical revelation of The One's Community of Life. Jesus, a peacemaker who planted seeds that overthrew Caesar as an imperial god, today is nourishing green seeds that can help undermine Taker culture's imperial attack on our Living Earth.

In the first five chapters of this book, I examine, for example, how Jesus' emphasis upon The One compares to what today in physics we call the first law of thermodynamics. Energy *is* — it can't be added to or subtracted from. Energy is one. Within this oneness, forms change, die, and are reborn. Jesus urged people to die, like a grain of wheat, to their dysfunctional ways and to birth healthy ways within the security of this eternal Oneness.

Children, Jesus said, are greatest in the Presence of The One. Today adults need to learn from the vitality of children and create programs that put them in the forefront of the green social movement.

A satirical thing Jesus said was, "Love your enemies," which is oxymoronic. If you love like sun and rain, he said, that love will wipe out the whole concept of enemy. Who is the enemy of sun and rain? Within Earth Community today, we need to love and to show compassion for every ecological dimension, mineral, plant, animal, and human within our global village and to welcome them into a comprehensive "we."

In chapters six through eight, I examine sayings of Jesus and their settings in relation to the wild community of Earth. For example, Jesus said that Earth decides to produce plants whether humans are conscious or unconscious. In mockery of the mighty cedar of Lebanon as a symbol of regal rule, he said that the weed seed of the mustard plant is the indicator both of the Presence of God and of untamed eco-diversity.

In the last three chapters, I look at sayings of the Rabbi and their settings in relation to a kind community. Jesus asked people to wash each other's feet, to share food in community potlucks, to live in modest dwellings, and to give up possessiveness about clothes and money. Jesus did not own a house, and in this respect, had a zero carbon footprint.

Throughout the book I present Jesus within the context of biblical tradition, including the sustainable theme of the Garden of Eden story, the cosmic green vision of the book of Job, and the ecological splendor and muskiness of the greenest book of the Bible, the Song of Solomon. God in Leviticus 25 asked for people to proclaim liberty throughout the land to all human, animal, plant, and mineral inhabitants. These same green biblical resources are available for us today.

Methods used in writing to accentuate greenness

Certain words, like Earth, are capitalized. Look in the Revised Standard Version of the Bible and you will find Earth capitalized in Gen.1:10. Proper nouns refer to particular and unique persons, places, or things. Without question Earth fits this description. I capitalize Energy when it refers to the oneness of reality and capitalize Ocean (the Mother of Life). Other capitalized words include proper noun phrases such as Earth Community. All capitalized words are nouns and subjects with value, not inert, passive objects. I use the proper noun phrase, More-than-Humans, to refer to the soil, water, plants, and animals who (like our family dogs are "who," not the impersonal "which") deserve intrinsic value as our companions within Earth Community.

It's conventional to capitalize such Hebrew names equivalent to the name God as Yahweh (the favorite Hebrew name), and as *Elohim, El, El Shaddai,* and *Adonai.* Throughout this book, I use such God equivalents, based on the Aramaic, as *Allaha* (masculine) *Allahta* (feminine), The One, and the Presence of The One. Using science I select such names parallel to The One as Creating Process, Community of Life, and Energy. It is crucial to remember that God is more fundamental than language. Jews acknowledge this reality by not voicing Yahweh when reading the Torah, the Hebrew Bible. The Christian Bible says that "the Spirit maketh intercession for us with groanings which cannot be uttered" (Rom. 8:26, KJV), or groanings too deep for words. God cannot be encompassed, only symbolized by vowel sounds and consonants produced by air pressure, as the popular writer Eckhart Tolle explains in *A New Earth.*

It is as futile to argue about the right name for God as to argue whether Sonny, Joseph, Big Guy, Papa Joe, Grabill, or *Nonno* (several grandchildren address me with the Italian word for Grandpa because one of them was born in Italy) is the right form of address for me. These names are all correct. A rose by any other name still smells like a rose. Islam celebrates ninety-nine names for *Allah,* which is the Arabic derivative of the name Jesus preferred, *Allaha.* By any other name, The One is still The One.

I will use throughout the book a mix of secular and religious terms, typically capitalized, to symbolize the full Energy system within Earth Community and within the universe at large. This mix models our need to heal the split between science and religion. We need to see the complementary more than the adversarial aspects of diverse images representing whole systems. Some of these terms are familiar, and others not. Here's a sample: Being, Creating Process, God, Presence, and Stillness. I suggest you consult at the end, as you are reading, the entire list of around sixty terms in the section Whole Systems Terms.

I believe in God, a whole system being, like I believe in breathing. He's the infinite fresh breath, the I Am who is a prankster, now hidden, now flaring into sight. This Being is our abode who offers the company and hospitality of galaxies, of a plate of rice, and of bacteria. God is amused when we think there is a place and time where he is not. Honest to God, she knows everyone in the universe, like my dogs know my scent.

A goal of this book is to make Green Jesus accessible to folks from all cultures. I chose not to use or emphasize some words and concepts that are distinctive to Christian vocabulary, so as not to be off-putting to those who are not familiar or comfortable with Christianity. Best-selling author Deepak Chopra, coming from the Hindu tradition, writes in *The Third Jesus: The Christ We Cannot Ignore* that there are three manifestations of Jesus: first, the historical Jesus; second, the Jesus of church history; third, the living, cosmic Jesus, who is a potential spiritual guide for anyone. This third Jesus is available to interact inclusively with all folk. I am focusing primarily upon the first and third manifestations. As a professional historian, I am presenting the first Jesus using reasonably verifiable evidence as I would if were writing about such other figures from two thousand years ago as Augustus Caesar and Herod the Great. I simultaneously present the third Jesus.

My views about the historical Jesus, Mary Magdalene, and first-century Galilee come from multiple sources. At times I present ideas that may seem to you unconventional, partly because it is not well understood how profoundly unorthodox first-century Jesus was. He wasn't crucified because he conformed to the mores of his society. We live in the midst of a crisis which cries out for his culturally revolutionary style. Consider this book a menu. Sniff and partake of ideas that whet your appetite, and pass by items on the menu of ideas in this book that do not stimulate your taste.

My sources on first-century Palestine are multidisciplinary and for the sayings and deeds of Jesus are multi-gospel. We have available today twenty-two gospels, and I draw upon the seven that best reveal the historical Jesus: Matthew, Mark, Luke, John, Thomas, Mary Magdalene, and Judas. In my use of the Aramaic language, I seek to translate Aramaic culture into English-speaking culture while being faithful to the Aramaic language and culture of the first century and the thought forms of contemporary English. The English translations of the Bible that I favor are the Revised Standard Version (RSV) and the Scholars Version (SV). Occasionally, I use the King James Version (KJV). I also at times paraphrase the Aramaic ecological, cultural, and linguistic context for what Jesus said and did in the first century.

Each chapter begins with a green principle related to the sayings and deeds of Jesus, followed by applications of the principle to green practices and attitudes for us today. At the end see lists of sayings of Jesus, green principles, green practices, and green lyrics. This book is intended to inspire you to see and to apply connections between Jesus and green living that you have never seen before.

HarperOne published in 2008 an unprecedented New Revised Standard Version of the Bible called *The Green Bible*, with a Tree of Life on the cover made of cotton linen. The sub-title, *Understand the Bible's Powerful Message for the Earth*, reinforces a goal of *Green Kingdom Come!* Also on the cover of *The Green Bible* is the verse, "God saw everything that he had made, and indeed, it was very good" (Genesis 1:31). This recycled-paper bible has over 1,000 ecological verses printed in soy-based green ink and includes essays by such figures as Archbishop Desmond Tutu, Pope John Paul II, and evangelical leader Brian McLaren. Over 25,000 copies sold within a few weeks. It has taken two-thousand years for our culture to underline that God and the Bible are green and earthy.

I am not writing a handbook in sustainability, although I provide examples and suggestions. Excellent handbooks exist, including *The Live Earth Global Warming Survival Handbook* by David de Rothschild. Another I recommend is by Yvonne Jeffrey, Liz Barclay, and Michael Grosvenor: *Green Living for Dummies.* An important reason for not trying to be comprehensive about green practices is that innovations are increasing at a geometric rate. By the time this book is published new sustainable processes will exist. Hopefully, within a few years, the novelty of green practices will be as astonishing as autos and airplanes were to those who thought around 1900, when my parents were born, that horse and buggy travel would forever be a mode of transport.

More deeply, my aim is help rebirth a powerful Leaver dream within the human species, a dream more foundational than any yet stated by Al Gore and by many green spokespeople. Only by our species embodying a dream, not focusing primarily upon political and economic changes, will we develop the will and commitment to renege on Taker behavior and restore Leaver behavior.

This introduction section, "OnEarth," has a title inspired by the Lord's Prayer in the Bible. Jesus said, "Thy kingdom come, on earth" (Matt. 6:10, RSV). I leave out the space between the two words, on and Earth, to remind us that we have one home — onEarth.

The title of this book, *Green Kingdom Come!* also comes from the Lord's Prayer. I imagine that Jesus could not help but sense, when he said, "Thy kingdom come," his total immersion in his green, lush, and eco-diverse Galilee. I say out loud by myself emphatically, "Green kingdom come!" It's a request which I hope you too voice. It's also an acceptance that greenness is built into our living Earth. The phrase evokes good news about the degree of sustainability already present today, and about a fullness anticipated.

"Green kingdom come" has an appeal that can revise our use of such phrases as "Don't wait until kingdom come," and "Blast to kingdom come." To make possible this revision we can dedicate ourselves to the following pledges:

1. We "blast" to kingdom "departing" our Taker addictions and welcome a united kingdom of one Earth, under God, with liberty, justice, and equal green opportunity for all.
2. We pledge ourselves to relate with neighborliness to members of the human and the More-than-Human mineral, plant, and animal kingdoms.
3. We don't wait for but act to create the wholeness of green kingdom come.

Sketch based upon a painting by
Ralph Kozak, www.jesuslaughing.com

Tea for Three: A Conversation

Linus: So I had to tell the teacher that I just didn't know...
Charlie Brown: Maybe some questions don't have an answer.
Lucy: Like what?
Snoopy: Like did Jesus ever own a dog?
— Peanuts *comic strip*

After sunset tonight, I lay on my back on the ice shelf above the gurgling Lake Superior at Many Cedars Beach watching the Long Nights Moon get rounder. Around me were sextillion snowflakes. I was happy to have drafted the "Introduction." I reflected on preparing to write what I imagined would be a sketch of the socialization of Jesus in what feels like a "New Earth Symphony."

Right now, I hear loons sing and wolves howl on "American Wilds." Loon singing has many styles, like human vocalization. Loons hoot with eight to ten notes voiced rapidly in varied frequency and intensity. Loons wail at night so loudly that they can be heard for many miles. These ancient birds, among the first on Earth, also yodel.

Now I am ready to type about Jesus, but first I heat water for tea. The kettle boils, and I unconsciously put a tea bag in each of two cups. I am barely aware of what I am doing. No one else is in the house or expected to come. I carry the two steaming cups to the southern exposure sun room. I touch the computer keys. At that moment of contact, a figure darkens the door to my right. Who appears to my wandering mind? Who? Can it be? It can't be. But it is. It's Jesus. He's the "third" Jesus, the spiritual Jesus mentioned earlier, present in our time, who is a potential guide for anyone.

I am somewhat startled by his appearance. He is in his early forties, graying around his temples. He is around five-and-a-half feet tall and has an open face, black curly hair and beard, and brown skin tone. He doesn't have a robe. He wears a casual turtleneck, slacks, and Birkenstocks. While he does not look like the sketch above of Jesus laughing, he exudes its spirit.

In my mind an interaction with Jesus unfolds. I offer him the tea I had unwittingly prepared. He takes both hands to pick up the ceramic mug. He says, "Ouch! Hot!"

"Sorry. I should have warned you."

I welcome him with "*Marhabah*" in Arabic since I can't think of the word for welcome in Aramaic.

Jesus says, "I feel welcomed. My English, as you can tell, is excellent. Don't be surprised if I use slang. Over the years, I've gotten used to being the most popular cultural icon in America. I keep track of your media. I've also looked at some of the thousands of books having me as the theme — twice as many as about God, as you may know — in the Library of Congress. This tea tastes good. Refreshing. Tangy. Thank you."

Having recovered a bit from the startling, but unconsciously prepared, visit, I tell him that I recently found something that primed me for his appearance. "The Internet," I say, "has a computer-generated image of what a Jewish male in your time would look like based upon a comparative study of first-century skeletons. You look remarkably like that computer image."

Jesus smiles knowingly. "I am what you see," he says.

"Would you mind letting me interview you, including about your time growing up?"

"Happy to do so."

What was your childhood like?

I was born around 10 Before the Christian Era (BCE). Mother, like scholars today, was not quite sure of the year. But it was some years before Herod the Great died in 4 BCE.

My home village, *Natsrat* in Aramaic, was a farm town of about three hundred Jewish people belonging to three clans. It measured ten acres, 2,000 feet by 650 feet. No synagogue building. No scrolls or schools. Little or no literacy. No fortification. No palace. No bathhouse. One well. No paved streets. Limited use of coins. We lived in a dirt floor house made from fieldstones plastered with straw and dung and a flat roof made with reeds, branches, mud, and dung. We slept with our animals. My father had his workshop in a cave. About half of our neighbors lived in limestone caves.

Nazareth, as you can see today, sits within a bowl of hills on the watershed heights between the Mediterranean Sea and the Jordan River. In my time, it was on the southwestern slope of the bowl. We had terraced fields with vineyards, olives, figs, pomegranates, wheat, barley, millet, vegetables and legumes. Steep, winding footpaths connected the town to the large Jezreel Valley, several hundred feet down below to the south. Large landowners controlled the Jezreel Valley, thirty by ten miles. Footpaths at first and then a road led to the northwest to the capital of Galilee four miles and a two-hour walk.

Tell me about your parents.

We had our ups and downs. Their names in Aramaic are *Maryam* and *Yousef.* One thing they used to say to my brothers, sisters, and me was, "It's easier to grow olives than to raise you."

Did you help your parents grow olives?

Yes. Our whole family harvested ripe, black olives at the autumn end of the dry season. We used long poles to knock clusters of olives off trees. We put olives in a hollowed-out limestone pit, rolled a stone over them, and crushed out the oil for eating and for fueling our lamps. Then, we took lye to remove bitterness from uncrushed olives and cured them by soaking them in salty brine.

How did you celebrate the harvest?

We celebrated the festival of *Sukkot*. We gave thanks for pomegranates, figs, grapes, olives, dates, and citron fruit. We dipped bread in olive oil and in hyssop, a dried herb. We sang, circle danced, ate, and drank wine. We built temporary lean-tos against our houses or against the slopes using date palm fronds and willow and evergreen myrtle branches. The blackish-blue berries of myrtle gave off a sweet scent that I can still smell. We lived and slept in the lean-tos for seven days to remember the Israelites who lived in similar booths during the forty years before they entered Canaan. West winds gusted between the fronds and fragrant myrtle, and at night, we watched the stars through the cracks. We also prayed for adequate rain in preparation for planting barley and wheat.

Sounds like my farm boy lifestyle growing up. Were you scared of the Romans?

Was I scared? Not really. Romans never came to Nazareth. It was too small and separated by high hills from the main roads around us. When I was about six years old, Herod the Great died. Anti-Roman riots broke out in the nearby town of Zippori, partly because Romans had been stealing from the temple treasury in Jerusalem. We didn't protest in Nazareth. A Roman legate from Syria, Varus, marched with troops to Zippori, torched part of the town, and killed and deported rioters. We went to the top of our bowl of hills on our northwest and could easily see Zippori burning for it was a city on a hill. But when my brothers, father, and I helped rebuild Zippori and make it Sepphoris, the new capital, the ornament of Galilee and residence of Herod Antipas (son of Herod the Great), we heard stories about the cruelty of Varus and the Roman centurions.

Did you have a class society in Nazareth?

No. We had little difference materially among our families, unlike the stratified society in Sepphoris and the Jezreel Valley below us. But patriarchs of our Nazareth clans had more power than others, including the power of life and death. If someone brought dishonor to our clan, he or she could be stoned. Women generally could not travel to Sepphoris unless in the presence of clan males.

When I was young, we were unable to travel the several days' journey to Jerusalem for Passover, because we did not own a donkey to carry provisions. Occasionally, dispossessed peasants, beggars, day laborers, slaves, and bandits would wind their way up to our village. We had free food kitchens for them. Nobody went hungry unless there was a season of drought, and then everybody suffered about the same.

We were, what you would say today, a sustainable community.

How did you celebrate the Sabbath?

From Friday sunset to Saturday sunset, we observed *Sabbat*. We stopped bartering and working. Mother and my sisters prepared food during the day on Friday. As *shemesh* set over the Mediterranean on Friday, we villagers gathered in a large cave during the rainy season or in the open-air plaza beside the well in the dry season. Adults and youth sat on benches around the perimeter, and youngsters moved about freely looking for hugs and playing with homemade toys. Odoriferous olive lamps lit the circle. We said the *Shema* (Hear, O Israel), sang, prayed, argued, and gossiped. If a rabbi or priest from Sepphoris or elsewhere was visiting, he would stand in the middle. If he could read and had a scroll of the Torah, then we heard Hebrew, a language no longer in common usage. Less than one percent of the people in Galilee were literate or even semiliterate. Our stories and discussions were in Aramaic with a few Greek words thrown in.

Jews and Christians have never observed the Sabbatical Year of Jubilee, commanded in the Bible in Leviticus 25, to give folks and animals rest from agricultural and pastoral duties for a full year and to allow poor people and wildlife free access to Earth Commons. Do you think it would be a good idea today, to observe something like a Sabbatical Jubilee, not for one year, but for fifty years, to make restitution for this command never having been obeyed?

I recommend it heartily. Don't wait until kingdom come to be and act green. Begin plans for a fifty-year Sabbatical Jubilee now.

You mentioned earlier working in Sepphoris.

Yes. Starting in my teens, my father, a *nagara*—an artisan, my brothers, and I did carving for and plastering of an aqueduct to Sepphoris. The aqueduct began just an hour's walk east of our village on the heights. We also did stonemasonry and woodworking, and met some of the few Greeks among what were eventually ten thousand Jews in Sepphoris. There I met other artisans who came from throughout Galilee. I also met Pharisees, scribes, tax-collectors, rabbis, magistrates, scholars, and itinerant therapists and storytellers. Sepphoris provided me with a cross-cultural education.

The gospels never mention Sepphoris directly, but say that Joanna, the wife of Herod Antipas's steward Chuza, was part of your group. She lived in Sepphoris.

Yes, Joanna and others in Sepphoris were part of my group.

In addition to my upbringing in the village of Nazareth and in the city of Sepphoris, other training for my itinerant ministry came from being an apprentice with my cousin, John the Baptist, who lived in *madbra*, or as you would say, wilderness. We members of his group ate locusts and wild honey. Many areas near Nazareth were forested, like Mount Tabor, and many areas in the Jordan Valley were thicketed. Gazelles, foxes, lions, and snakes lived in *madbra*. It was in *madbra* and with my relations to itinerants like John that I got much of my young adult training.

Your recorded parables, sayings, and deeds are witty and clever. Where did you learn these traits?

My four brothers—James, Joseph, Jr., Jude, and Simon—and I entertained each other with pranks. We could see in the cosmopolitan city of Sepphoris that the Nazareth people were considered country bumpkins. Being in the underside of society, we saw through high-class pretense. We made fun of ourselves, people in general, and, especially, the elite. We knew the code, an eye for an eye and a tooth for a tooth. We could see that if we knocked out an elite person's tooth, we would not have a tooth knocked out in response. We would have our head smashed.

Instead of physical violence, we turned to satire. I became a mimic. I found ways to entertain and educate. I learned from itinerants. In my ministry group, as we traveled about, we exchanged our teachings and healing therapies for a bed roll and a meal from a hospitable family.

You say in the Sermon on the Mount that if someone hits you on your right cheek, let him hit you on the other cheek as well.

In my traveling group, we would demonstrate and teach people through what you might call guerrilla theater. I had Peter face me and try to slap my *yaminah pakah*, my right cheek, with his right hand. Peter would come at me, turn himself into a pretzel trying to twist sideways to figure out how to flat-hand or backhand my right check, and would lose his balance and flop into the dirt.

"OK, Peter. Wipe off your robe. Come on now. Hit me on the other cheek."

By then, I would have turned and had my back to him. Now my left cheek was on the opposite side of his right hand, just as the right cheek was opposite his right hand before when I faced him. This time he'd try to stretch his arm around in front of my neck to whack my left cheek and would end up hugging me from behind instead of clobbering me (Matt. 5:39).

Then I'd address the crowd. "Practice this so that when the occasion arises with an unjust overlord, ask him to smack you on your right cheek, then about face, and ask him to slap you on the other cheek. The flabbergasted overlord, not at first getting your trick, may eventually see that you are pulling his leg. Even if he doesn't get the joke, at least you will empower yourself to develop creative ways to cope with injustice."

I used to say, "Let's continue, folks. Play the same game as I have done with Peter."

What a scene. People would pair up, tip over, get red dust all over their garments, and eventually cackle.

In one Beatitude, you said that people who weep will laugh (Luke 6:21). What did you mean?

Here's how it is in Aramaic. *Tubva becha hasha, gehech,* which means that people who bawl and wail are lucky because they will also laugh. Notice the Aramaic word *gehech,* which means laugh. *Gehech* is onomatopoetic, like the sounds ha, hee, and haw. Put your tongue down and back and forcefully say ha. You'll get close to the guttural "h" and "ch" in Aramaic. Ge-hech. If you hang on to and repeat the last "ch" sound, the word becomes a laugh. Listen. Ge-hech-cha-cha-cha. Try it.

Ge-hech-cha-cha-cha.

Not exactly the way I sound in Aramaic, but close enough.

Once, you invited a man to accompany you, and he said, "Let me first go and bury my father." You replied, "Leave the dead to bury their own dead" (Luke 9:59–60, RSV). You, of course, knew that for a son not to bury his father was the unspeakable height of dishonor, bringing shame and retribution on him and his family forever. Why did you say such a preposterous thing?

Well, the gospel text you are citing does not give you the contextual picture of the corpse of a dead son unable to chisel a burial spot out of limestone for his dead father. Imagine a stiff failing to put ointment on another stiff. See the corpse of a son rigid with rigor mortis, unable to wrap linen about his dead father. Look at the son's cadaver, wrapped in linens, improperly burying his dad. My saying is a parody, helping people to see the irony of letting honor rituals about the dead prevent them from honoring equitable life for the living.

How did the audience respond to that saying?

Well, what's written in the gospels is just a snippet from a much longer repartee with the crowd. I learned to play the audience, and the audience played me. People often caught my caricatures and laughed.

The Gospel of Judas explicitly says that you laughed repeatedly in conversation with Judas. He thought you were laughing at him.

No. I told him I was not laughing at him. Rather, my lampoons and riddles amused me.

I like your caricature of people who want a cataclysmic outward sign before choosing to live a wholesome way motivated from the inside out. At least, that's how I read your sayings in Mark 4:21 and Luke 11:29–36.

I said to people that they didn't need to cover an olive lamp with a bushel basket, an outward act, to realize that lack of air would snuff out the flame.

"You folks," I said, "don't put olive lamps under the bed pallets to realize that the pallets would catch fire, burn a hole in the dried dung and branches of the flat roof, and stink up the house." What people primarily needed then, and need now, is enlightened awareness and the will to act on evidence that the Presence of The One, her or himself, is the sign, not an outward suffocated flame or a conflagration turning bed and roof to charred stench.

You seem like a Zen Buddhist.

I've read Zen sayings. Here's one I like. A Zen student says, "A master once said to me, 'Do the opposite of whatever I tell you.' So I didn't."

I like enigma and hyperbole. I have read an American comic strip in which Adam says to his son, "As the Earth's temperature continues to rise, what will happen to the deserts?

    A. They will become grasslands.
    B. They will remain the same.
    C. They will expand.
    D. They will disappear and become water bodies."

The son says, "I choose D. Global warming will raise sea levels and cause entire continents to be submerged."

Good one.

Jesus, did you catch an image that is circulating on the Internet? A clothesline has panties hanging left to right. Panties of the 18th century on the extreme left are baggy and down to the knees. Panties from 1900 go to mid-thigh, and ones from 1950 go to the upper thigh. Panties from 1990 are bikini briefs. Ones from 2006 are a nearly invisible thong. The caption: "Positive proof of global warming."

Gehech-cha-cha-cha.

I am curious about your relationship with Mary Magdalene.

I was closer to her than any of my associates. She was the widow of a sardine merchant in Magdala. Wealthy widows could travel with men in public without shame or dishonor. She used her resources, both money and dried sardines, to help our mission of empowering everyone to regard themselves as members of the Presence of The One.

Without her, you would never have heard of me. The names of all but the tiniest fraction of one percent of first-century residents of Galilee are lost to history. After my crucifixion, only her living vision of me, whom she called *Rabboni*, My Rabbi, stirred a social memory of me and an opportunity now for me to visit you. No Mary Magdalene, no written gospels. No Mary Magdalene, no Christianity. No Mary Magdalene, no Apostles' Creed.

Mary woke up the Sunday morning after my crucifixion. She walked to my tomb. Arriving, she saw me as stunningly as you see me now. Her first look at me imagined me a gardener and continued with other visions of me as stated in the Gospel of Luke and in her Gospel of Mary Magdalene. My presence with her was so intense that she was able to convince my skeptical male associates that my companionship was alive for them also. Her visions of me and those of Peter, John, and Thomas, which included scenes of talking, eating, and touching, were like Paul's vision of me on the road to Damascus. Her powerful visualizations led to a social movement that makes me a household name around the world. Without her, you wouldn't be having your own vivid vision, so real it seems physical, of me drinking tea and conversing with you.

If you don't mind, I'll invite Mary Magdalene to join us. She can tell you about herself directly.

Fabulous.

(I heat up more water and prepare a third cup of tea. Within moments, Mary Magdalene comes into the sun room and sits down. She is around sixty years of age with gray hair, intense, sparkling, deep golden brown eyes, and dressed in today's style.)

Welcome, Mary Magdalene. I would love to hear how you came to meet Jesus.

Word spread around the Sea of Galilee about a young rabbi from Nazareth, and I knew he had to go through Magdala on his way between Capernaum and his hometown. So I invited him to dinner. As an older, wealthy widow, I was free from the purity rules that forbade nearly all other women from associating with men at meals and in public. After that dinner event, he and I often talked, walked, and meditated. His whimsy tickled me. The despair that I felt before my husband died began to recede.

It says in Luke 8 that you had seven demons.

Seven symbolizes fullness, and seven demons means that I was full of despair. The sardine business, with its day and night presence of fish smells, consumed my husband. He always wanted more goods and insisted, not requested, that I want more too. But I didn't. He persisted, with violence. My husband told his cronies that I was an idiot not to want what he wanted. A breaking point came when he planned to build bigger storehouses than we needed. Servants of wealthy Jews in Sepphoris, in Tiberias just south of Magdala on the Sea of Galilee, and in Gamla on the heights northeast of the Sea picked up dried sardines regularly, so we didn't need more storage space. I was very unhappy.

Then one night he had a dream. *Allaha* appeared to him and said, "Fool. This night your soul is required of you. And the things you have prepared, whose will they be?" My husband woke up, told me the dream, clutched his heart, and died.

Your story about your husband's dream sounds like the parable of the rich landowner in Luke 12:17–18.

Rabboni and I disguised my personal story in the parable by having the fool own a landed business instead of a fishing business. In the parable, as you know, an active, abundant Earth produces a huge harvest and the passive fool does nothing but daydream about bigger barns and about lavish eating, drinking, and being merry for many years. In absurd contrast to the lavish, productive Earth, his heart becomes un-lavish and unproductive, and his dream of merriment collapses in his unexpected death.

May I say that many of you folks today are behaving like my former husband?

He always thought I would become like him, so he had a lawyer write a will that I was to inherit the business if anything happened to him. Widow inheritance was common among merchant and landowner families. Peasant and village women did not get inheritances. The assets of their husbands went to sons or brothers.

My husband's death brought a strange turn. I regularly provided dried sardines from my stores for the poor. Inconspicuously, I became a female rabbi. A number of prominent Jewish women—Joanna, who was the wife of the steward of Herod Antipas, Susanna, and others—traveled with us and materially helped support all of the members of *Rabboni's* group.

Do you mind if I call you by your Aramaic name?

Certainly not.

Maryam Magdala, I would like to hear more of your stories. Thank you for the ones you have told.

Jesus, what do you suggest we do today in particular to learn from you about sustainability? What would you say?

With a green heart, examine my teachings carefully. For example, I said, as quoted in Matthew 5, that the sun rises on bad and good. I was teaching Jews and Greeks that there is only one Earth under the rule of the one sun. Like the sun which favored both ritually impure and pure people in my day, spread today your favors locally and internationally without partiality. Use the resources of the sun and Earth to care for all people and all species, not just a few.

Do you think we need a green dream?

Yes. Here's one for the human community to voice.

We dream of the sun smiling upon our sustainable Earth home.

We dream of the rain falling upon a revival of species.

We dream of valuing an equal right to life and liberty for all species.

We dream of being one mind with Mother Earth.

We dream of renewable energy from east to west.

We dream of singing, "Green at last. We're green at last."

(I look down at my tea cup, thinking that I will offer to get more tea. When I look up, Mary Magdalene and Jesus have vanished.)

FOR A LONG time, I think about my visitors and the green lifestyle Jesus had, both in his youth and in his itinerant ministry. I write up the interview with Jesus and Mary Magdalene. Then, I notice that Long Nights Moon has set. Darkness shrouds the sun room. I am still surrounded by sextillion snowflakes, each one seeded by a microscopic dust particle and each grown by icy water vapor and by Earth's air. The hexagonal snowflakes, so inscrutable that no theory yet fully explains their endless uniqueness and beauty, lie around me in this silent night.

PART ONE

One Community

During the American Revolution, Thomas Paine's *Common Sense* was a best seller. His ideas resonated with a significant number of people in the varied colonies who sensed a view they had in common. The destiny of the united colonies was to start an experimental government in a new world.

Today, what do you sense you share with others about Earth's destiny? The common sense of astronauts and cosmonauts is that they cannot see any boundaries, of species, nations, or religions, from Earth's orbit. There is one green and blue planet. John Glenn traveled in Friendship 7 around the Earth in 1962. For him, the setting sun melted into a thin rainbow that hugged the horizon. The sky was black as tar. No differences existed among people at all, as Connie Schultz reports in a column titled "John Glenn: Our Similarities — From a Distance."

Rabbi Jesus taught that there is The One, a teaching that is both a religious and scientific truth. All religious views, whether arch-conservative or arch-liberal, and all sciences, whether traditional Newtonian or post-Einsteinian, require a dialogue between humans and other members of the cosmos. All knowledge and belief systems are alike in that they share this indispensable dialogue process.

What does make self-evident sense is to treasure what we have in common. Today, what we need is to embrace Earth Commons as our home and clean it up.

What does it mean to embrace our Earth Commons? Thomas Friedman in *Hot, Flat, and Crowded: Why We Need a Green Revolution and How It Can Renew America* writes that it means more than producing clean electrons and energy efficiency. It means no one left inside with faces pasted to electronic screens. It means whole people submerged in whole ecosystems with all senses paying attention to More-than-Humans. Thomas tells a story of the indigenous guide Gilbert in the humid Peruvian rain forest. Gilbert led the way and had no phone, binoculars, iPod, or radio. He did not suffer from the first-world disease of "continuous partial attention." Gilbert heard chirps, whistles, howls, and crackles, and identified sounds of birds, insects, and animals. With immaculate vision he spotted a spider's web, a butterfly, a toucan, and a column of marching termites. "He was totally disconnected from the Web, but totally in touch with the incredible web of life around him."

The vocalist Della Reese sings about a dream of hope on the Epic Records Christmas album, "Touched by an Angel." Her song, "If I Can Dream," is by W. E. Brown. Let's absorb her passionate optimism and apply it to our green agendas. "If a man can dream of a better land, where all his brothers walk hand in hand, Lord, tell me why, oh why, oh why, why can't their dream come true?"

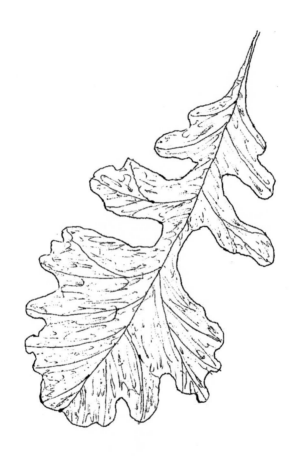

Leaf of bur oak

1

DEAD AND REBORN

WOULD JESUS DRIVE A HUMMER?

Dear God, instead of letting people die
and having to make new ones,
why don't you just keep the ones you got now?
— *Jane, quoted in* Children's Letters to God

You know, there is a heaven for girls and a heaven for boys.
But mice are so small they can get in either one they want.
— *Grandson Erik, age five*

Tonight after sunset, I lay on the ice at a place on the shore a mile west of Many Cedars Beach that I've named Great Waters Beach in remembrance of the Native Americans whose village was close to this beach for two centuries. Today, Ojibway folk live on two nearby reserves called Red Cliff and Bad River. The Ojibway word for marsh, *Mushkizibe*, was mistranslated as "bad." Thus, this reserve is better called Marsh River. These Native Americans have several names for this island, including Spirit and Yellow-Bellied Woodpecker. On the ice shelf, snowflakes landed on my nose and face. I inhaled several. I heard a deep sucking sound periodically when a wave came under the nearby ice floes and my ice shelf. A slightly fatter Long Nights

Moon, now a bit larger than half, fuzzily shone through the filmy cloud cover. There were no stars. I thought about death and rebirth as I anticipated writing the first chapter.

PRINCIPLE—The death of over-consumption produces greenness.

A fascinating question Jesus asked was, "What will it profit a man, if he gains the whole world [*alma*] and forfeits his life [*naphsha*, breath of life]?" (Matt. 16:25–26, RSV). Let's examine the word, *alma*, translated "whole world." *Alma* refers to the ageless, eternal world, not primarily the material world. *Alma* refers to the entire world system or the universe. It is analogous to the word Energy in the first law of thermodynamics. This law says that the whole universe of Energy cannot be created or destroyed. Energy is.

Energy does not need to be sought as profit or gain, but is a sustainable and constant, ageless given. In contrast, breath is not a given.

Let's rephrase the question of Jesus for us today. "What is the profit in seeking to gain what is a given and forfeiting what is not a given, one's breath?" Or rephrasing the question in green terms, "What is the profit in gaining control of the whole Earth Community and forfeiting sustainability?"

What is given and what is not given are two aspects of the universe. Physicists speak of the immeasurable, black, dark energy and black matter of the universe that totals an estimated 97 percent of the universe and interacts with the 3 percent of energy in the universe that is measurable by weight or by speed. The comic Stephen Wright wonders, "OK, so what's the speed of dark?" Dark energy, of course, has no speed, but its power and that of measurable particles together produces a nonstop dance. Energy in general does not die, but Energy's measurable aspect, the 3 percent of the universe, includes forms which come into being and which die. Thus Energy is simultaneously stable and changeable.

The aspects of Energy that change are described in the second part of the first law of thermodynamics. Energy cannot be created or destroyed, but it can change from one form to another, for example, electricity to heat.

Those of us who want to compare traditional theology with the first law of thermodynamics can see a similarity between the concept of Creator and the concept of Energy, and between the concept of Creation and the measurable aspects of the universe. Creator (Energy in general) is changeless (can't be added to or subtracted from), as in the first part of the law of thermodynamics. In the second part of the law, Creation (measurable energy) is full of change.

The dualism of Creator and Creation, as if they are opposites, poses problems for those of us who see the universe as one, seamless system. Certainly Jesus spoke of The One [*Allaha*] as seamless. The words Creator and Creation leave the impression that the universe involves an active subject and a passive object. But constituents of the universe — black energy, black matter, and measurable matter — are each active and passive, pulsing in mutual influence. Rumi, the thirteenth century Sufi Muslim, said it well: "A great mutual embrace is always happening between the eternal and what dies, between essence and accident."

The Harvard theologian, Gordon Kaufman, in his book *Jesus and Creativity*, has influenced me to come up with a concept that harmonizes the two parts of the first law of thermodynamics. The name I have made up is Creating Process, which honors the mutuality of creating and created Energy. The concept of Creating Process is similar to the Buddhist concept of Dependent Co-Arising. Another comparable name, in a book by physicist Brian Swimme and historian Thomas Berry, is Unfolding of the Cosmos.

Now let's return to Jesus, and what he said that is connected to the statement about seeking to gain the whole world. He was with his friends Philip and Andrew when he said, "Unless the kernel of wheat falls to the Earth [*Ar'ah*] and dies, it remains a single seed. But if it dies, it produces a great harvest" (John 12:24). *Ar'ah* includes soil, the smell of decaying leaves, and Mother Earth in general.

The sayings of Jesus about death and rebirth and gaining and forfeiting are comparable to the second law of thermodynamics, also called the law of entropy. The second law says that Energy spontaneously tends to flow from being concentrated in one place to dispersing, not vice versa. For example, a hot frying pan, when taken off the stove, disperses its energy out into the cooler room. The dispersed cooler energy cannot ever reassemble itself into the hot frying pan. Entropy says that as concentrated forms disperse they eventually fall apart, and once they fall apart, they cannot be put back together. Once the kernel of wheat falls into *Ar'ah* and dies, it cannot reconstitute itself again as a seed.

Once we drill for two hundred years into concentrated deposits of oil and natural gas within Mother Earth and consume them, using them to power machines and heat buildings, the burned oil barrels and gas BTUs cannot reconstitute themselves again.

The lessons are several. Energy, in general, is sustainable. *Allaha*, The One, is sustainable. Creating Process, as a continuous flow of Energy, is also sustainable. Forms separately and in certain combinations are not sustainable. What may or may not be sustainable are the overall ratios, numbers, and sizes of particular kinds of energy within Earth Community.

If we increase unsustainable uses of forms within Earth Community, we reduce the capacity of Earth Community for sustainability. And vice versa, when we reduce unsustainable actions, sustainability within Earth Community increases. We can let the over-consumption "kernel of wheat" habit fall to the Earth and die, and produce "a great harvest" habit of greenness.

Japanese people have been pioneers in reducing the over-consumption habit. The two thousand people in the mountain town of Kamikatsu have focused on banishing all waste by 2020. They have set up a Zero Waste Academy that has pushed recycling to an 80 percent rate (the American average is around 30 percent), perhaps higher than any community in the world. They have 34 categories of trash, from batteries, to fluorescent lights, to bottle caps. Toyota's plant for producing the hybrid Prius in Nagoya has 800-kilowatt solar panels blanketing the tops of buildings. It draws 50 percent of its electricity from solar panels and 50 percent from capturing waste heat. Carbon dioxide emissions are half what they were in 1990, despite increased production. Beginning in 2009, government laws require telecommunication companies to recycle all cell phones. Japanese companies long have hated waste.

> **PRACTICE—We seek to keep deaths and rebirths of varied forms in sustainable proportion by practicing the three Rs of reduce, renew, and redouble.**

Let's return to the concept of death as mentioned by Jesus in the saying about the kernel of wheat. We humans have not liked some aspects of death and change applied to us. We often repress the reality of our personal death. We use embalming to make corpses look like they are asleep and still breathing. In America, we emphasize the right to life, liberty, and happiness, and project that our bodies will happily live forever free, even though we have never shaken hands with a resuscitated cadaver.

We think of ourselves as gods who can shape Earth Community like a lump of inert clay to keep our species alive, no matter the cost in life, liberty, and happiness to other species. Ten millennia of the Agricultural Revolution have created the illusion that we humans can divide the Earth into two parts: spaces and times that we control for our own food, housing, and consumption purposes and the rest of the wild, natural world. Control means to increase extractions and products, to waste energy, and to destroy eco-diversity, the opposite of reduce, renew, and redouble.

In reality, no times and spaces are under our ultimate control. Wildness, in the end, controls us. In our obsession to bring more of Earth's resources under our thumb, we have brought ourselves to the point of extinction — the ultimate loss of control. It is folly to seek to rule other species and to domesticate wildness. It is impossible, a fantasy.

Jesus said to Philip and Andrew, after the comment about a kernel of wheat dying, "Those who love life [*naphsha*, breath of life] lose it, but those who hate life [*naphsha*] in this world [*alma*] will preserve it for unending, real life [*alma*]" (John 12:25; Luke 17:33, SV). On the surface, this statement is a nonsensical paradox. The sub-text of this statement is that those who hang possessively to the breath of life will, at death, lose it. Those who non-possessively breathe will experience unending life and agelessness.

An important footnote is that in Genesis 1, both humans and cows have *naphsha*. Both humans and cows have the breath of life. By inference, all members of Earth Community have intrinsic value.

The Rabbi was implying, "Humans need to be willing to give up possessing forms, like the kernel of wheat gives up possessing its form." For us today, we need to give up possession of ecological forms for the purposes of our own exclusive welfare. We need to let that kind of possessiveness end, so that wildness can bring forth essential life in a harvest of eco-diversity.

We can learn to let go of possessiveness by observing the way our bodies function all the time. There are 1,000 trillion cells in our bodies, and three billion cells die per minute. Stomach lining cells last two days on average before death and replacement. Brain cells last years, but still die. A gene that aids the dying cell process is called protein 53. Every year, not only cells die, but also 98 percent of our body's atoms pass out of our body and are replaced by new atoms.

Like incoming waves dying on the beach and new ones rising to take their places, my body is continuously eliminating atoms and cells and birthing new ones. Breathing is a constant reminder that I am inhaling atoms and exhaling them. Atoms in my body at this moment have been in the bodies of millions of my cousins in Earth Community before me and will depart and be within them in the future. My body is uninterruptedly departing and arriving. I die physically all the time, until my last breath.

As a species, if our total numbers shrink (for example, giving incentives to encourage adoption of children rather than reproduction), there will be a larger ratio of energy for other species within Earth Community. If we wholeheartedly imagine a collective human tombstone reading "See, we told you we were sick," then we have a chance as a species to get well.

The human species is gambling against the waning of the coal, oil, and natural gas bonanza. These three fossil fuels have been cheap, abundant, versatile, and easy to get. What we have used has died, and what has been reborn is not a harvest of cheap oil and gas deposits.

Humans have sucked energy forms from the Earth, and what has been burned and broken down has engorged us. According to the first law, the energy in oil and gas deposits did not disappear. Oil and gas forms were reborn in the energy required to extend agricultural and grazing processes—to increase food for the rising numbers of our species, from less than one billion of us before the fossil fuel era to over six billion of us today—and to mass produce consumer goods. The possibilities in technology took over our human imagination and impelled us to eat from the Tree of "Mechanization." In the Bible the Tree of the Knowledge of Good and Evil infers that the knowledge of technology and mechanization is good and anything that interferes with our technological innovation is evil.

The human species seems to defy the law of entropy. Our species is not appearing to fall apart, because it is using the falling apart of fossil fuels, animals and plants, and other forms within the Earth's closed system. The Earth is closed because no new forms of energy are arriving from the sun or other regions of our solar system. Our species has enlarged our share of energy in the Earth's closed system and presently imperializes, according to some estimates, around 40 percent of photosynthesis production.

Instead of seeking to monopolize photosynthesis production, we need to practice proportionality, as in the lyrics of the song, "Enough for Everyone," by Bryan Field McFarland (www. songvault.fm). He sings, "There's enough, there's enough, enough for everyone. More than enough, enough for us, enough for everyone."

Here are twelve ways to support actions that can result in enough for everyone, developed by the Carbon Mitigation Initiative, jointly sponsored by Princeton University, British Petroleum, and Ford Motor Company (www.princeton.edu/~cmi), and organized under the three Rs of reduce, renew, and redouble.

We humans need to reduce extractions in mining and in fossil fuel. We can

1. Increase car fuel economy to 70 mpg by 2050.
2. Reduce car travel from 10,000 miles a year to 5,000 with increased mass transit, telecommuting, and urban design conducive to walking and biking.
3. Develop zero-emission vehicles.
4. Develop bio-fuel from waste materials as a short-term

replacement for fossil fuel until carbon-free technologies are invented.

5. Increase efficiency of current coal plants from 32 percent to 60 percent and permit no new coal plants.
6. Increase building and appliance efficiency to achieve zero emissions by 2050.
7. Sequester CO_2 underground.

We humans need to renew energy. We can

8. Increase natural gas use fourfold as a short-term move until renewable technologies can replace natural gas.
9. Expand wind power to 75 times the current capacity.
10. Expand solar power to 1000 times the current capacity.

We humans need to redouble and multiply eco-diversity. We can

11. Decrease deforestation to zero and double the rate of new tree plantings.
12. Stop soil erosion with conservative tillage at ten times the current usage, and expand local, organic agriculture.

The Carbon Mitigation Initiative believes its steps are possible. Studying the list encourages us to think about the death of over-consumption.

The well-known head of the Goddard Institute for Space Studies at NASA, James Hansen, argues, in a recent speech I attended, for certain priorities within the Carbon Mitigation Initiative list to address what he calls our "planetary emergency." Hansen says that we can possibly bring the proportion of CO_2 in the air down to ratios that would prevent a "perfect disaster" if we stop building coal plants, sequester all coal plant CO_2 by 2030, use no till agriculture, and store CO_2 in the soil by employing charcoal biomass (also called agrichar, or terra preta). We can make agrichar from millions of tons of agricultural waste, municipal and yard waste, manure, and sewage. About 50 percent of char, if buried in soil, remains stable for thousands of years and creates a carbon sink more substantial than no-till farming and tree planting. Byproducts of agrichar are biofuels. These methods could possibly stabilize ice melt, species extinction, and regional climate change.

James Hansen and his wife Anniek have updated his lecture prescriptions in an open letter of December 29, 2008 to Michelle and Barack Obama posted on the website blog of Grist. James and Anniek write as fellow parents concerned about the fate of their grandchildren and those yet to be born. Their sense of urgency is large. They have a three-point plan. One, establish a moratorium and phase-out of coal plants that do not capture and store carbon dioxide. Two, reject a carbon emissions cap-and-trade system which generates special interests. Instead, establish a clear carbon tax on all oil, gas, and coal production at the well-head or port of entry, and use the dividends to support no-carbon innovative energies and products. To continue burning fossil fuels will destroy the planet and civilization. Three, introduce quickly fourth-generation, nuclear power reactors. These reactors use 100 percent of the energy in uranium, unlike present reactors which waste 99 percent of the uranium energy. James and Anniek write that presidential leadership is essential.

Both conservative Texas oilman Boone Pickens and Al Gore want an investment of $1 to 3 trillion over the next ten years in wind power and other renewable energy. Those who argue these goals are not possible should remember that computing power on a chip has doubled every two years and that Wikipedia, with over two million articles, did not even exist seven years ago. The cliché is sometimes true: where there's a will, there's a way.

The Obama administration appears to have the will to provide green leadership. A coalition of 28 environmental groups has sent a 359-page wish list, entitled "Transition to Green," of hundreds of issues to stimulate a green surge. The Obama team has received this report which recommends changes in 95 core issues involving 29 federal agencies. The report's recommendations fit the broad categories of energy and jobs, environmental justice, science-based decision-making, and integrity and transparency.

One additional method to practice the three Rs is to end our wasteful burial tradition. I intend for my body to experience a green internment. We have sustainable options. Burial without embalming may be done by placing the body in an Ecopod, a container shaped like a kayak and made of recycled newspapers, which costs as little as $100. The Natural Burial Company says its services provide composting at its best, with no formaldehyde embalming, no cement vaults, and no laminated caskets (www.nationalburialcompany.com). I would like my body to fall to the Earth within an Ecopod, hopefully near a favorite bur oak. Falling like a kernel of wheat, I would like to be reborn in a harvest of mosses and ferns, of the earthy smell exuded by fungus and humus, and of a bur oak tree with its deeply-corrugated bark and its gorgeous lobed leaves.

ATTITUDE—We have heart and hope about our own death.

We have some fear, rather than heart and courage, about our personal death, which underlies our fear about giving up overconsumption. Best-selling author Bill Bryson writes tongue in cheek in *I'm A Stranger Here Myself* that he is afraid of death. Reading statistics on death odds, Bryson notes that there is a 1 in 250 million chance that something falling from the sky will conk him on the head. The odds are 1 in 450,000 that, even staying away from the window, something will kill him before nightfall. Singing "The Star-Spangled Banner," he is twice as likely to die in a mangled heap as Prince Philip of the United Kingdom. The United States is dangerous, unlike England, with possibilities of crashing his car into a moose, being eaten by grizzlies, butted into oblivion by a bison, or being terminated by tornadoes and blizzards. Guns bump off 6.8 per 100,000 Americans annually, as compared with a nonenterprising 0.4 per 100,000 in the United Kingdom.

Jesus dealt with death, as noted, by parody. The Rabbi pictured a son's corpse, rigid with rigor mortis, unable to wrap linen about his dead father. Let me offer you a Jesus-like contemporary parable built on his satire about the dead burying the dead.

Grieving children stand around the bed where their father, a smoker, has just died. The three young adults feel sad about their dad's passing away. But they also want to celebrate his habit of playing practical jokes. So they hire two clowns to act dead and to bury their dad.

On the day of the funeral, one clown wears a skintight, black body suit with a white skeleton image on it. He drives a hearse down a street past pedestrians. He waves his skeleton at bystanders. The hearse's loudspeaker sounds forth the black spiritual, "Them bones, them bones, them dry bones. Now hear the word of the Lord." The three children follow in a convertible behind Skeleton Clown.

After going through the cemetery gate, Skeleton Clown parks and opens the back door of the hearse. Getting back in the vehicle, he briefly pedals the gas. The coffin lurches out the back and tumbles to the ground. The coffin lid opens. The convertible behind the hearse, tires squealing, comes to a stop to avoid smashing the coffin. The convertible driver blasts her horn and up from the dead pops a person out of the coffin dressed like her dead dad.

Reaching in his coat pocket, Dead Dad pulls out a cigarette. In a cloud of exhalation, he sings lustily, "Tell St. Peter at the

Golden Gate that I hate to have him wait. But I gotta have another cigarette."

Dead Dad hands three cigars to his children, who light up. When the cigars explode, Skeleton Clown's dancing bones fly.

Then Dead Dad gets back in his coffin, and Skeleton Clown closes the lid. Skeleton Clown takes a bow and addresses the coffin. "Thanks, Dead Dad. You've helped me show that burials of the dead, by the dead, and for the dead shall not perish from the Earth."

This modern parody reinforces what Jesus taught about not fearing death. Jesus said, "Do not fear those who kill the body but cannot kill the soul. Are not two sparrows sold for a penny? And not one of them will fall to the ground without your Father's will. But even the hairs of your head are all numbered. Fear not, therefore" (Matt. 10:28–31, RSV). *La dechel.* Fear not.

Fear, at its base, has to do with loss of breath and consciousness. Rumi said, "Don't let your throat tighten with fear. Take sips of breath all day and night." The moment we fear, let's deepen our breath, remembering that The One boundlessly envelopes the bounded dimension of sparrows, the one hundred thousand hairs of our heads, and our bodies. I breathe through my nose with intentionality, either intense short breaths or deeper and longer breaths, for five minutes daily. This exercise reduces anxiety, increases vitality, and gives my lungs and diaphragm an internal massage.

Is it possible to have fearless resolve about what happens after our bodies pass away and breath forever ceases? The essence and Spirit of the universe and its members exist before the birth and after the death of bodies. Essence and Spirit cannot *not* exist. Humans universally sense that babies come from the Spirit world and that our bodies pass away at death into the Spirit world.

Our soul, our measureless energy, continues forever. So heaven, a soulful reality, for boys, girls, mice, one hundred thousand hairs from our heads, everyone, and everything is assured. We humans can entrust our post-body, soul existence to Creating Process. We can expect a mysterious presence within the unending Presence of The One, who cannot be added to or subtracted from.

What time is it?

2

HERE NOW

WOULD JESUS FORECAST AN ECOLOGICAL DISASTER?

Our Father, who does art in heaven.
Harold is his name.
— *Reese, three years old, quoted in* Children's Letters to God

Taste the *here* and *now* of God.
— *Rumi*

Cold, frosty gusts exhilarated me while I walked at sunset on Great Waters Beach. Layers of clothing kept my body toasty, so I was not shivering. Nippy breaths chilled my nostrils. Crisp inhalations made my lungs vibrate with the immediacy of the frosty air. I love frigid weather, because I feel alive and in the moment, listening to winter with my whole body. Back in the sun room, I think about how Jesus emphasized that the Presence of The One, the Kingdom of God, is indeed with us, like my sensing cold wind is with me throughout my walk.

PRINCIPLE—Earth Community is here now, within and without.

Jesus said, "The Kingdom of God [*Malkuta Allaha*] has come upon you" (Matt. 12:28, RSV). How do we enter into the King-

dom of God? We don't have to enter, because the Presence of
The One is already here. Jesus said, "The Father's imperial rule
[*Malkuta*] is spread out upon the Earth, and people don't see it"
(Thomas 113:1-4, SV). The door to the Presence is now. Today
Earth Community is everywhere, and we often don't see the
web of life. The ecosphere surrounds and dwells within us, no
matter how our preoccupations distract us from recognizing its
constant company.

Malkuta is a noun in the feminine gender, and thus could be
translated as Feminine Presence. The quote from the gospel of
Thomas could read, "The Father's Feminine Presence is spread
out." *Allaha* is in the masculine gender. The word *Allahta*, which
is the feminine form of *Allaha*, occurs in the Aramaic Christian
Bible three times, and I will occasionally use this word instead
of *Allaha*. The One, of course, is gender-full, not gender specific.
But the five-thousand-year reign of patriarchy has tipped the
balance so far in the masculine direction that we need reminders
that The One is as much feminine as it is masculine.

The Feminine Presence, so often hidden from our consciousness, is as near as our ear. The Muslim Sufi, Rumi, taught us to
let this current breath slap us and wake us up. He said, "*No need
to announce the future! This now is it. This.* Your deepest need and
desire is satisfied by the *moment's* energy here in your hand."

Just as people often do not experience the Presence slapping
them awake, Jewish people, before and after Jesus, also often did
not experience the Presence slapping them awake. The prophets
frequently daydreamed about a not-here, not-yet future messiah,
a messenger of Yahweh. The name Yahweh means, ironically, I
Am Who I Am or I Am Here Now. Many Jews in the first century superimposed on Moses and King David glories that would
return in an even more glorious future. John the Baptist and the
Apostle Paul projected an apocalypse and judgment day in the
future. Christians predicted a second coming of Jesus that had

already come in Mary Magdalene's vision of the living Presence of *Rabboni*, My Rabbi, after his crucifixion.

Jesus spoofed the idea that the Presence was somewhere else and sometime else. "If your leaders say to you, 'Look, the Father's imperial rule is in the sky,' then the birds of the sky will precede you. If they say to you, 'It is in the sea,' then the fish will precede you" (Thomas 3:1–3, SV).

The Presence envelops us, like Earth Community, and embraces us like gravity. Today, we can dream that spaceships, UFOs, or comets will save us from our damaged planet. We can project that the return of Christian or Muslim savior figures will rescue us from our failure to live sustainably. We can theorize that reincarnations will give us another chance to act morally.

Or we can look to the Rabbi who was acting out the meaning of his name, *Eshua*, in Aramaic, which means to restore the Presence of Yahweh, of I Am Who I Am. *Eshua* means to restore the cornucopia of today's here and now, not to invoke the threat of a judgment day, nor promise the arrival of a Presence that is already present.

Happily, the Vatican today is reducing emphasis on future escapist theology. Under Pope Benedict and his predecessor, John Paul II, the Vatican is emphasizing that now is the time to be green. A Vatican spokesperson has announced a new commandment, "Thou shall not pollute the Earth. It is a sin to cause environmental blight" (www.reuters.com).

Pharisees in the first century, hoping for a future rule in which their purist morality system would control all Jews, tried to trap Eshua into showing allegiance to the emperor in Rome in order to ridicule his teaching that the rule of *Allaha* is already present in Palestine. They asked, "Is it permissible to pay the poll tax to the Roman emperor or not?"

Eshua wanted to see a coin. They handed him a silver *denarius* coin. "Whose picture is this?"

They said, "The emperor's."

Pharisees claimed no deity but *Allah(t)a* and were forbidden by Jewish law to have any graven image in their possession. But here the forbidden image of Augustus Caesar gazed up at everyone in the circle from the silver coin in Eshua's hand with the engraving, "Caesar, Son of God."

Rome had minted nondescript coins with no image of Caesar on them so that scrupulous Pharisees wouldn't have to break one of the Ten Commandments. But Eshua trapped the trappers breaking one of the Ten Commandments.

He responded to their riddle with his own riddle: "Render therefore to Caesar the things that are Caesar's, and to God the things that are God's" (Matt. 22:15–22, RSV). The subtext of his riddle was not to urge the separation of church and state, something that would be impossible to imagine in the first century, but to show the Pharisees that Caesar has only a silver coin, whereas *Allaha* in the eternal present has everything. He implied, "The One's Presence is here now abundantly, even though you think it's not because your narrow code of ethics is not practiced abundantly. By the way, thanks for the silver coin, which I'll keep to recall your failure to entrap me."

The present is palpable and discoverable from within. Eshua said, "Be on guard so that no one deceives you by saying, 'Look over here! or Look over there!' For the seed of true humanity exists within you. Follow it! Those who search for it will find it" (Mary Magdalene 4:3–5, *The Complete Gospels*). He also said, "The Kingdom of God is within [*legau,* within and around] you" (Luke 17:20–21, KJV). The word *legau* is simultaneously an adjective, adverb, and preposition, and means fully common among, around, and inside, like one's belly or guts.

God is fully common among, around, and inside our guts. Literally, God is our guts! S/he is also the guts of everyone and everything. Humans have misused the word God to connote by it someone other than us. Three year old Reese in the epigraph says, "Our Father, who does art in heaven. Harold is his name."

By age three, Reese already views God as somewhere other than here. The startling thing is not that we can become conscious of The One, but that we are unconscious of The One. Sleepwalking unawareness of the Presence of The One is like my saying that I am not conscious that I am writing at the computer right now. God is Being her/him/itself, not a being. This Being is in the guts (cannot not be) of every being — rock, molecule, plant, galaxy, and human. Every being lives and moves within Being, and Being lives and moves in a continuous now within every being.

PRACTICE—We cultivate the habit of letting here and now envelop our green behavior.

Rumi said, "You are the source of milk. Don't milk others! There is a milk fountain inside you. Don't walk around with an empty bucket. There is a basket of fresh bread on your head, and yet you go door to door asking for crusts. Knock on your inner door. No other. The horse is beneath the rider's thighs, and still he asks, 'Where's my horse?'"

Today, some of us don't sense the perspiring horse of the present beneath our thighs. We have the delusion that a future horse will rescue us from our problems.

Some of us nostalgically think that by digging holes in remaining wild habitats in the fifty states and Canada and under the Gulf of Mexico and Arctic Ocean or blasting off the tops of mountains with coal seams in Appalachia, we can again have energy independence and abundant fossil fuels.

Some of us, worried about doomsday, accept evidence that 70 percent or more of Florida will be underwater from melting icecaps by 2100 if we continue business with carbon dioxide emissions as usual, and we look helplessly toward an ecological Armageddon.

Some of us believe the *Left Behind* novels by Tim LaHaye and Jerry B. Jenkins and yearn for the rapture.

Some of us believe that, since there is no significant warming in the troposphere over the equator, global warming is caused by increased magnetic resonance of the sun, not carbon emissions. Others believe that the sunspot cycle is not on schedule, and we are in for global cooling. Regardless, we think that human life will turn out all right.

Others of us ride the horse of the creative present tense about sustainability and carry out green activities. An example of this is in Erie, Pennsylvania, where John Dineen leads a factory called General Electric Transportation that employs 4,500 people (www.globalerie.com/blog/category/ge-transportation). This factory employs world-class engineers and manufactures cleaner, and more efficient, exportable locomotives than anything produced in China or India at a much lower labor cost.

Another example features the founder of an environmental business-strategy group called GreenOrder, Andrew Shapiro, who is teaching companies how to integrate green activity into their whole business (www.greenorder.com). Shapiro has been a consultant with General Electric, General Motors, and British Petroleum. He says that the green revolution is as transformational as the digital revolution.

Prime examples would be our own daily green habits. David Gershon in *Low Carbon Diet* describes twenty-four practices to reduce unsustainability, which, if we are not doing them, we can begin now to join others who are doing them. I've culled some practices from *Low Carbon Diet*.

We practice "Dumping on Garbage." Instead of producing four pounds of solid waste today, we take paper, glass, aluminum, and cardboard to recycling. We take our own cloth bags to shop. We buy in bulk, purchase items with less packaging, and buy reusable items. We end junk mail by using a website (www.directemail.com/Junk_Mail).

We play the game "Plug Your Electricity Leaks." Instead of wattage-wasting appliances being plugged directly into wall sockets, we plug TVs, DVDs, lamps, and other appliances into power strips, which we switch off when the appliances are not in use. We roam the house looking for switches and gizmos to turn off. We save two pounds of CO_2 going into the air today.

We end glare-bomb and sky-glow lighting outdoors by installing downward directed lights, and less of them. It is impossible for many urban dwellers to see stars against the blackness of space. Light pollution is the most visible form of energy waste. If we compare it to air pollution, it would be like being able to see only 25 percent of the way across the Grand Canyon. Security lighting is only partially accurate because two-thirds of all crimes occur during the day.

We play "Scrub-A-Dub-Tub." Instead of using the dishwasher daily, we use the dishwasher once a week and save one-hundred pounds of CO_2 polluting the air yearly. Instead of waiting until the water becomes hot, we reduce the use of hot water for washing our hands. I washed my hands in cold water today and saved half a pound of CO_2 from zipping up the stack.

Instead of going the shortest route, we "Drive Earth Smart" and take the route that involves the least idling, saving up to 30 percent in fuel. We hypermile, taking off slowly from stops, gliding slowly to stops, avoiding using the brake as much as possible, and thus getting the most hyper miles per gallon we can. Instead of driving seventy-five miles per hour on the highway, we drive sixty and save 20 percent in fuel. I recently drove a thousand miles in my Windstar at the speed of 60 and found it relaxing. My wife just got a hybrid, and out on the road I got 40 mpg at 65 mph and 45 mpg at 60 mph.

Low Carbon Diet suggests broadening our diet and becoming less dependent on meat ("Chew on This for a While"), saving over ten pounds a day in CO_2 emissions. In "Light Up Your Life," Gershon suggests installing compact fluorescents, which use 75 percent less energy than incandescent bulbs and last longer. "A Cool School" concerns teaching children to develop sustainable habits.

Some American households are reducing their daily carbon use by fifteen pounds (5,000 pounds a year) by such additional *Low Carbon Diet* tactics as scraping, not washing off plates, hand washing dishes in two tubs (one for soap, one for rinse), and not using dishwashers. Today is the day to help lower the average American household generation of 55,000 pounds of carbon dioxide annually compared with Sweden's 15,000 pounds.

Like John Dineen, Andrew Shapiro, and David Gershon, we accept the challenge of acting with Earth savvy now.

ATTITUDE—We feel wholehearted and gutsy while being green today.

Eshua (Jesus) said, "So don't fret about tomorrow. Let tomorrow fret about itself. The troubles that the day brings are enough" (Matt. 6:34, SV). Eshua asked, "Can any of you add an hour to life by fretting about it? So if you can't do a little thing like that, why worry about the rest?" (Luke 12:25, SV). My grandson Drew says, "Don't let tomorrow be the recovery from today." In the Lord's Prayer, we say matter-of-factly, with no hint of anxiety, "Give us this day our daily bread." We don't say, "Give us fretfulness about getting tomorrow's bread."

There is urgency about setting up a worldwide effective green system. But we need today to change any habits of hectic stress if we want to have maximum green effectiveness. We can say no to some responsibilities and duties and events on our calendar. Occasionally, we can reduce the agenda to zero. We tune out busyness when we've got more to do than hours in a day.

Let's clearly and calmly, day by day, see ourselves partnering with the basic unfolding of the universe in its Creating Process and with a renewable energy revolution. We bank on it that when we get to the next appointment or responsibility, we will have all the energy and insight we need for the moment. We let the appointment worry about itself. We are not in charge of the clock or the movement of the sun. We do not own time. Time does not exist except as a projection of human desire to turn life into a measurable commodity. Let's not be control freaks. If it's not enjoyable at some level within, let's not do it. We can't do things perfectly and can give up that neurotic notion. We let regrets about the past drop like weights. We don't bemoan because it is over, but breathe now and thank it for happening.

We are here within the river, not upstream or downstream, and can think of ourselves as Cultural Creatives, a term coined by sociologist Paul Ray and psychologist Sherry Anderson and also the title of their book. Cultural Creatives make up about 25 percent of Americans and Europeans. Cultural Creatives, according to Ray and Anderson, see reality as one integrated whole system. Reality is not seen as a dualistic system with opposites of past and future against each other. Reality is seen as a Creating Process both scientific and religious. Cultural Creatives let go of the anthropocentric notion that humans are the crown of creation, set dualistically apart from inferior nonhumans, and do not identify with a cartoon showing an American astronaut standing on the moon holding a banner that reads "Finders Keepers."

Polling suggests that hundreds of millions of Cultural Creatives live throughout the world, and my sense is that the existential spirit of cultural creativity is fueling technological breakthroughs in the renewable energy revolution. Cultural Creatives come in about the same proportion from all races, religious beliefs, classes, and political parties, with only one demographic bulge: women constitute 60 percent of Cultural Creatives.

Men and women in Europe, Asia, and the Americas are giving themselves to innovation in the areas of solar, biomass, geothermal, wind, algae, and other technologies to make a renewable energy system work. Let's look at solar energy. By 2050 solar energy could supply ten times more energy than the Earth needs, if conversion of sunlight to electricity becomes competitive with coal conversion. Solar companies that are moving in that direction include Japan's Sharp Corporation, California's Innovalight, China's Himin Solar Energy Group, and a multinational firm called Ausra. A book by Fred Krupp and Miriam Horn, *Earth: The Sequel,* tells numerous stories of entrepreneurs in enterprises like these solar companies who are acting wholeheartedly on behalf of renewable energy.

At the core of being here now for Cultural Creatives is the gutsy pulse of the eternal Present, more powerful than any fixation on the past or future.

Let's assume that you are a Cultural Creative. For you and me it makes sense to align our full attention to what is happening here and now, within and without, as greenness unfolds. We realize that nothing in the universe is more powerful than the evolving present, the Creating Process. Upon this fulcrum rests space and time. We practice nonresistance to the presence of the green kingdom awakening, like our olfactory nerves cannot help but attend to the wood smoke in a campfire. We die to unawareness of and rise to awareness of wherever and whenever the green kingdom is coming.

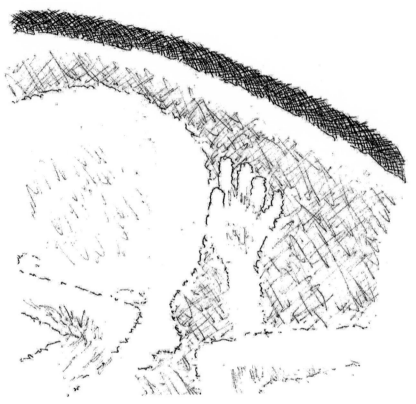

Nearly four-month old baby inside water of womb

3

Inside Water, Out

Would Jesus honor a chimpanzee baby?

> Outer world is not my hub,
> I am right now passing through.
> Within is my center,
> and Spirit fills what I do.
> Heart currents guide me,
> 'round inside's ocean core.
> And I here make my axis,
> in my core ever more.
> – *My lyrics for tune of Albert E. Brumley,*
> *"This World Is Not My Home"*

Tonight it has been cloudy. I just walked down to Many Cedars Beach, and, to my astonishment, the ice shelf was gone. The temperature today was up to around thirty degrees. Two-foot wave crests, lined up four or five deep, rolled successively onto the shore, pushed by a southern wind. I looked at Lake Superior, which some call the "largest inland ocean" in the world, and remembered that its granite bottom is the lowest place in the Americas, seven hundred feet below sea level. The bottom of Lake Superior is one-fourth of a mile below its surface. Some of the water molecules in the waves plunging toward the shore had once been down there in the depths, and were leaping with brisk ions nearly up to my face. Now, I'm back at my computer. Long Nights Moon, in an egg shape, is glimmering through haze and tree silhouettes into sun room.

IN THIS CHAPTER, we recognize that water births new life forms inside out. New forms issue from within the water of wombs out into the world, from inside the Ocean out onto land, and from inside the snow of the winter solstice out into spring. We can celebrate the inside-out principle by valuing babies that come from animal mothers' wombs. Another opportunity pertains to the health of Mother Ocean out of which all organic forms have come. Our hope for green success entails an examination of our psychological wombs, our biological and emotional hearts, and our cosmological stories. We need new stories to appeal to children that show the central import of the Ocean in the sustainability of Earth Community.

PRINCIPLE—Life flows from inside water out.

On one occasion, Jesus saw some babies nursing. He said to his disciples, "These nursing babies are like those who enter the Father's domain." Defying the norms of first century culture, Jesus shocked his listeners by holding up suckling, pristine babies, who had just emerged from womb engulfment, as guides within the Kingdom of God, the Presence of The One. At that time, babies were the property of the father and had no legal rights. The mother had no legal power. If the father disliked the gender of the baby, disliked his wife, or felt he could not afford the baby, he could legally decree that the baby be exposed naked to the elements to wail, wither, and die. He could sell the baby into slavery or give it away. He could keep it to abuse or to nurture. That shows how worthless a nursing nonperson was in first century patriarchal society.

Here was the Rabbi holding suckling babies forth as guides within the Presence of The One above scholars and clergy. The listeners of Jesus were incredulous and said, "Then shall we enter the Father's domain as babies?" (Thomas 22:1-3, SV). The remark of Jesus was so politically incorrect and memorably inside-out that in some early Christian carvings Jesus appeared as a nude infant amid adults.

Writer Anne Lammott in her *Operating Instructions: A Journal of My Son's First Year* describes life in the womb and at the breast in reference to her own child. With ultrasound, she was able to look at her fetus in its fourth month, as in the drawing above. She pretended to identify legs, arms, and the bottom of the baby. She didn't want the doctor to think she was a lousy mother, because she was already anxious about a kid who might not be photogenic. Eventually, the delivery occurred out of the inner ocean of amniotic fluid. Baby Sam came out with his fist balled up beside his head like a power salute, tearing Anne. She shivered, even though she had a fever. While the doctor stitched her up, her heart was about ready to break with mixed feelings, because she couldn't hold Sam and nurse. Then Sam came to nurse at her breast, and he became the most bewitching sight she had ever seen.

My daughter, Tamyala, talks about nursing her baby, Celia. "Nine months ago, there was nobody. Now here is my special somebody, my baby, who is like butter melting into my heart and constructing the strongest bond imaginable. A marriage takes years to bond deeply. But a baby bond is like fast food, right here and now. Celia latches onto nursing easily. She is pretty, perfectly formed, mild, sweet, and tender."

Jesus had an astonishing talk in a womblike cave with the Pharisee Nicodemus (*Niqodimaw*), which was as culturally jolting as his saying about nursing babies. Jesus was in Jerusalem at the end of the rainy season when pilgrims from throughout the Roman Empire attended the spring Festival of *Pesach* (Passover).

There were few inns, so Jesus and his associates had taken shelter in a cave. Nicodemus walked on streets of yellow-red rock toward the cave where Jesus was staying. It was night. Heavy dew in the cool night, pushed inland by a Mediterranean wind, gave relief from dryness. Nicodemus pulled his robe around himself to keep warm and entered the cave. There olive oil lamps glowed, and a rug softened the hard Earth. Jesus offered him a drink of wine.

The Pharisee began the talk. "Rabbi, we know that you've come as a teacher from God."

Jesus said, "*Ameyn ameyn amar ana lakh.*" *Ameyn* is the word amen that we use today at the end of prayers. Jesus used amen at the beginning of the conversation, not in a prayer. The word *Ameyn* means grounded. So, the Rabbi emphasized that what he was going to say was doubly grounded (*Ameyn ameyn*) like rocks and wells of water. Then Jesus said, "Unless a man be born again, he cannot see the Kingdom of God."

Dumbfounded, Nicodemus said, "How can a man be born when he is old? Can he enter the second time into his mother's womb and be born?"

Jesus said, "Except a man be born of water and of the Spirit [*yiled men Mayah Ruha*], he cannot enter into the Kingdom of God." *Mayah* means water, and *Ruha* means simultaneously spirit, wind, and breath.

Nicodemus said, "How can these things be?" (John 3:1–9, KJV). The Pharisee ultimately walked out of the cave into the night, baffled. He trudged back to his house, breathing in *Ruha* and feeling humid *Ruha* gusts made humid by *Mayah* from the Mediterranean Sea.

The Rabbi was teaching that new life does not emerge from Pharisaic rules about rituals, nor from John the Baptist's baptismal practice (Jesus never baptized anyone) but emerges physically from *Ruha* breath, emerges mysteriously from *Ruha* spirit and wind, and emerges physically and spiritually inside out.

The writer, Joanna Macy, who has bridged Christianity and Buddhism, explains a born-again experience as expanding her breathing and awareness to the point where everything outside was also inside: "I had turned inside out, like a kernel of popcorn shaken over the fire. My interior was now on the outside, inextricably mixed with the rest of the world."

Joanna's inner core, creating the sense of connectedness to the outer world, is how nature works. If there is no interior water core, like the Mediterranean Sea, then there is no exterior life! No spirit and wind, no life. No breath, no animal life. The beginning of the Hebrew Bible recognizes Creating Process, energized by spirit, wind, and breath, stimulating newness from inside Ocean out onto land. The planet's Ocean was stirring "without form and void, and darkness was upon the face of the deep; and the Spirit [and Wind and Breath] of God was moving over the face of the waters" (Gen 1:2, RSV). Out of this salty matrix came the dry land, plants, animals, and humans.

Over four billion years ago, ice chunks bombarded fiery Earth, creating our living hydrosphere. Steam, vapor, and clouds formed above and rain fell in between. Ice chunks cooled our planet and pooled into Ocean whose watery circumference brought forth, from inside out, rivers, lakes, and land. She birthed, out of her oceanic uterus, organic bacteria and other aquatic life after the icy bombardment. Wetland plants later colonized land. Today, Ocean occupies 70 percent of our ecosphere.

A sack full of water, like Ocean, immerses mammal fetuses. In a mini-ocean, I spent my first nine months, and then I came inside out. Even out of the womb, water fills 70 percent of my body.

Water is indispensable for life. The 2.3-million-square-mile Coral Triangle in the Pacific Ocean, including waters around the Philippines, Indonesia, New Guinea, and the Fiji Islands, provides a powerful illustration. The Coral Triangle includes 75 percent of the reef building corals and twice as many fish species as any other coral region in the world. This Triangle maternity ward, sometimes called the Ocean's Amazon, generates the greatest biodiversity of any reef system on the Earth. Two of the most powerful equatorial currents on the planet traverse the Triangle and invigorate larvae, mollusks, and other species, as described in the article, "Can Ocean's 'Amazon' Be Saved?" in the *Christian Science Monitor*.

The place where I sit now was immersed in two hundred feet of frozen water during the last Ice Age fifteen thousand years ago. When the ice shield receded, the Earth sprang up after the weight melted off. Thus, the twenty-two islands of the Apostle Islands, including eco-diverse Spirit Island on which I reside now, came inside out of melting ice water.

In the many instances of rebirths issuing from water, there is the regenerative ice and snow of the winter solstice. The pregnant northern hemisphere of the Earth makes merry during the lengthening nights awaiting, with expectant breath, the rebirth of the sun. Christmas is about birth. The Christ Child's birth date was put on December 25 in the fourth century to compete with the Roman winter solstice festival, Saturnalia.

The Christmas crèche symbolizes new birth coming to Earth. At the age of five, my grandson, Erik, arranged a Christmas crèche from the Caribbean. In school at the same time, acorns were a topic. The manger scene with Mary, Joseph, and Jesus was inside a coconut with one end chopped off. Outside the coconut were sheep, angels, shepherds, wise men, and camels. When all the figures lined up just right around the coconut manger, Erik called his mother to come and see. "Look," he announced triumphantly, "I've fixed it so they all can see Jesus in the nuthouse."

Here on Spirit Island in the long dark nights of Christmas season, snow swathes the trunks and branches of every red oak, elm, and maple trunk and branch. Icicles line up on the eaves. White crystals on the greens and browns of the forest concoct a mind-blowing, wet snow extravaganza. A light breeze helps snow clusters fall lazily in happy whiffs here and there to the Earth. Snow decorates the twenty-foot high totem pole to my left, sculpted from top to bottom with a thunder bird, eagle, raven, bear, salmon, and a frog resting on a turtle's back, symbolizing the Native America view of life growing atop the North American Turtle Island. This season is an exquisite time, promising that purple lupine flowers will come out of their snow cocoon in three months.

PRACTICE—We value water in animal wombs and in the Earth's hydrosphere as we promote sustainability.

Since Jesus scandalized his first century world by saying that nursing babies, rather than scholars and priests, were guides within the Presence of The One, he would likely say something scandalous today.

I imagine him being asked by the Nobel Peace Prize committee to recommend a prize winner. The Rabbi addresses the Nobel committee in Oslo, Norway. "Ladies and gentlemen, there have been many political figures and academics, almost no women and no nursing babies on the Nobel Prize list. In our day, we need to regain a more varied ecosystem, and one way is to remind ourselves that humans are not alone in the ability to think. It's clear that primates, African gray parrots, border collies, scrub jays, and other More-than-Humans think. My spiritual brother Rumi said, 'We began as a mineral. We emerged into plant life and into the animal state, and then into being human, and always we have forgotten our former states, except in early spring when we slightly recall being green again.'

"I recommend that you let an expert on chimpanzees like Jane Goodall help you find a baby chimpanzee nursing in the Congo rainforest. Gather TV footage. Don't take the infant out of its ecological home and bring it to Oslo. Award the prize sym-

bolically. Humans are turning our Earth neighbors into domesticated objects. Chimpanzees in zoos are property, don't have
civil rights, and are not held forth as models. Let's value the inside water out process of this chimpanzee baby — 98 percent of
her DNA overlaps with ours — to fashion a new world in which
babies of all threatened species have a chance to be born."

It might help us identify with this Nobel Prize recommen-
dation of Jesus if we consider the latest research about animal
intelligence. A recent experiment shows that a chimpanzee has
better mental retention than the British memory champion, Ben
Pridmore, according to the article by Fiona Macrae in the *London Daily Mail*. In less than thirty seconds, the British champion
can memorize the order of a shuffled deck of cards. Pridmore
spends evenings memorizing numbers that include four hundred digits.

A seven-year-old chimpanzee male, Ayumu, did three times
as well as Pridmore in a computer game recalling the positions
of numbers on a screen. Ayumu and Pridmore both watched a
computer screen in which numbers in various positions flashed
for a fifth of a second. White squares appeared after a fifth of a
second and obscured the numbers. The participants had to touch
the white squares concealing the numbers in order from the lowest to the highest. Ayumu was right 90 percent of the time and
Pridmore only 33 percent. This accomplishment by Ayumu is
breathtaking. The researcher, Professor Tetsuro Matsuzawa of
Kyoto University, says that people are prejudiced to think that
chimpanzees are inferior to humans in every area of intelligence.
Young chimpanzees remember patterns and sequences with astounding accuracy.

Other primates and a variety of species, including birds and
octopi, show amazing thinking skills, according to the article
"Minds of Their Own: Animals Are Smarter than You Think" in
National Geographic. An orangutan named Azy, whom Rob Shu-
maker has befriended for twenty-five years, communicates with

abstract keyboard symbols and shows an understanding of the emotions of others. In the wild, orangutans use tools to extract insects from tree holes and twist leaves into bundles and use them like dolls. A bonobo primate named Kanzi uses more than 360 keyboard symbols and understands thousands of words. Kanzi communicates in sentences, makes stone tools, and plays the piano. According to a theory of researcher William Fields, Kanzi speaks English too high and too fast for human ears to understand.

In addition to valuing the womb water birthing animals, we value Earth's largest fresh water resource, Lake Superior. The water temperature of Lake Superior is warming twice as fast as the air temperature. An article in the *Christian Science Monitor* states that less of Lake Superior is freezing over in winter, reflecting less sunlight and absorbing more heat. The ice road, solid enough to carry cars, that has formed annually in the winter during the last century between Bayfield and Spirit Island has not frozen solid enough for car traffic twice in the last decade. The advent of warmer water layering on top of cold water is now taking place in mid-June instead of early July.

Lake Superior's water around Spirit Island, a geographic neighbor of over twenty islands in the Apostle Islands National Wildlife Refuge, is evaporating more rapidly than it used to. Recently, it was eighteen inches below its normal level. There is less rain and ice, and evergreen trees are turning burnt orange and dying. South of here, a state forest caught fire a few months ago. The head of the Apostle Islands Wildlife Refuge, Bob Krumenaker, says that if global warming continues, dryness will cause half of all tree species more than ten miles from Lake Superior to die out in thirty years. Heat will cause walleye fish to disappear from northern waters.

The Apostle Islands and wetlands on shore are among the most bio-diverse in the world, mixing coniferous and deciduous forests. Mammals include wolves, black bears, otters, raccoons, fishers, foxes, and coyotes. Among the over two hundred bird species are cormorants, loons, and bald eagles. A wide selection of national park personnel, historical preservationists, and conservationists in Canada and the United States recently voted this wildlife refuge area their favorite in the United States, above Yellowstone and Yosemite, as reported by Hope Hamashige in the *National Geographic News*. People cannot purchase any part of the Apostle Islands, except a number of properties on thirteen-mile-long Spirit Island. Part of the appeal is that both Bayfield, Wisconsin, from which people take a ferry to Spirit Island, and Spirit Island have no suburban pollution. There are no franchises like Wal-Marts and no subdivisions. In addition, 25 percent of the island is devoted to a wilderness preserve, and we recycle all solid waste. We have no traffic lights. There is no place to rush to.

My wife, Donella, and I consider our second home of Eagle Moon on Spirit Island a dream. It's a nine-sided, cathedral-ceiling home with sun room extension to the south, floor to ceiling windows, and a nine-sided and windowed cupola set within a gorgeous forest. We feel deeply contented in this place.

We also feel uncomfortable with the more than thousand-mile round trip from our Illinois home and with the double burning of fossil fuels at two houses. My carbon footprint is large. If every human on Earth used as much energy as I do, it would require the resources of six Earths. Our discomfort has become so strong that we have decided we cannot live with ourselves and set an example for our grandchildren and others if we continue to own two homes. We have put this house on the market, and before this book has gone to press, it has sold.

Lake Superior is not the only body of water with problems. The Colorado River watershed is in trouble. Lake Mead and Lake Powell, which supply water and power to millions in California, Arizona, Nevada, and New Mexico, stand a 50 percent chance of running dry by 2021, according to a study by the Scripps Institution of Oceanography in La Jolla, California. Overuse by humans and a reduced snowpack are causing a reduced river flow on the Colorado. More reservoirs are not the answer. Changes needed include xeriscaping (low water use) for homes and commercial buildings, fewer water intensive crops like alfalfa, and miserly irrigation techniques.

The largest ocean in the world, the Pacific, has over two million fishermen and women extracting more than sustainable numbers of Ocean species and using dynamite fishing on the reefs in the Coral Triangle. The heat of the east to west El Niño current of 1998 has bleached and destroyed a significant number of reefs. Over 150 million people live on and pollute the shores of the Coral Triangle. To address these issues, a consortium of international environmental groups, banks, and six nations in the area are developing an action plan, which the World Ocean Conference likely will approve in 2009.

We who reside in the richest countries of the world need to reduce our carbon footprint to reduce the risks of a rising Mother Ocean, Robin Bell reports in an issue of *Scientific American*. On the ice sheets of Greenland and Antarctica, heat is causing the surface ice to melt and puddle in lakes. The lakes find crevices and siphon water to the bedrock, which creates slippery skids for huge sections of the ice to slide toward the Ocean. The thawing of either the West Antarctica ice sheet or the Greenland ice sheet would raise Ocean levels around twenty feet and inundate south Florida. If the East Antarctica sheet slips into the Ocean, the sea rise would be 170 feet and inundate nearly all of Florida.

Additionally, three highly significant climate changes are occurring in the hydrosphere with a connection among them. Investigators have no consensus about the connection, as explained by climate journalist Fred Pearce in the book *With Speed and Violence*, but the dangers are large in each of three categories of change:

1. There are possible major shifts in the worldwide under-water Ocean currents, influenced by thawing in the polar ice regions. These shifts may cause unusual and unpredictable weather everywhere.
2. There is a possible reduction of the humidity and rainfall production of the Amazon rainforests. This reduction may cause major droughts in South America and elsewhere, and catastrophic fires in a tinder-dry Amazon basin.
3. There are possible major shifts in the wind currents and temperature of the equatorial Pacific that may cause unusual and unpredictable weather in Indonesia and the Andes of South America.

A specific threat to Mother Ocean is her rising acidity caused by the absorption of increasing amounts of carbon dioxide. Historically, eroding limestone creates large proportions of calcium carbonate in seawater, which neutralizes acid and provides carbonate for marine creatures to build shells and reefs. Acidity off the tip of the state of Washington's Olympic Peninsula is rising ten times faster than projected. In the Southern Ocean, where cold water absorbs carbon dioxide faster than in warmer water, the diminishing ratio of carbonate is threatening the existence of tiny sea snails which are food for a wide variety of fish. Sea creatures are finding it hard to form shells and corals. Existing shells and reefs are beginning to dissolve.

Finally, the hydrosphere is in crisis because the amount of water available on Earth is fixed and finite, and human consumption is going up (www.worldwatercouncil.org). The human population has doubled since 1900, but water use is up sixfold, with 66 percent of that going to irrigation for agriculture. Over-irrigation from the 1960s to the 1990s diminished the Aral Sea (the fourth-largest lake in the world) in Kazakhstan 75 percent, killing off fish and other marine life and causing what some have called the worst ecological disaster of the twentieth century. Recent efforts by the World Bank and the Kazakh government have restored the north part of the Aral Sea to 40 percent of its original size. Farangis Najibullah writes about this in "Central Asia: Aral Sea Shows Signs of Recovery," on Radio Free Europe online.

The shrinking Dead Sea in Israel and Jordan is down significantly and has become two separate bodies. When I saw this split in the Dead Sea directly, it was traumatic for me. I expected the Dead Sea to look like it has looked on maps since my childhood. I was shocked and frustrated by the overuse of water in irrigation in the upper Jordan Valley and in Israeli cities.

Globally, the water available per person is down 33 percent, with half the Earth experiencing a water crisis. Americans consume two times more water per person than Europeans and six times more per person than sub-Saharan Africans.

Ways to conserve globally are set forth by Peter Rogers in *Scientific American*. Set high prices for water in the areas of highest use, so as to give incentives for saving water. Reduce irrigation water by drip and other methods. Adopt low-water sanitation as, for example, Stockholm does by separating excrement from urine and using both for fertilizer. Exploit such new, more economical desalinization technologies as reverse-osmosis and carbon nanotubes, as Singapore and Tampa Bay are doing.

What can we Americans do as individuals to protect the hydrosphere source of life? Let's collect rain in barrels rather than draw down central utility sources for lawns and gardens. Let's plant a rain garden to hold moisture and prevent soil erosion. Let's use leaves and other mulch, and water less outdoors. Let's put in low-flow showerheads, and shorten our showers. Let's use buckets rather than hoses or car washes, and reduce water consumption at least fivefold. Let's put in a low-flush or a composting toilet. Let's reduce the number of times we use a dishwasher or a washing machine, and for the latter, let's use a front-loader rather than a top-loader. Let's put in a permeable driveway.

And, let's stop wasting money on the manufacture, transport, and disposal of plastic containers used for bottled water. Americans spend on average $400 a year for bottled water, whereas drinking tap water costs on average 51 cents a year, 800 times less. San Francisco has banned bottled water, the city of Seattle refuses to buy it, and Chicago taxes it. The high tide of drinking bottled water, which is not a health benefit, has occurred. Americans have begun going back to the tap.

In addition, let's remember that water does not primarily come from a tap or a bottle, but from the precious Ocean, the mother of life.

ATTITUDE—We increase heart and hope for green action by self-examination and by telling stories to children honoring Ocean's creativity.

The theme of this chapter is to experience water—within a womb, a breast, a lake, and the Ocean—as the physical and spiritual source and inspiration for reducing products, renewing energy, and redoubling eco-diversity. Jesus said something fascinating about the most important water organ in our bodies. He said, "Blessed are the pure in heart [*lebah*], for they shall see God" (Matt. 5:8, RSV). In Aramaic context, the Rabbi was saying, "Contented folk experience their *lebah* radiating energy and seeing The One everywhere outside."

The *lebah* is a juicy pump, circulating watery blood throughout intricate veins and arteries. Being born again is to let this miraculous, internal organ inspire our emotions, thoughts, and actions to radiate a fantastic awareness of *Allaha* and Earth Community inside and outside.

The heart of a fetus begins beating within three weeks of conception. The heart beats before the brain of the fetus even starts to form and can beat after a person's brain dies. Inside the chests of both mother and fetus, their hearts go in syncopation "th'boom, th'boom, th'boom." The heart of the embryo develops nerve bundles. Anne Lammott looked at the ultrasound of her four-month fetus and gaped at the heart, beating as boldly as the intense bursts of a pulsar. She started to cry.

At the birth of any baby, there are more heart nerves sending signals to the brain than vice-versa (www.heartmath.org). The electrical waves produced by the beating heart in general are fifty times the amplitude and a thousand times the strength of a brain wave. The brain and other organs synchronize their waves with the heart's wave.

To have heart, or, as some Christians say, to invite Jesus into one's heart, are not necessarily clichéd expressions. To participate in life fully, we start with our heart, not our head. Our heart is in the middle of our body, not at the periphery in our head. Wisdom begins inside water and flows out.

It has been a formidable challenge for me to learn how to mother myself from within. That is one of the lessons Jesus tried to teach the Pharisee, Nicodemus. Traditionally, I have projected onto females my demands for them to nurse, take care of, and wait on me. Patriarchal attitudes cling rather tightly to my skin. One afternoon, I was on the table of my energy therapist who was opening up my chakra energy centers, from my feet to crown chakra at the top of my head. The therapist, Gretchen, sang in a fluted manner on several pitches close to my head. Then silence.

I went to sleep on the table and had one of the most preposterous, stunning, and wondrous dreams of my life.

Look with me at my dream field of vision. Not more than a foot away from my dream eyes appears the opening to *my* womb. I stare at it, thinking it will disappear. But here it lingers like a still photograph. It's strikingly clear, and I speak in the dream, "I can't believe it. It's my entrance to *my* womb. Not someone else's. Mine."

The image faded, and I woke up. Today, I claim that dream to empower me to mother my experiences from my internal water organs, both symbolic womb and physical heart, inside out.

Letting our insides mother us is tricky as we attempt to green our behavior. We can hide behind our anonymity as weirdos of the planet, because no intrinsic and external systems make us individually accountable. Green incentives, carbon taxes, and other systems are not in place to reduce our guzzling of energy. Our peers are acting the same as we, so we have implicit permission to be wasteful. In a fuzzy way, responsibility belongs to everybody. We cannot sense easily our portion of liability in our daily decisions. Thus, unsustainable behavior is not exactly our fault.

In our hearts, we sense some personal responsibility, but shadows inside mix ignorance, feeling, and fantasy. The shadows include secret, dangerous, and irrational energies. For some of us, the shadows are driving us powerfully to cook scientific evidence. Some of us are arguing that global warming is not taking place, or if it is, it is not because of human activity. Others argue that global cooling is on the way, ignoring the catastrophes being caused by unsustainable human acquisitiveness. In the shadows are also floating anxieties about the long struggle ahead for our descendants. An informally adopted nephew, Paul, is angry that my generation is leaving him vulnerable. Paul's goal is to go into politics and make the hard decisions about changing our addictive consumerism as a species.

One attitudinal shift we can make concerns the kind of stories we tell our children and grandchildren. We need to concentrate on stories that teach the fundamental truth of the primacy of the Ocean in our lives.

I offer two such stories. These stories make this chapter comparatively longer than other chapters, and at first you may feel that the stories are peripheral to the green aim of this book. But I encourage you to let yourself sink into the stories, and to recognize that we need to reclaim a green cosmology that the indigenous tradition has known for thousands of years. One story comes from the Onondaga Native American tradition and the other from Japan.

It might help to imagine that you are telling the following Onondaga story to children at bedtime. You might want to read it out loud, so as to let the resonance of your voice help you embody the primal value of the Ocean in nourishing a green perspective.

Once upon a time, before there was land, there was Mother Water. Sky Woman fell down toward Mother Water from Sky Tree, holding in her hand just a few of Sky Tree's seeds. Down, down, down she fell. Water animals, like Swan, Duck and Beaver saw that she was in trouble. Two swans flew up, touched wings, and caught her. Slowly, they brought her down where water animals were watching.

"She is not like us," said Duck. "She doesn't have webbed feet. She can't live in Mother Water like us."

"What shall we do?" said Beaver.

"I know," said Loon. "In my dives, I have gone very deep and have seen that there is mud below me. Let's bring up some mud so that Sky Woman will have a place to stand."

All the water animals thought this was a great plan.

First Duck dove down far beneath the surface, but he could not get to the bottom and floated back up. Then Beaver went deeper where it was very dark, but he could not get to the bottom. Loon tried, swimming with strong webbed feet. She was gone for what seemed forever, but she too failed. Other water animals also failed.

Finally, a small voice spoke up. "I will bring up some mud or die trying."

The water animals looked around. It was Muskrat.

He dove and swam and swam. Muskrat went so deep that he thought his lungs would burst. He swam deeper still. At last, just before losing his strength, he reached out one small paw and grasped at the bottom. Muskrat barely touched it, and then floated up, almost dead.

The water animals looked at Muskrat, thinking he had failed. Then they saw that his right paw was tightly shut.

"He has some mud," they shouted. "Now what shall we do with it?"

"Place it on my back," said a voice. It was Turtle, who had watched Muskrat's dive.

The water animals took the exhausted, nearly dead Muskrat and placed his right paw on Turtle's back. To this day, you can see the scratches of Muskrat's paw on Turtle's back. These scratches mark the thirteen sections on the shell. Each section stands for one of the thirteen cycles made by the moon in its travels from new to full and back again during the year.

While Muskrat scratched, the tiny bit of mud fell from his paw onto the back of Turtle. Immediately, the back of Turtle began to grow. His back grew larger and larger. The mud grew larger too until both back and mud space were big enough for Sky Woman. She stepped onto the Earth, opened her hand, and let seeds fall into the mud. From the seeds, trees came up. Many Native Americans call North America Turtle Island.

Eventually, Sky Woman scooped up some Earth, breathed into it the breath of life, and made Dog. Finally, she made Human. Then all the water, sky, and land animals sang a song to celebrate new life on Earth.

Well, we say to our kids, "That's a bedtime story for tonight. Now you know that Earth and land animals, including humans, came from Mother Water. What part of the story do you like? Who is your favorite figure? Would you like to hear another story, this time about how Mother Water feeds us? You would? OK."

So, we tell another story to children at bedtime. I got the basic ideas for this next story from Japan. In Japan every child learns about two figures who are as famous as Mother Goose is in America. The names of these two figures are Otohime and Urashima Taro. In the 1990s, I bought in a bookstore in Nagoya, Japan an illustrated children's version, written in Japanese, of the story of Otohime and Urashima Taro. I have translated the name of Otohime to one of its meanings, Radiance, and the name of Urashima Taro to Youth, and I have named three sea characters who don't have names in the Japanese version.

The Japanese story begins.

A young girl named Youth walked one fine morning along the Ocean's beach. Youth waved goodbye to her human mother. "I'm going fishing," she said.

With her pole and lures, Youth got into a rowboat in a lagoon, and rowed out through the surf. Soon Turtle appeared, and offered to give Youth a ride. Youth rowed back to shore, and tied her boat to a tree. She waded out to get on the back of Turtle who had followed Youth. Turtle said, "I want you to meet my queen."

"What's the queen's name?" said Youth.

Turtle laughed. "Radiance."

Youth, chuckling, did not believe her good fortune. Youth rode on the shell of Turtle, who dove down into the water. Down both of them went until they saw, swimming up to meet them, three unusual figures.

Turtle introduced them. "Youth, I'd like you to meet Ashray."

Ashray, its body as clear as glass, swam up and met Youth nose to nose.

Next was Selky, a sea lion that had a tail and a human form from the waist up. And, third, there was WaterLeaper, a winged toad. The five of them continued down together until they saw in the distance below them a gleaming labyrinth with thousands of passages. They swam inside and met many more figures, each fascinating and unique. Youth could scarcely believe her senses.

At the center of the gleaming labyrinth was a large room with foods gathered from every place in the Ocean and arranged in a circle. In the center was Queen Radiance, who had the form of a human and was beaming with shining colors from within the Ocean. Queen Radiance had links to the networks of life in the Ocean.

Radiance took Youth by one hand and swam with her and Turtle to a treat. "Take one bite. Now ride on Turtle's back around the circle. Ashray will offer you a bit of another treat."

For hours, Youth took a bite (none the same as another), made a round, and then repeated a round, sampling an indescribable array of sour and sweet smells and tastes. Ashray, Selky, and WaterLeaper swam with Youth.

Finally, Radiance said, "Youth, I have enjoyed your visit very much. You are a wonderful young person. I am going to give you a beautiful box on one condition. You must promise never to open it."

Happier than she had ever been, Youth said, "Queen Radiance, I thank you with all my heart. I will never open your gift."

Taking the box, Youth got on the back of Turtle and waved goodbye to Queen Radiance, to Ashray, Selky, WaterLeaper, and to the many other attendants at the banquet. The gleaming labyrinth got fainter as Turtle swam up to the beach where Youth had tied her boat. Youth couldn't wait to tell her tale to her mother.

"Thank you, Turtle. Going with you was so much, much more fun than fishing in my boat. Goodbye." Turtle flipped a leg and said, "Farewell." Then Turtle dove down.

Youth looked at the box and the Ocean and felt terrible. Youth missed Queen Radiance. Without thinking, Youth pulled off the wrapping of the precious gift from Radiance and opened the box.

The instant the box opened, Youth choked, coughed, and saw that the wood in her boat had rotted. The tree, stripped of its leaves, had died. The house where her mother had been a few hours before had vanished. Youth looked down at her hunched and wrinkled body and was shocked almost to death. She was now ninety years old and had white hair.

We conclude this story by saying, "Children, that's it for stories tonight. I'll tell the stories again later to remind you and me that Earth herself and all of us who live on land come from Mother Water."

We often forget that our food is a gift from the Ocean and from rain. Food is not a gift from a box. We must not partake of the food of life with forgetfulness. If we think that food comes from containers in stores, we will get sick, age, and risk death. No water, no food! Daily with gratitude let's remember Radiance, queen of the Ocean.

Life moves from inside the water womb out!

*Image of Jesus as child from the Roman sarcophagus of Junius Bassus,
357 Common Era
(www.religionfacts.com/christianity/history/jesus.htm)*

4

DOWNSIDE UP

WOULD JESUS LAUGH 400 TIMES A DAY?

Dear God, I am Amearican. What are you?
— *Robert, quoted as misspelled in* Children's Letters to God

You can always tell a family with a five-year-old in it. You have
to wash the soap before you use it.
— *Anonymous*

In this chapter, we marvel at the upside-down view of Jesus
that kids are, as he would say today, the coolest members of
the human species. Imitate them! We examine embryonic development of experiential green education for youth. We learn
why and how laughter can be therapy for the world, if adults
would model themselves after children who laugh on the average of four hundred times a day.

PRINCIPLE—Children are the greatest humans.

The associates of Jesus wanted to know who is greatest in *Malkuta Shemaya,* the Presence of the Web of Energy. The word *shemaya,* as mentioned earlier, connects sight and sound represented
by the sun (*shemesh*) and by the call to hear (*shema*) in a Sabbath

gathering. The associates wanted to know who is greatest in the Kingdom of Heaven.

The Rabbi called a child over and had her stand in front of him. He then spoke emphatically. "I swear to you, if you don't do an about face and become like children, you will never enter Heaven's domain [*Malkuta Shemaya*]. Therefore, those who put themselves on the level with this child are greatest in Heaven's domain" (Matt. 18:1–4, SV).

This statement was as outrageous for its time as what Jesus said about adults needing to follow the guidance of nursing babies. Here we listen again to a saying of his that is culturally bizarre. Children in the first century, like nursing babies, had no status in law or custom. Until Jewish boys came of age, the oldest males had by far the most power, including the power of life and death in their own families.

Imagine the president of the United States during a State of the Union Address. In the company of members of Congress, whose average age is sixty, he brings in children under twelve to stand around him. We hear him announce that his address is not about the economy, energy policy, or education. "My fellow citizens, unless you do an about face and become like these children, you will not embody what it means to be an American citizen. Put yourself on the same level as these children if you want to be the greatest in American society." Can we picture a standing ovation?

A child's sense of smell is sharper than adults and more like a dog's, who can smell one hundred times better than adults. One of the most advanced senses babies have at birth is smell, far more advanced than sight, as discussed by Anita Sethi in the article, "Your Baby's Sense of Smell," in *Babytalk*. At two weeks, a newborn smells the difference between his mother's and another woman's breast milk. For the first two months of life, a tot prefers the scent of his mother to anyone else's. Mom, even unwashed, smells like roses.

As adults, many of us miss most of the richness of the smells in nature. We have, to coin a phrase, Smell Deficit Disorder. We have names for thousands of colors. Dictionaries contain over one hundred thousand words. But an ancient and powerful sense is aromatic. We can differentiate only a few hundred smells in odor identifications tests, and usually we can name less than half of these.

Compared to adults, children are the greatest in the Presence of the Web of Aromas.

On one occasion, Jesus was laying his hands on children, perhaps stroking their shoulders, while his associates were scolding the kids for bothering the Rabbi. Jesus scolded his associates. "Let the children alone. Don't try to stop them from coming up to me. After all Heaven's domain [the Presence of the Web of Energy] is for children such as these" (Matt. 19:13–15, SV).

A baby's sense of touch is also more extensive than adults. A fetus receives jostling touches by total immersion in amniotic fluid of five million sensory cells on the largest and most complex organ on its body, the skin. Touching is such an amazing and powerful sense in infants and children that a child who is not stroked and massaged either dies or grows up stunted in emotions, mind, and body. The healthiest babies receive massages head to toe daily. Children, often into their teens, keep around a special blanket, a pet, or a cuddly toy animal. My grandson, Karl, when age ten, loved to cuddle with his toy animal, Ducky, and cried when he thought that it had gotten lost in the mail after Aunt Sandy had sewn a reincarnation of his Ducky. Hugs are as natural as breathing for children, and we notice that Jesus laid his hands on kids. Roger Dobson discusses "How the Power of Touch Reduces Pain and Even Fights Disease" in the The Independent (London).

At five months old, Anne Lammott's son, Sam, was brilliant at exploring by touch. With all five fingers of his hands, he clawed and rubbed at available nooks in his universe. He probed and investigated his feet (which he also sucked), his mother's chest, and his plastic-covered pad. In the silence of his room, the only sounds made were by the moving of his wee fingers. The sounds were like a person buried alive in a coffin, scratching the top from the inside. Anne wanted Sam to stop because he was getting on her nerves. But Sam was not about to end his perpetual fact-finding. Scritch, scritch, scritch.

Compared to adults, children are the greatest in the Presence of the Web of Touch.

When I was growing up, after the age of ten there was little or no hugging. My aunt Esther was the exception. Her presence was uncomfortable when I was a teen, because I was not used to a full body-press embrace. Not until my thirties did hugging a person become part of my life.

A child typically is more spontaneous, playful, curious, and imaginative than an adult. It's not likely that an adult would write like the child's epigraph above, "God, are you Amearican?" A child, not an adult, is curious enough to see if he can pour milk, ear to ear, through his own head. Children get soap filthy, so it has to be washed. Children, untainted by taboos, picture themselves picking the lice off God's clothes.

The best-selling author of *Expecting Adam* and of *Leaving the Saints*, Martha Beck (who was raised a Mormon), asked her son Adam, who has Down Syndrome, "Where does God live?"

"God lives in pizza. God lives in Mexico."

Martha foresees a day when all members of our species will give up on a fragmented God who is present in some people and not others and will toast Muhammad, wave to Buddha, and high-five Jesus and Rabbi Hillel.

I am imagining while I write that Jesus in 2003 was in the presence of me and my three-year-old grandson, Alexander Joseph, and that Jesus said to my grandson, "Don't try to stop Alexander Joseph from coming up to me."

That summer, Alex and I went into a canyon in Texas hill

country, two blocks from his house. Alex announced that there were real lions in the canyon jungle. I growled and roared like the big male lion in the zoo we had seen the day before. The lion had charged at us toward the fence until his massive head and paws were only three feet away. In the canyon Alex grabbed my hand as my growling continued. "Be careful," he warned as we crawled up a slope in the jungle. Eventually we pulled back, because Alex said, "It's too scary."

Back on the canyon floor, we picked wild flowers. Alex used one as a pretend phone. He pushed numbers and said, "We're OK, Mom. Don't worry, Mom."

We walked on small limestone boulders hauled in and placed randomly beside a dam. Each jagged boulder pile became a mountain climbing expedition. Alex said regularly as his feet slipped and he was about to fall down, "I can do it! Don't help me. Don't hold my hand!"

Soon wild flower stalks became fishing poles. We stood by the lake behind the dam, and he used his stalk fishing pole to catch, he said triumphantly, "bigger fish than yours." He knocked a fish I caught off my pole. Then his pole, dreamlike, became a weapon, and he challenged me to a duel.

After a standoff sword fight, he took my plant-stalk weapon out of my hand, and it changed into an enchanting clock, which he wove into a chain-link fence. Alex said, "You are my daddy, and we have seven more minutes to fish before we go home." So we fished some more. "OK, Daddy, it's time to go" he said. "When we get home, we'll get in the car, and go out to get an ice cream cone."

Compared to adults, children are the greatest in the Presence of the Web of Imagination.

Jesus took children in his arms one day, and again his associates objected. This time, Jesus got indignant (Mark 10:13–15). Jesus did not say to the children, You must believe some religious doctrine, or I am going to tell you to go get lost, like my temple-socialized associates who have been trying to shoo you away. Religious leaders said children were the least in the Presence of the Web of Energy. The associates of Jesus thought he was foolish to extol children.

A child absorbs learning by osmosis in the school of life. A child does not have to say, "Lord, Lord," to be in the Presence of the Web of Energy. Jesus explicitly noted this: "Not everyone who says to me, 'Lord, Lord,' shall enter the Kingdom of Heaven" (Matt. 7:21, RSV). Many indigenous groups see children as the freshest and wisest souls from the Spirit world. In earlier centuries, aborigines in Tasmania had a custom of letting children tell their dreams first thing in the morning to instruct the whole community.

In the gospels, Jesus so frequently emphasized the role of children within the Kingdom of Heaven that the Christian community for several centuries remembered him as a child with curly hair, as in the sketch I made above, and not as an adult and not on a cross. A new book skillfully documents this century-long regression from the Presence of the Web on Earth and from children to the cross (see Brock and Parker, *Saving Paradise: How Christianity Traded Love of This World for Crucifixion and Empire*). In the sarcophagus of Junius Bassus, which I used as a model for my sketch, Jesus sits on a pedestal with his head higher in elevation than bearded Peter standing to his right and bearded Paul to his left. On another sarcophagus, Jesus appears standing as a nude toddler with the hand of John the Baptist on his head.

PRACTICE—We build the green movement downside up.

In the comic strip *Hi and Lois*, a boy says to his dad, "Kids today have it tough."

"In what way?"

"Your generation protested against the war in Vietnam. We have to save the entire planet."

Since children are going to be around to face ecological dilemmas longer than adults, they are the ones to whom we should give priority in the greening of our educational systems. To help symbolize this priority, I recommend that we return to picturing Jesus as a child as his earliest followers did for nearly half a millennium.

Experiential education is the most effective, efficient, and powerful way to learn. We cannot continue to treat children as empty heads to receive a formal education still conceived of as the traditional three Rs of reading, 'riting, and 'rithmetic. We need to treat youth as full-bodied learners (as we can see with kids and electronics today), since they possess greater dexterity and keener senses of smell, touch, imagination, and other skills than adults. My granddaughter, Brianna, aged ten, text messages and phones daily an incredible network of family and friends. Kids have the potential to be the best teachers in a world needing to advance a green revolution that practices the new three Rs of reduce, renew, and redouble. Children are our latent teachers in developing love of biodiversity.

Preschool kids who touch, smell, and grow their own vegetables learn to taste and eat different vegetables. The Early Sprouts program, which has spread from Keene State College in Keene, New Hampshire, to preschool centers throughout New Hampshire, has kids growing carrots, tomatoes, green beans, bell peppers, chard, and butternut squash. Surgeon General Steven Galson has recognized that this Early Sprouts program involves children modeling for us all how to deal with obesity.

We have other models like the Journey for the Planet program. Thousands of students in hundreds of schools and youth programs throughout the United States have used this curriculum to teach a low-carbon diet. I hope some of you readers of this book will become inspired to provide leadership for this program. It requires a few hours to prepare and then to meet with a school or youth organization representative. To get started, visit www.empowermentinstitute.net/lcd.

In my community of Bloomington/Normal, Brigham Elementary School has Living Green teams of Eco Kids who push blue recycling bins around and write about environmentally friendly topics in the school paper. One of our two school districts, Unit 5, is installing geothermal systems and has saved more than $2 million in the last two years by turning off 3,800 computers when not in use, shutting off lights, and turning down thermostats.

An organization in New York has developed a fledgling, eight-page magazine, *Conservationist for Kids*, and has carried out a test distribution run in March 2008 to five hundred fourth grade classrooms throughout the state. The aim is to give a little shove to kids to go outside. The inaugural issue deals with students keeping a field journal, recognizing tracks and droppings of animals, and finding places where animals feed. A teacher's supplement correlates to math, science, and technology learning standards for fourth graders. The three-times-a-year magazine, in its next two issues will deal with birds and with climate change, writes William Kates in an article in the *Pantagraph*.

We have another model, the course "Wilderness 101," in the 843 acres of New York's Central Park. This is an after-school and summer course that since 2002 has involved over two hundred teenagers from around New York City. The kids are intern horticulturalists whose varied roles include planting and weeding, giving tours, picking up garbage, and making films and creating comic books about the park. The films are twelve minutes in length. One film, for example, is based on interviews of people who fish in the eleven-acre pond in Central Park. A place the teenagers treasure is the Hallett Nature Sanctuary in the southeast corner. The interns wear with pride green

T-shirts that say Central Park Conservancy and bring family and peers to what one intern calls "teenager-hood." The kids develop roots in this green section of their city, and they often return to Central Park after they have graduated. See www. monitorweek.com/2007/0726/p13s03-legn.html?page=2.

Another example is university student volunteers designing solar-powered homes (www.solardecathlon.org). In October 2007, the U.S. Department of Energy sponsored its third Solar Decathlon. This third Decathlon involved twenty teams from across the United States and around the world building homes that met ten criteria, including running all appliances and an electric car solely on solar energy and using materials that were already on the market. One student on the Massachusetts Institute of Technology team was Samina Ali, who plans a career in designing and building green homes. "I've done carpentry for Habitat for Humanity," she says. Another volunteer was Amy Tighe, who plans to be a green real estate agent. The Department of Energy's aim is to mainstream solar housing by 2015.

We can give incentives for green youth community service. The United States can take the lead in forming an international network of Green Corps organizations that stress experiential education. The commitment needs to be a global crusade, like the wholehearted commitment of every person in the United States to the winning of the Second World War.

Only this time, the mobilization of resources in a network of Green Corps organizations is for people in all nations to win a victory over our own human inertia and our own denial about being at war with Earth Community. Now is the time for brave, daring, audacious, and nervy commitment for us to become the greatest, greenest generations in human history since the beginning of the Agricultural Revolution.

In addition to experiential green education for children, we need an activist revolution with young people at the forefront.

Today's youth can give downside up leadership to what needs to be the largest social movement in the history of the human species.

Bill McKibben's Step It Up campaign (http://stepitup2007. org) conducted a five-day, fifty-mile march from the Green Mountains to Burlington, Vermont around Labor Day 2006 involving one thousand people, many of them youths. The result was that Vermont legislators pledged to back an 80 percent reduction in carbon emissions by 2050. Step It Up, with high participation by youths, helped organize two thousand demonstrations for cleaner energy in all fifty states in 2007.

In another activist example, youths in over seven hundred campuses and high schools created Campus Climate Challenge and held the first national youth summit in Washington, D.C. in November 2007. Over six thousand youths gathered and lobbied for five million new green jobs, a moratorium on coal plants, and a 80 percent reduction in fossil fuel emissions (the same goal as Step It Up) by 2050. A twenty-year-old leader of this movement, Shadia Fayne Wood, says that her generation, outnumbering baby-boomers by three million, are fighting for their lives. This movement plans active lobbying in every congressional district during the election in November 2008, Shadia reports in the Spring 2008 issue of *Yes!* magazine.

A civil disobedience event on Monday, March 2, 2009 at the Capitol Power Plant in Washington DC, co-sponsored by Greenpeace and other green groups, involved thousands of young people. The weekend before this Monday the biggest national conference for students and youth dealing with climate change, called PowerShift '09, convened, and then demonstrated at the coal-fired plant that powers federal government buildings. The message is that coal (50 percent of electricity comes from coal) is bad, and is now driving our atmosphere above a safe ratio of 350 parts per million of carbon dioxide. Coal is filthy at its source, removing mountaintops in West Virginia and Kentucky, and making everything that breathes sick. The idea of "clean coal," unless plant emissions are sequestered, is a lie. (See www.capitolclimateaction.com)

ATTITUDE—In sustainable action, we have hilarity like children.

We adults can better complement youth green action if we laugh like children. Adults laugh on average fifteen times a day, twenty-five times less than children. These are mind-boggling statistics. Laughter is inner calisthenics, with a torrent of air coming out as fast as 70 mph. Natural laughter enhances resilience in creating sustainable communities. See a fuller discussion of laughter exercise in Chapter Nine.

In the *Piranha Club* comic strip, there is a discussion about carbon offsets.

A character says, "Ernie, did you know that just by breathing you add tons of carbon dioxide to the atmosphere? As a citizen of Earth, do you know what you can do to fight global warming? You can buy a carbon offset! Give us a dollar, and Enos and I will hold our breath for a full sixty seconds!"

Ernie says, "If I give you sixty dollars, will you hold your breath for an hour?"

Looking down on three raindrops on a dollarweed leaf

5

Dropping Rain

Would Jesus picket against warfare?

Dear God,
Maybe Cain and Abel would not kill so much if they had their
own rooms. It works with my brother.
— *Larry, quoted in* Children's Letters to God

Who would Jesus bomb?
— *Bumper sticker*

I n this chapter, we recognize that rain drops indiscriminate-
ly. Rain drops on roses, a process reminiscent of the phrases
"raindrops on roses, and whiskers on kittens" from "My Favorite Things" in *The Sound of Music*. Rain falls on all species.
Rain plays no favorites among soils, plants, animals, primates,
and humans within Earth Community.

PRINCIPLE—Rain drops have no enemies.

In a *Peanuts* comic strip, Lucy says to Charlie Brown on a bus
driving in the rain, "Why do we have to go on a field trip?"
"So we can learn more about nature."

Charlie Brown, Lucy, and Linus get off the bus and stand in a downpour.

Lucy says, "Just what I need. A chance to study rain up close."

Jesus said, "God causes the sun to rise on both the bad and the good, and sends rain on both the just and the unjust" (Matt. 5:45, SV). *Allaha* causes sun and rain to bless clan insiders and outsiders, righteous and unrighteous, and Jewish groups and Roman conquerors.

Sun and rain are wildly inclusive. Sun and rain bless American soldiers and Al Qaeda jihadists. The sun doesn't shine on one region of the world and not on the other. The realm of sun and rain is cross-species, cross-chemicals, and cross-particles, including sharks, E coli bacteria, and zebras.

Rain treats people without prejudice and behaves like mixed-race kids treat each other in Anne Lammott's church. One Sunday, her son Sam was in his walker for the first time, and the preschool kids pushed him repeatedly across a room. The preschool, interracial kids and Sam howled with glee and were beyond being in love with each other and with fully captivating romps.

Most people, whether in the first century or today, unlike sun and rain, are inclined to separate the good people from the bad and relatives from nonrelatives. Once when the family members of Jesus went to meet him, people informed him that his mother and brothers were at the edge of the crowd. Jesus raised his eyes toward the sky, I imagine, in mock puzzlement and said, "My mother and my brothers—whoever are they?" I suppose he winked at his brothers at the edge of the crowd, signaling that his exaggeration was blatantly sardonic. Pointing to his associates in the inner circle, he said, "Here are my mother and my brothers. Whoever does God's will, that's my brother and sister and mother" (Matt. 12:48–49, Mark 3:31–35, SV). Possibly he kept joshing. "Look at James and John! Here are my sisters!" The tomfoolery of Jesus was to challenge people's clan and gender shibboleths and to expand the idea of family to include anyone.

Let's look at another daffy saying of Jesus. "If any come to me and do not hate [set aside is the meaning of the Aramaic] their own father and mother and wife and children and brothers and sisters, they cannot be my disciples" (Luke 14:26, RSV). In Thomas 55:1–2, Jesus asks associates to set aside pop and mom, brothers and sisters, but leaves out wives and children. In Thomas 101:1–3, it's just pop and mom.

Set aside mom and pop as if they are enemies? Now that doesn't make sense, some of us muse. But Jesus was using hyperbole to strip off the sanctity around the manipulative patriarchy, not attacking his parents and siblings. Clan rules preferred that first cousins marry first cousins to keep clan boundaries sharp. He was using wit to help people break free from their clan and gender imprisonment.

My grandson Drew likes to say, "Family is a relative term."

Jesus said another thing that is especially oddball, zany, and deviant and goes outside a strand of Jewish historical logic. "As you know, we once were told, 'You are to love your neighbor,' and, 'You are to hate your enemy.' But I tell you, [*Hab b'eld'baba.*] Love your enemies" (Matt. 5:43–44, SV). Tight clan customs in the first century encouraged a violent mentality of us versus them. Male elders in the first century had, as we have noticed, the power of life and death. The Aramaic word for enemy, *b'eld'baba*, did not refer just to people outside the clan but also referred to arbitrary, patriarchal rulers inside the clan.

Let's reflect for a moment on how deeply imbedded the practice of hating one's enemy was in Hebrew tradition. Isaac's first-born son, Esau, hated his brother, Jacob, who was loved more by their mother, Rebekah (Genesis 27:41). Maybe Jacob and Esau didn't have their own rooms when they were growing up. King David asked God to slay the wicked. David said, "Do I not hate them that hate thee, O [Yahweh] Lord. And do I not loathe them that rise up against thee? I hate them with perfect hatred. I count them my enemies" (Psalms 139:21–22, RSV). David didn't pray, like the child in *Children's Letters to God*, "I wish that there was not no such thing of war."

Clan ethics in Hebrew culture encouraged revenge against those who brought dishonor or shame to anyone in the clan. An example involves a Canaanite clan leader's son, Shechem, who had sex with Jacob's daughter, Dinah, before a betrothal. Afterward, Shechem asked Jacob for permission to marry her. The sons of Jacob, Simeon and Levi, said to Shechem that if all his clan men circumcised themselves, he could marry Dinah.

After Simeon and Levi made the marriage pledge, Shechem believed them. Shechem got all of his clan's males to cut off their foreskins. On the third day after the circumcisions, while the men were sore and scabby, Simeon and Levi got revenge for the violation of clan rules, never having intended to keep their pledge. The two deceivers ambushed and slaughtered the unhealed men of Shechem's clan and stole their cattle, donkeys, sheep, household belongings, wives, and children (Gen. 34:1–31).

Stephen Wright's one-liner, "I'd kill to get a Nobel Peace Prize," fits this horrible clan story. Simeon and Levi lied and killed. At the end of their murderous rampage, there was the peace of death. Jacob's clan had restored honor, not by an eye for an eye, but by hundreds of corpses and hundreds of stolen goods and wives.

Now let's return to the spectacularly unexpected saying of Jesus, "*Hab b'eld'baba.* Love your enemies." The Aramaic word *hab* evokes affinity reaching out from our inner recesses to penetrate, like a blaze, unconditionally whoever and whatever is in its path. *Hab* is something like that kinship we feel for all those cheering for our basketball team. *Hab* is something like the loyalty we feel for all those sharing our nationality, singing our national anthem, and reciting our pledge of allegiance. But *hab* is deeper than kinships and loyalties that are not inclusive of the entire Earth Community. *Hab* is the feeling of astronauts and cosmonauts who, from space, embrace the whole blue-green planet, all people, species, and locations.

The category of enemy, from the heart habit of *hab*, is an absurdity. Martin Luther King's "inescapable network of mutuality" describes a *hab* world. Within love there are no bits and pieces of separate selves and private salvations, but only relationship. To follow Jesus and to be saved from the sins of hate and of the war narcotic means to join his peace insurrection and to resist governments that promise peace through violence.

Do we have fears, hurts, and losses in our relations with our human and More-than-Human neighbors? Of course. We can honestly acknowledge fears and losses and also turn to a deep default setting of our core that knows that *hab* does not hold grudges and forgives self and others.

Hab is at the heart of the teaching of Jesus about the inclusive nature of the Kingdom of God and of Earth Community. A *hab* heart has no bad blood.

PRACTICE—We develop cross-cultural and cross-species friendships around the globe.

Today, Jesus says to us to love elementally so that those who appear to be enemies disappear. In his career, he never taught anything that would support military institutions. The bumper sticker asks satirically, "Who would Jesus bomb?"

I picture Jesus today looking to our primate cousins, the bonobo, who live on the left bank of the Congo River and who do not practice enmity. What would Jesus say about our cousins?

The Rabbi would say, "Consider the bonobo primate." (Consult the bonobo references listed in the sources.)

These cousins of ours, whose DNA is 98 percent identical to ours, cooperate with each other. Field researchers have never seen a bonobo deliberately kill another. Embraces between and within genders and ages occurs daily in their communities. Bonobos do not polarize between good and bad bonobos or good and bad bonobo clans. Bonobos have no enemies inside or outside their species, and thus follow the Rabbi much more fully than humans.

We need to imitate our bonobo cousins and abolish the uneconomical and unhealthy institution of human warfare. Right now, the world's annual military budget is 1.1 trillion dollars, and the American military budget is over six hundred billion dollars, more than all the rest of the world put together. In the United States, military spending proposals are usually separated from the regular budget and do not receive careful analysis for more cost-effective alternatives. Conservatively, American contractors and bureaucrats waste 25 percent (some say over half) of these resources. For example, the twenty American B-2 stealth bombers cost over $40 billion dollars, and they have never served a clear military purpose. Each plane takes 124 hours of maintenance for one hour in the air. The antiballistic missile system has also been a stupendously expensive boondoggle. In the United States, we spend $1 on education and health for every $5 on the military. In the long run, military expenditure does not boost employment or the basic economy. Military organizations take young people out of families and communities where they have been taught that killing is murder and forces them to commit ritual murder of whomever the government and public opinion tells them is an enemy. Veterans have a disproportionate higher rate of suicide, divorce, and homelessness.

Warfare involves ecological destruction. In Vietnam, the United States sprayed Agent Orange, which included a deadly carcinogen, on forests. Agent Orange defoliated large portions of the Quang Tri and Tay Ninh provinces, turning them into moonscapes. Vietnam veterans in the areas of the spraying developed unusually high rates of skin cancer.

Ninety percent of our 200,000 year *homo sapiens* history involved no institutionalized warfare. During that time was there infanticide? Yes. Sporadic killings? Yes. But platoons and companies whose primary duty was to annihilate other platoons and companies on command? No. Institutional warfare began about six thousand years ago in Central Asia and the Middle East. But it can be repealed, as legal slavery has been.

Today, Jesus says, "Consider the bonobo."

A male bonobo may briefly chase another male away from a female, but the assertion does not end in violence. Immediately after the chase, the two males hug. A female may strike a juvenile, and its mother may lunge at the striker. The two females then immediately hug to release anxiety and to affirm cooperation. That's it. These close cousins of our species make a lie of the theory that our violent genes made our species invent war and that war is natural.

Today, we can invest some of the trillions of dollars spent year after year on worldwide military budgets to expand conflict management education, green community service, and international police, special, and peacekeeping forces. Cooperative social skills in nurturing the human community, cultural anthropologists tell us, made our human species more ubiquitous that any other mammal species. A mother holds and caresses her baby for years. Friendly gestures like smiles, handshakes, back patting, and hugs build trust. Social dancing, drumming, singing, and telling stories around the campfire link hearts and minds. We need training in interpersonal and intercultural listening and in experiential community education. We especially need community service in a form I mentioned earlier, an international Green Corps program.

Today the Rabbi says, "Consider the bonobo."

Bonobos, our cousins, are hospitable in daily interaction. Females are on the same footing as males. Female elders act in concert to end male power displays. When stress arises in gathering and eating food, in jealousy, and in meeting another bonobo community, bonobos express free and consensual body-to-body, odor-to-odor embraces. Juveniles cavort imaginatively and play a game like blind man's bluff.

We are beginning to show the same kind of bonobo hospitality through the onset of international networks of green home stays, including access to local biodiversity. A combination of people-to-people and people-to-species friendship on a worldwide basis is a way to advance sustainability.

Considering the bonobo, we can move from the Industrial Revolution to the Eco-Effective Revolution that would bring benefits to all the species around us by the way we make our products. A company called MBDC (McDonough Braungart Design Chemistry) is consulting with companies to put into practice a new design philosophy that is changing the world. Instead of cradle-to-grave products dumped in landfills at the end of their life, MBDC creates cradle-to-cradle cycles. For example, Nike is beginning to make leather that composts. MBDC certifies companies that do three things: recycle or compost environmentally safe products, employ renewable energy, and use water efficiently. The end result of eco-effective products is a healthy ecology. The founders of MBDC—an architect, William McDonough, and a chemist, Michael Braungart—have written a book, *Cradle to Cradle: Remaking the Way We Make Things*. These two authors have worked with the Ford Motor Company to redesign the original River Rouge plant in an eco-effective manner and with Mayor Richard Daley to seek to make Chicago the most environmentally friendly city in the world.

ATTITUDE—We renew our hearts by making restitution for the abuse our species has wreaked on the world.

The extent of the abuse is reflected in recent records of rising CO_2 levels and rising temperatures. The year 2005 was the hottest on record. The next hottest years have been 2007 and 1998. I remember 1998 vividly, watching roadside grasses catch on fire, seeing pictures of the Mississippi dry up so that no barges could navigate, and sweating through a record number of days in June above 100 degrees. The third hottest years were 2002 and 2003. In 2003, over thirty thousand people died from the heat in Europe, most in France. The fourth hottest year was 2001, and the fifth hottest, 2004. For evidence, look to the website of NASA's Goddard Institute for Space Studies. Carbon dioxide levels are higher today than at any time in the last 420,000 years, and the rate of extinction of species will not decline until green living increases.

Our need for wholehearted restitution for living unsustainably connects to a perception of Jesus in his day. At one point, his friends believed he was mentally ill because he was driving out demons. They thought he was out of his mind. Scholars from Jerusalem said that the prince of demons possessed him (Mark 3:21–22).

Some people will think that those of us who want to make restitution for our nongreen behavior are out of our minds. But to address the responsibility that we feel for our human imperialism against our own and other species and their habitats, we need a collective event to help expel our malignant spirits and refurbish our hearts.

Jesus gave us a clue about an atonement ritual. "If your hand gets you into trouble, cut if off! If your foot gets you into trouble, cut if off! If your eye gets you into trouble, rip it out!" The Rabbi continued, saying that it's better to be one-handed, one-footed, and one-eyed, than to have your whole body burn in a hellish garbage dump (Mark 9:43–47, SV).

We don't need species-wide atonement gore like that signified by the hand and foot amputation metaphors of Jesus. We've had more than enough gore already in the last century. Rather, we need green atonement action!

I envision an international atonement event near Kilimanjaro

National Park in East Africa accompanied by the launching of a movement I have imagined called Ecoholics Anonymous. The highest free-standing mountain in the world and the tallest in Africa, Kilimanjaro, is losing its glacial cover rapidly. At the current rate, ice will disappear from it within a generation, and the loss has been causing drought throughout the area. The Deep Rift region of East Africa is the birthplace of human primates. An international gathering here would signify a going home to the tropical Deep Rift valley where human primates became *homo sapiens*. The Deep Rift, including the cities of Jerusalem and Mecca, marks the cleavage between African and Asian tectonic plates and extends from Turkey to South Africa.

Here in East Africa, representatives would symbolically amputate and rip out papier-mâché hands, feet, and eyes and toss them into a purification fire. Through an Internet site, people could participate in communities everywhere. At the Kilimanjaro gathering, the representatives would ratify processes promoting an Eco-Effective Revolution and establishing international Green Corps and Ecoholics Anonymous groups.

Ecoholics Anonymous groups could use sayings by Jesus. The Rabbi said that if you love those who love you in your clan, what merit is there in that? After all, even non-Jews love those who love them in their clans. "Do favors for those who hate you, bless those who curse you, pray for your abusers." (Luke 6:27–28; Matt. 5:47, SV).

Green Jesus today says, "Why do you think you are exceptional when you keep your favors and love within the human clan? If you don't bless and pray for those who are in other species, how are you exceptional? Have you prayed for threatened species and habitats today? Have you asked forgiveness for poisoning your Earth home for your great-grandchildren, an intergenerational form of taxation without representation?"

Members of Ecoholics Anonymous would dedicate themselves to ending the human warfare against the Earth and to create sustainable communities. Here are five pledges I propose for members of Ecoholics Anonymous. These pledges are modeled on those in Alcoholics Anonymous, the most successful self-help group in human history:

1. I admit that I often act to enlarge product consumption, to waste energy, and to reduce eco-diversity.
2. I make a list of the attitudes and actions that make me insensitive to More-than-Humans and seek to remove these attitudes and actions from my character.
3. I pledge allegiance to The One, by any name, and I ask for the will to reduce products, to renew energy, and to redouble eco-diversity.
4. I make amends to More-than-Humans by being in awe of and praying for threatened species and habitats and doing Green Corps projects in my community and around the world.
5. I volunteer to help form and mentor Green Corps groups.

PART TWO

Wild Community

In the spring of 1960, I had a primal walk in the rain. I walked the circumference of the city of Bloomington, Indiana at night. It was right before talking my prelims for my doctorate. I left my green bungalow just after dusk on the east side of the Indiana University campus at the headwaters of the city of Bloomington's Jordan River which meanders through the campus. Dressed in shorts, a T-shirt, and sandals, I was heading north when both a cool drizzle and a haunting spell began. I prayed and asked for divine guidance and assistance.

An inner voice, so pronounced it seemed audible, said, "Taste me in the rain dripping down your face. Stick out your tongue and sip me. Smell me in the humidity." I forgot that hours were passing as I tasted, smelled, and walked. I was not conscious of being cold. "Watch me in the dark shadows of the trees. Listen to me in the silence. My name is I Am Who I Am. Feel my wetness on your body." Rain trickled down my body onto my striding feet. Eventually, after going west, south, east, and then walking north on the "circumurban" highway, I came out of my meditation zone and realized dawn was near. "Sense wild nature with all your senses, and then you will know me."

A monumental irony of this all-night walk was that what I got from seeking guidance about my prelims, which propelled the walk, was not what I expected. What I received had nothing to do with academic knowledge but with wildness. The huge stash of academic knowledge in my tamed head at that point was Piled Higher and Deeper (PHD) than at any time before or since. The all-night walk did not have an ongoing effect on my habits, for I proceeded to focus upon academic research and teaching. But, over time, that primal walk has echoed in my consciousness.

While sitting at my computer, one sound sequence on the "American Wilds" CD that repeatedly surprises and pulls me in is thunder and rain. Hearing thunder for the first time in the spring, Kickapoo Native Americans in the region around Eagle Pass, Texas, leave their jobs to gather for a festival. Thunderstorms rumbling, cracking, and splashing on the roof and skylight of my Illinois home, Tree Haven, irresistibly amaze me. One exciting, wild night in Wisconsin, I was in a tent partly afloat in rainwater. Lightning divided the air, followed by long, booming cadenzas bringing the atmospheres back together. I was spellbound by the sensory overload.

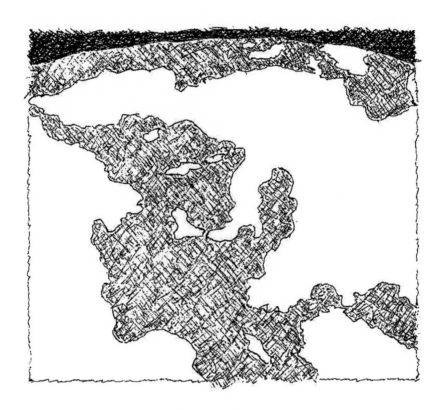

Earth as seen from space

6

SOILED GOODS

WOULD JESUS GROW VEGETABLES IN THE FRONT YARD?

Someone sent me a postcard picture of the Earth. On the back it
said, "Wish you were here."
— *Stephen Wright*

Earth's here for everyone,
and feeds upon our sun,
of trees we sing.
Globe where many species died,
globe of blue Ocean's pride,
under each mountain side,
let Earth's gong ring.
— *My lyrics to the tune of "My Country, 'Tis of Thee"*

Last night and today have been cloudy and I could not see
Long Nights Moon or the sun. A while ago, I went fifty yards
from my door to a special space between two trees, red oak
and maple. Around me were red and white pine, ash, and cedar.
Last year in this special spot, I used eye-screws to put in place
horizontally a six-foot pipe between the red oak and maple eight
feet above the fungi, leaves, needles, and soil of the Earth. Before

going to this location today, I put two metal sleeves, each with a hook on the front and with padding inside, around my boots at the ankles and snapped the sleeves in place. When I got to the two trees, I grabbed the pipe, pulled my feet up with their inversion boots, and hooked them over the pipe. Then I swung upside down. My head was in the breathtaking, or was it breathgiving, position of inhaling ions of snow close to Earth.

Upside down, my field of vision capsized. Hundreds of trees hung from Mother Earth above and dangled into cloudy sky below. Inversion swinging never fails to remind me that it is wise to get my head out of superiority attitudes and down lower into connective attitudes with the iron and nickel core of gravity in the center of our planet. Having finished my skull-in-the-Earth gravitation experience, I sit now at the computer looking through the window in the sun room at the inversion site from which I just came. I am remembering words I just have sung upside down, words inspired by a traditional folk song, "Standing Like A Tree" (quoted in the Green Lyrics section at the end).

Hanging like a tree, with my feet straight up,
    my branches wide and open.
Come up rain, come up sun, come up fruit to my heart
    that is open to be hanging like a tree.

THINGS WE HAVE—ORANGE juice, sweaters, houses—come from the Earth. In the story told in Gen. 1–2, the storyteller mentions the Earth twenty-six times. The first male's name, *Adamah*, means Red Earth. Palestinian soil is red. Each creative day when Earth brought forth someone new, God said, "It's good." The word Earth occurs over seven hundred times in the Bible.

PRINCIPLE—Earth produces by herself.

One day Jesus stood on a boat off shore in a cove of the Sea of Galilee near Capernaum telling parables. "Suppose someone sows seed on the ground, and sleeps and rises night and day, and the seed sprouts and matures, although the sower is unaware of it." *Ar'ah geir eta pira.* Earth produces grain by herself (Mark 4:26–28, SV).

The Rabbi lived during a time when the calendar year included many festivals about the generative power of the soil. The people of Nazareth planted and pruned, but whether they were awake or asleep, the Earth kept on bringing forth vegetables and fruit on her own.

The annual rhythm of wet and dry season festivals, set at various dates according to agricultural and moon cycles, helped ground Jesus. Let's review the festival cycle in the first century and see the links to the rhythms of the Earth. *Pesach* (Passover) introduced the dry season around the end of March and beginning of April. Another name for *Pesach* is Festival of the Barley Harvest. Fifty days after Pesach, near the end of May and beginning of June, came *Shavuot*. Another name for *Shavuot* is Festival of the Wheat Harvest. As the dry season was ending around the end of September and beginning of October came *Sukkot*. This festival celebrated the harvest of grapes, figs, and olives and the sowing of barley and wheat. During December, Hanukah occurred. It was the time of the return of the rainy season and the rebirth of the sun. Another name for Hanukah is Festival of Lights, celebrating a military victory by the Maccabees. This festival lasted eight days with the lighting of a candle on each of eight stems on a candlestick holder called a menorah. The stem patterns of Jerusalem sage plants were a model for the menorah design. Around the end of February and beginning of March during the last weeks of the rains came *Purim,* marking the deliverance of Jews from massacre by the intercession of Queen Esther.

Songs for these festivals originated in the earthiest book,

Song of Solomon (Song of Songs), in the Bible. It's the only book in the Bible in which the names of *Allaha,* Yahweh, and God in their myriad forms do not appear. In Song of Songs, what does appear are members of Earth's wild community who demonstrate vividly varied textures, tastes, and fragrances.

Both the Song of Songs and the parable of Jesus about Earth producing by herself highlight that the Creating Process of The One is materializing day and night diverse plants, animals, topographies, and water expressions whether we humans are aware of this or not. Turning upside down agricultural images that feature the farmer, the Good Earth parable of Jesus in the boat declares that farmers are not the prime movers in the soil's productions. Mother Earth is.

Today, we often honor the same principle. We have Earth Day. During the Halloween festival, we feature the harvest of pumpkins and at Thanksgiving, the harvest of cranberries, goods of the soil—soiled goods.

PRACTICE—We redouble eco-diversity by raising food in our yards.

Given the need to increase the biodiversity of the gifts of the soil, we have the opportunity to think about our grass lawns in a new way. Here is a dialogue about lawns from www.richsoil.com/lawn/god.html.

God: "St. Francis, you know about gardens and nature. What is going on? What happened to the dandelions, violets, and stuff I started eons ago? I had a perfect no-maintenance garden with plants that grow in any soil. I expected to see a vast spectrum of color, but all I see are grass rectangles."

St. Francis: "It's the tribe of Suburbanites, Lord. They started

calling your flowers weeds and went to great lengths to
kill them and replace them with grass."

"Grass? But it's boring. It doesn't attract butterflies, birds,
and bees. Warm weather makes grass grow fast. That
must make Suburbanites happy."

"Apparently not, Lord. As soon as it grows a little, they cut it
with incredibly polluting lawn mowers, sometimes twice
a week, and bag it."

"Bag it? Is it a cash crop?"

"No, Sir. Just the opposite. They pay to throw it away."

"When it gets hot in the summer and the growth of grass
slows, Suburbanites must be pleased for it saves them a
lot of work."

"You are not going to believe this, Lord. They drag out hoses
and pay more money to water it so they can continue to
mow it and pay to get rid of it."

"Enough. I don't want to think about this anymore. St. Cath-
erine, what movie have you scheduled for tonight?"

"*Dumb and Dumber*, Lord. It's a really stupid movie
about—"

"Never mind. I think I just heard the whole story from St.
Francis."

Can we stop fixating about the soil around our houses and buildings being postcard-perfect, mono-cultural grass rectangles?
Yes, we can. During the Second World War, Americans grew
40 percent of their food in home Victory Gardens. I helped tend
them at that time. How many quarts of peas and beans and corn
did I help can? Hundreds. Today, an utterly essential transfor-
mation is occurring, one in which I am participating, that will
shift the way we get our food. This change has the potential to
reduce our carbon footprint by as much as 30 percent and to
increase biodiversity.

People are taking out some or all of their lawns and planting dinner. Books are appearing with such titles as *The Year I Ate My Yard*, by Tony Kienitz and *Edible Estates: Attack on the Front Lawn*, by Fritz Haeg. People are rewriting landscaping codes that forbid the front yard going into food crops. Protests occurred at a public hearing against landscaping codes in Sacramento, California, where twin, eleven-year-old boys dressed as a carrot and a tomato. The city changed the law.

A graduate student in Santa Monica, California, Nat Zappia, grows 35 percent of his food in his yard and spends only about $100 on plants. He explains that his front-yard garden is like walking a dog. "None of our neighbors talked to us," he says, "until they saw vegetables going in where there used to be sod." A landscape designer, Rosalind Creasy, keeps eight hens and one rooster in her yard. Creasy says that at least once a day a child visits her yard, experiencing reality instead of reality TV. Some people are putting grape arbors in their yards. Leigh Anders of Viroqua, Wisconsin, says, "This movement can start with simply one tomato plant."

Best-selling author Barbara Kingsolver in her book, *Animal, Vegetable, Miracle: A Year of Food Life*, demonstrates vividly that we are what we eat. Barbara, her husband, Steven, and nineteen-year-old daughter, Camille, left the Sun Belt and its fossil-fueled food pipeline and headed for the rural "promised land" in Appalachia. There they ate only food they had grown themselves or bought locally. Kingsolver's good-humored narration of her experiences reveals surprises about zealous zucchinis and the sex lives of turkeys. Her family has put the kitchen table, local foods, and their neighbors back at the center of their lives.

The principle that "Earth produces by herself" can teach us to increase conservation tillage more than ten times our current use and to stop pumping nitrogen and pesticides into the soil. We can increase wild prairies, forests, and wetlands, and thereby decrease the amount of topsoil that erodes into streams and waterways. Let's expand local, organic agriculture and stop importing food from thousands of miles away and paying exorbitant transportation costs. I moan, "Do I have to give up bananas?"

ATTITUDE—With courage, we reduce unsustainable uses of our yards and make our music more green.

Today, we can use the spirit of an earthy parable Jesus told about a woman and yeast to revise conventional uses for our yards. Jesus said, "Heaven's imperial rule [the Feminine Presence of the Web of Energy] is like leaven [yeast] which a woman took and concealed in fifty pounds of flour until it was all leavened" (Matt. 13:33, SV).

In the centuries before the time of Jesus, Jews had come to believe that unleavened flat bread without yeast was a metaphor for upright, moral living, and leavened bread with yeast was a metaphor for polluted, immoral living. In the first century, many people washed, mopped, and scoured their houses before Passover to eliminate yeast to show how moral and righteous they were. Male heads of households presided at the Seder Passover meal.

Listeners gasped at the parable of Jesus. They couldn't believe this unimaginable, politically incorrect saying. I assume they talked back to the Rabbi. "You can't have a woman taking the lead at Passover time. You can't put yeast in the Passover barley flour. The bread won't be flat." As in his other sayings, Jesus turned conventional morality upside down with extreme hyperbole.

I picture the woman in the Rabbi's parable to be a solid mature, broad-shouldered and muscular woman. With strong arms, Woman Elder thoroughly stirs yeast into one measure of flour weighing about fifteen pounds until it mixes into every part of the barley flour.

Woman Elder next gets another large container, measures

out another fifteen pounds or so of flour, and vigorously stirs yeast into it. Then she gets a third container as large as the other two, puts in flour and pounds yeast into it.

Now Woman Elder lifts up each container, dumps its leavened flour onto a large table, and sculpts a gargantuan blob weighing fifty pounds. She pounds and smashes the single dough blob. Punch. Poke. Pound. The blob rises into a mass as large as her body. Woman Elder divides her immense heap of leavened bread into small portions. She checks on her children, and leaves flour tracks throughout her house until no place is free from "corruption."

She puts her small portions of leavened bread in the oven, and inhales the pleasures of baking. Then she puts her "polluted" buns, permeated with yeast, into large bushel baskets. She lugs her buns up and down lanes, and gives them to mischievous kids to distribute throughout her entire neighborhood.

Through this parable, Jesus taught that the Feminine Presence of the Web of Energy fills the Community of Life regardless of religious rules prohibiting leavened bread and regardless of propriety demanding the scouring of houses to free them of yeast. Using the Woman Elder parable, the Rabbi encouraged an awareness of a moral sense that transcends conventional morality or immorality. Jesus burlesqued narrow-minded literalism.

Are we ready to transcend the conventional impropriety of tearing up our lawns? Are we ready to plant vegetables in the front yard where grass used to grow? Are we ready to build a greenhouse beside our driveway and grow food at home rather than have it imported from thousands of miles away?

In addition to challenging convention about our yards, we can create greener music by using earthy lyrics from the Song of Songs, sung and danced during the festival season in first-century Nazareth. During the festivals, there was circle dancing and drinking of wine. These events were not a single day, but spread over many days.

The theme of Song of Songs, a poetic allegory, is passion for Earth Community. Lyrics ooze delight in wild animals — doves, gazelles, foxes, lions, leopards, and ravens.

The dominant singers in Song of Songs are a dark and enchanting Woman and her male lover, both thinly disguised as two voices of Mother Earth. Enchanting Woman is wild. She sings, "In sandy Earth or in deep valley soil, I, a wild flower, grow" (Song of Songs 2:1-3, RSV). "The voice of my beloved! Behold, he comes, leaping upon the mountains, bounding over the hills. My beloved is like a gazelle, or a young stag." He echoes back, "O my dove, in the clefts of the rock, in the covert of the cliff, let me see your face, let me hear your voice." (2:8-14). He hastens to her presence, marked by aromatic myrrh, frankincense, and spices (4:6-14). Earth Community members clearly are actors in the musical ensemble. "Living Water, you are a fountain, a well, a river. Come, north winds and south winds! Breathe upon my garden" (4:15-16).

Images in Song of Songs involve an array of numerous More-than-Humans. There are twenty-five kinds of trees, flowers, herbs, fruits, nuts, and spices. Water manifests itself in torrents, floods, streams, and dew. The hills, clefts, caves, ravines, valleys, groves, and stones of Earth appear, along with cultivated pastures, orchards, gardens, grapes, and vineyards. Elemental sun, moon, wind, air, and fire figure in the allegory.

The Song of Songs, the book most diverse with More-than-Humans in the Bible, is saturated with the sense of smell. Here is a guide to explicit mentions of aromas. We smell the fragrance of anointing oils, of nard (a perennial herb), of myrrh, and of henna blossoms. Fig trees and vineyards give off their essence. The traveling retinue of King Solomon exudes zippy odors of myrrh, frankincense, and powders of merchants like a column of smoke. The male lover in the allegory seeks a mountain of myrrh and a hill of frankincense. He says of Enchanting Woman that her love is more fragrant than any spice, the scent of her garments is like the scent of the cedar of Lebanon, and her garden emanates wafts on the wind. She replies that her hands drip with liquid myrrh and that her male lover's cheeks and garden are like beds of spices. She smells the blossoms of pomegranate and nut orchards. The male lover says the breath of Enchanting Woman is like apples. Mandrakes (plants of spring) offer their flavorsome whiff. The beloved makes haste like a gazelle upon a mountain of spices.

Today, we need to use our biblical tradition in the Song of Songs to encourage musical ardor and love for Mother Earth, who produces from the soil the good plants and animals among whom we move and have our being. It is not as if we have not celebrated nature in our musical history. In our waltz tradition we honor trees in "Tales from the Vienna Woods" and a river in "The Blue Danube." Throughout this book I have written lyrics for popular tunes that reflect our human membership in Earth Community. I give these examples partly as a way to stimulate a green creativity in our bluegrass, country, rock, rap, and other musical idioms. In this creativity I urge you who are songwriters to include earthy lyrics from the most green and sensuous book in the Bible, the Song of Songs.

Approximate size of black seeds in pods (I took away the lining of the pod in my drawing to reveal the seeds) and of golden, four-petaled mustard flowers in a cluster with buds waiting to open in the center of the cluster

7

MUSTARD AND DANDELION

WOULD JESUS SPRAY WEEDS?

What did the skeleton say while riding his Harley?
"I'm bone to be wild."
— *Anonymous*

Too many bugs and leeches and spiders. Please spray the
wilderness to rid the area of these pests.
— *National Park visitor comment*

Tonight, December 21, is special. It is the winter solstice. It is the longest night of Long Nights Moon. For me, the winter solstice season lasts from before Thanksgiving to Valentine's Day, and it typically includes all or part of Christmas, Hanukah, and Kwanzaa festivals. Here is the time when the Earth is readying herself to be reborn. The winter solstice also symbolizes the six months of the year, from the autumn equinox to the spring equinox, when nights in the northern hemisphere are longer than the days. It also represents an idea I have that, for a fifty year period, Earth Community will take a sabbatical rest, like trees in winter.

The weather has turned cold again. I walked down to Many Cedars Beach and heard what sounded like crashing waves. But

I knew that couldn't be true. The crashing was not spasmodic, but continuous. Getting closer I heard riotous percussion. Tinkling. Clinking. Jingling.

Lake Superior and the wind were pushing ice floes and ice sheets toward the shore. The floes were breaking up and trying to make ice stacks of pieces that wouldn't hold still. The orchestral composition in several keys simultaneously was chiming. Pinging. Dinging.

No composer could write down a polyphonic score like this. Standing on the bluff, I saw shards jumping, turning, and sliding. Long Nights Moon, nearly full, enjoyed the ceaseless motion. I got down within the symphonic players and clanging, ringing, and pealing noises popped up here and there. Each clink, tiny by itself, teamed with other clinks. Collectively, primal clinking created an omnidimensional, powerful, surround sound.

PRINCIPLE—Wildness manifests itself everywhere.

One day, the associates of Jesus were curious, as they must have been most of the time, wondering about the next cockeyed thing he would say or do. They asked him, "What is *Malkuta Shemaya* like?" What is the Presence of the Web of Energy, the Kingdom of Heaven, like?

Jesus said, "It's like a [*hardeta*] mustard seed. It's the smallest of all seeds" (Thomas 20:1–3, SV; Matt. 13:31–32; Mark 4:30–32; Luke 13:18–19). The Roman biologist of the first century, Pliny the Elder, wrote that the mustard plant grew contagiously, and once sown, it was virtually impossible to get free of it. Spindly stalks of mustard with golden, four-petaled flowers and black seeds grow one to three feet tall and attract birds where people do not necessarily want birds that might eat barley or wheat seeds.

For the first sixty years of my life, I did not want to experience Israel and Palestine from a tour bus where the tour guide would offer speeches at sites where masonry shrines mark the life of Jesus. The Rabbi didn't ride a bus. His feet got filthy. His sweat stank. He was, like a skeleton, "bone to be wild." Memorial buildings did not exist in first-century Palestine. I was determined that, if I were to go, I would experience life along its natural byways the way he did.

Reading in the 1990s about the *hardeta* weed seed and its riotous character, I became convinced that Jesus must have been a riotous character as well. For the first time, I wanted to visit the Holy Land.

My wanting to visit the Holy Land reminds me of the story of three American-Jewish fathers who had different motives for sending their sons to the Holy Land than I had for going. The first said, "I sent my son to the Holy Land to study Hebrew, and he came back a Christian." The second said the same thing happened to his son. The third, a rabbi, said, "My son, like your sons, came back a Christian." The three decided to talk to God about their predicament. The rabbi prayed, "God, we come to you for help. We have sent our sons to the Holy Land to become learned Jewish men. And they come back Christians! We do not know what to do." Suddenly, a voice filling the heavens said, "I can't believe you are telling me this. The same thing happened to me!"

I went to study the Holy Land and came back wholly impressed with holy wildness. For example, I could never have imagined before going over that there was some connection between dandelions, which I have been digging up all my life, and the ministry of Jesus.

Both mustard plants and dandelions take over where humans do not want them to be and spread out of control. Like a *hardeta* seed or a dandelion seed, the Presence of the Web of Energy, the Kingdom of Heaven, sprouts all over the place.

I have observed mustard in Israel and Palestine in varied months of rainy and dry seasons since 1997. I have walked places during each trip that Jesus walked and have found *hardeta* growing untamed in every season. Once I was swimming in a concrete pool beside the Jordan River near Mount Hermon, and I couldn't trust my eyes. Right before me, out of a crack in the concrete side of the pool, a healthy mustard plant grew laterally straight out. I climbed an asphalt road on the Mount of Olives, and there, in a seam on the street, a mustard plant burst up.

Bill, a friend at a kibbutz on the Sea of Galilee, gave me black mustard seeds he had gathered from the wild. I scattered the seeds behind my Tree Haven home in Illinois, and they shot up exuberantly.

Let's imagine Green Jesus giving us a modern parable like the mustard seed one. He says: "The Presence of the Web of Energy is like a dandelion seed."

Dandelions grow wild throughout the world—Europe, Asia, Africa, and the Americas. Each yellow head consists of hundreds of tiny ray flowers. In early spring, honeybees feed upon the nectar of the flowers. Overnight, the yellow head can turn into the familiar white seed head. Hundreds of seeds soon become tiny parachutes, spreading far and wide. Dandelions proliferate exponentially, are difficult to exterminate, and grow under adverse conditions. Some American gardeners detest them, and the more gardeners try to weed them, the faster they grow. If gardeners do not completely dig up their taproots, dandelions regenerate themselves. Dandelion seeds germinate without a long period of dormancy. The plant is a hermaphrodite, cross-fertilizing itself. This gender fullness allows it to foil the gardener by dispersing parachute seeds as early as the day after the flower opens.

A dandelion asks another dandelion, "What is a dandelion digger for?"

"It is a human invention to help us reproduce."

The Presence of the Web of Energy and a dandelion-covered

Earth are irrepressible. I recall my visits to Russia where Russians adore *oduvonchik* (dandelion). In Russia the dandelion plant is taller and denser than in America, sometimes filling space between buildings in urban areas. Russians don't treat *oduvonchik* as a weed and often harvest wild dandelions as food for animals and themselves. During the Depression, my family ate dandelion salads. When I garden, I gnaw on dandelion roots, which Russians use for medicinal value.

The many comments by Jesus on *hardeta*, quoted in the gospels of Matthew, Mark, Luke, and Thomas, were lampoons. By calling attention to a madcap weed, he poked the religious and political ribs of his listeners. When people thought about the coming of a messiah who would usher in a fantasized, grandiose Kingdom of Heaven, they pictured a cedar tree on Mount Hermon as the proper symbol. The prophet Ezekiel compared messianic Israel to the mighty cedar. Ezekiel wrote that The One will plant a noble cedar on a lofty mountain, and all kinds of animals will live under it and in the shade of its branches all kinds of birds will nest (Ezekiel 17:22–23). Ezekiel likened the Pharoah of Egypt to the cedar of Lebanon, a tree whose top touches the clouds. All nations dwell under its shadow, and other trees in the Garden of Eden envy it (Ezekiel 31:2–9). The king of Babylon, Nebuchadnezzar, had a dream of a tree like the cedar rising in the midst of the Earth and people viewing it to the end of the whole Earth (Daniel 4:10–11).

The cedar of Lebanon, *cedrus libani*, grows best at elevations of around six thousand feet on western slopes facing the sea, much like the sequoia in the Sierra Nevada Mountains of California that grows at a similar elevation on slopes facing the Pacific. The cedar can reach an age of 1,500 years, a height of one hundred feet, with horizontal branches of fifty feet growing in every direction, and a trunk diameter of ten feet. It has male and female flowers on the same tree. Dropping needles every two years, the cedar forest creates a scented litter one foot in thickness. The Phoenicians axed trees in the cedar forest of Mount Hermon, used the logs to build ships, and created history's first, far-flung, seafaring empire by selling cedar lumber throughout the Mediterranean. The cedar symbol has had staying power, and today appears prominently on the flag of Lebanon.

As with nursing babies and with children, Jesus whacked another stereotype below the belt. Instead of saying the Kingdom of Heaven is like the most conspicuous, perennial, longest-living organism in the Middle East, he stunned his listeners by pointing to the pesky mustard plant living and dying annually. The Presence of the Web of Energy is like mustard seeds that reseed annually and keep on living perpetually, not like a single cedar tree that lives and dies. Today, instead of saying the Presence is like the sequoia, Jesus baffles us by celebrating the dandelion.

Jesus sacrilegiously mocked the cedar symbol. He said that if one has confidence the size of a mustard seed, one can uproot a mountain (like Mount Hermon with its cedar forest and the top-down rule for which it stands) and sink the mountain in the sea. In essence, he said about mountainous obstacles that obscure the pervasive Presence of the Web of Energy, "Flush them!" (Matt. 17:20; Mark 11:23).

Jesus knew the mustard plant well because he spent much of his time in *madbra* (wilderness) where he practiced *slotha* (meditation and prayer). The gospels mention his *slotha* experiences about a dozen times, occurring frequently when he spent the night on a hilltop away from his companions. The frequency of these "visions quests" suggests that wildness was in his cells. His creativity and unusual metaphors grew in *madbra*.

To get a better sense of what wildness was like for Green Jesus, let's accompany him near the beginning of his public ministry on an imaginary walk from a river bank below a plateau some twenty miles east of Nazareth. (See the map of Galilee.) There is some evidence that this plateau, with its village of Bethany Beyond Jordan, was the home of John the Baptist. The river bank we are walking along is on the Yarmuk River, a tributary of the Jordan River, and close to the Yarmuk's juncture with Raqqad Stream, which flows south from Mount Hermon. The Yarmuk gurgles within Holy Ravine.

We watch melted snow from Mount Hermon flow from the Raqqad into the Yarmuk. It's the end of winter and the rainy season. Pink and white blossoms of almond trees bud near the banks. Now we are climbing a switch-back path toward Bethany Beyond Jordan up on the plateau, hundreds of feet higher than the Yarmuk. When we get to the top, we see winter wheat and barley growing on what today is labeled the Golan Heights.

At the southern entrance of the village, we meet relatives of John and Jesus. We hear talk that John is to baptize his cousin the next day in the Yarmuk. As the sun sets to the southwest, deep shadows fill Holy Ravine.

The next morning, it's cool and windy on the heights, but it gets warmer as we descend. We are part of a line moving downward. When we near the bottom, we stop at a springs that fills a pool carved out of stone some yards above the coursing Yarmuk. Here, John immerses many people, including his cousin, Jesus. Doves give morning calls to each other.

After the baptismal event, Jesus and followers of John — Peter and Andrew from Bethsaida on the north shore of the Sea of Galilee — ponder the future of Jesus. Peter and Andrew decide to leave John the Baptist and join the new group around Jesus and accompany us as we walk west within Holy Ravine. Donkeys carry some belongings. The first night, we bathe in hot mineral springs at Hamat Gader, which is one mile before the Yarmuk empties into the flood plain above the Jordan River channel.

The next morning, we enter the plain, filled with winter wheat and barley. Here, local and migrating birds from Africa, including yellow-vented bulbuls, sing lustily. We walk four miles west across the plain until we come to the Jordan River ford. Four miles upriver to our right and north is where the Jordan exits the Sea of Galilee. We inhale and chew wild mint as we cross the ford. The water is shoulder deep. Spring rains make the cold water muddy and rocks slippery. We hold our knapsacks above our heads. Our robes become reddish brown. On the west side, Mary Magdalene joins us, having traveled south from Magdala.

Jesus, Peter, Andrew, and Mary Magdalene huddle. It becomes clear that Jesus does not want to go north to Tiberias, Magdala, and Capernaum. He wants to meditate on top of the high, wild plateau to the west.

In the Hebrew tradition, wilderness (*madbra*) produced foundational instruction. Moses and the Israelites wandered in wilderness. Elijah went into *madbra*, rested under a broom bush, whose yellow flowers goats found delectable, and meditated. The Psalmist exulted, "The pastures of the wilderness drip, the hills gird themselves with joy. The meadows clothe themselves with flocks" (Psalms 65:12–13, RSV). In *madbra* were lilies, henna blossoms, and thorns. *Madbra* included wild asses, ostriches, and wild grapes. The Hebrew Bible refers to *madbra* around three hundred times.

We say goodbye to Peter, Andrew, and Mary Magdalene, who start the trip to their homes a few miles north. We follow the trails of gazelles, ibexes, and foxes up the gullies and slopes. We munch on dried dates and locusts. We also carry bread and dried sardines that Mary Magdalene brought. There are small spring-fed oases for refreshment along the way, which we can easily spot by the reeds dancing around them.

We climb unhurriedly and often stop to get our breath. We turn around and look down and north at the waves of the blue Sea of Galilee, twelve miles long by seven miles wide, to our left. The end of Holy Ravine is straight ahead to the east. The Jordan channel, with its thickets of reeds, papyrus, and lions, zigzags to our right on its way south to the Dead Sea. We see cormorants, eagles, and egrets flying below us. To our upper left is snowy

Mount Hermon about forty miles in the distance. We resume climbing until we reach the summit of what I have named Madbra Plateau, six hundred feet above the Jordan River.

We find a spring protected by black basalt rocks. A light, variable wind dries our sweat. We look west and see the Jezreel Valley. Mount Tabor, a symmetrical prominence stands alone eight miles away in the Valley. We see fifteen miles away the hills of Nazareth on the north edge of the Jezreel Valley. The setting sun is low in the sky to the southwest toward Africa.

The next morning, Jesus says he wants to meditate alone. He knows that *slotha* meditation has taught him to do public ministry, but in what manner? He no longer wants to be an apprentice of his apocalyptically-minded cousin John, who specializes in baptisms as a sign of repentance. What shall he do? His first night on Wild Plateau, he lies down near a cave where foxes have a den. He prepares to align his heart with The One.

The Gospel of Mark says that the Spirit drives him into *madbra* among wild animals (Mark 1:12–13). Snakes and doves are among his companions. Inner voices clamor in one direction and subside in another. Should he imitate the ascetic Qumran Essenes? Should he seek to act out messianic images in the Hebrew Bible? Should he conduct a temple-focused ministry?

He receives guidance to turn away from these options. Like John, who lives in *madbra* and has sustenance from locusts and wild honey, Jesus does not lack for food here. Homim trees, with small fruit that tastes like apples, and the edible seeds of mustard plants grow wild.

Finally, his vision quest produces a strategy. Jesus will become an itinerant throughout Galilee. He will help empower people who follow or don't follow purity rules across the whole social spectrum. He will use parables and therapeutic touch to teach people to share healing, bread, and fish, and be like unruly mustard seeds that live freely and abundantly within the Presence of The One. He will invite women like Mary Magadalene to be full and equal partners with men. He will use satire rather than legal seriousness.

PRACTICE—We protect and expand the eco-diversity of forests.

How do we live today like mustard seeds in a world that is increasingly less wildly eco-diverse? So much of the world has the human mark on it that we typically think of wild as meaning without human impact. What is without that human mark? No living tissue on the surface of Earth Community has less than dozens of synthetic chemicals burrowing into the cells. Even the top of *Chono Lungma*, meaning Great Mother, but conventionally called Mount Everest, has lead and mercury industrial emissions in its ice. Humans have polluted every niche of the Earth, except the recesses where bacteria live thousands of feet below the surface.

The nonprofit group Nature Conservancy, which sets aside millions of acres of land worldwide, gives us some idea of the kind of relatively protected wildness left in the world. Protection, according to one Nature Conservancy analysis, exists for about 5 percent of temperate grasslands, savannas, and shrublands and for about 10 percent of temperate broadleaf and mixed forests. Officially protected areas on a global map are fractured and disconnected spots.

Only three relatively intact forests remain on the planet: the Amazon rainforest, the Russian boreal (meaning north wind) forest, and the North American boreal forest. This North American forest stretches from the eastern tip of Labrador to the Bering Straits in Alaska, according to a feature article in the Summer 2007 issue of *Nature Conservancy*.

This boreal forest contains 1.7 billion acres of spruce, tamarack, jack pine, aspen, and birch. This forest is home to three billion birds of at least three hundred species, many of whom visit some parts of all the lower forty-eight states at times during the year. Tens of thousands of lakes and ponds each provide a breeding place for at least one pair of loons. Hundreds of thousands of caribou still migrate. This woodland is the birthplace and residence of the healthiest remaining populations of wolves, moose, wild sheep, wolverines, lynx, and grizzlies. Such industrial activity as logging, mining, and fossil fuel extraction has impacted about 30 percent of the forest.

Currently, there is a colossal struggle in Canada between protectionists and industrialists who want to build an 850 mile highway and natural gas line along Canada's largest river, the Mackenzie. This river system drains 20 percent of Canadian territory northward into the Arctic Ocean. In ecological terms, the financial value of the Mackenzie River watershed has an estimated worth of about $400 billion a year in such green services as clean water, pest control by birds, and absorption of CO_2. The current industrial value of products in the watershed is ten times less, only $40 billion per year.

A Native American named Herb Norwegian has been the most vocal opponent of the highway and pipeline project. Herb says, "It's not as if you are running a garden hose across your backyard. You're talking about building something the equivalent of the China Wall."

Because of threats like these to the integrity of forests, overwhelmingly clear directives for the human species are to

1. Protect around five billion acres of forests
2. Discontinue deforestation immediately
3. Increase dramatically the planting of new trees

Skeptics can think of dozens of impractical reasons for these directives. But as the Mackenzie conundrum's bottom line dollar shows, ecological capital benefits are at least ten times larger than the industrial benefits.

One exceptional leader who knows about the ecological benefits of the Canadian boreal forest is the premier of the province of Ontario, Dalton McGuinty. He announced in summer 2008 that 55 million acres (a forest half the size of the Ontario province and half the size of Texas) will be off limits to development. Premier McGuinty relied on the science of the International Panel on Climate Change to make that decision. This unprecedented act increases the odds that the carbon currently stored there stays put and that a large, non-fragmented habitat will endure.

ATTITUDE—We develop heartfelt passion for trees and, with hope, plant billions of them.

One way to develop fervor and zeal for trees is to recognize their prominence in the Bible. Genesis begins with the story of the Tree of Life, a symbol for all the new life forms coming from Creating Process (Gen. 2:9). The last book in the Bible, Revelation, ends with the Tree of Life, with twelve kinds of fruit, one for each month, and with leaves for the healing of the nations (Rev. 22:2). The Bible mentions twenty-two species of trees over five hundred times, more than any category of species except humans.

My bond with trees began at a young age. An apple tree swing, a tire held by a rope that I twisted, allowed me at age five to spin while looking up at the tree's branches swirling under a cobalt sky. Climbing trees began with a cherry tree at the same age and today continues with a crimson maple in front of my Illinois house, Tree Haven. When granddaughter Celia visits, we have a ritual of climbing this maple tree. In grade school, I picked peaches and apricots in orchards. The redwoods of Santa Cruz and the sequoias of Yosemite were beyond grand. In Yosemite was an astounding sequoia tree older than Christianity.

In January 2000 I walked again, as I did in childhood, among sequoia trees in California. The sequoia species has been in

North America for fifty million years. Individual magnificent trees outlive human empires. Here, on the western slopes of the Sierra Nevada Mountains, with Pacific Ocean moisture blowing in from the west and condensing in fog, the Earth and sun create sequoia geniuses of the world.

I looked down into the San Joaquin Valley, parallel to both the Pacific Ocean and the Sierra Nevada Mountains, stretching from San Francisco to Los Angeles. In the 1940s when I lived here, the valley had no smog. Indeed, Los Angeles in those times had no visual smog for thirty miles from Mt. Hollywood to Long Beach. Today, a thick haze blocks the view.

But here among the sequoia species—a species existing only in the Sierra Nevada Mountains and nowhere else indigenously on Earth—an extinction story is in the making. Humans are filling the San Joaquin Valley, not only with grids of their own irrigated plants, but with toxic gases which waft up into sequoia groves and endanger seeds. Exhaust fumes from countless human machines heats the mountain air and dries climate. Sequoia trees cannot survive dryness.

One sequoia, which I have named Marvelous Marvel (conventionally called General Grant), lives beside a stream where it succulently sponges and sucks droplets of the King's River watershed. Under the asphalt parking lot of two acres and under asphalt trails near Marvelous Marvel Sequoia and near granite boulders, the roots of sequoias lace with roots of cedars, azaleas, and dogwoods. I call the mass of tendrils Root Village.

I was mostly speechless, only making the tiniest mutter or two. My boots crunching and squeaking on the snow broke a profound stillness—profound isn't the right word, but it's the best I can do. It was overload time. I, an almost seventy-year-old infant compared with trees over two thousand years old, felt overwhelmed. Sequoia giants touch a place, a place so tasty, that it is like no place that has ever existed. These are trees of matchless life.

Meantime, I kept walking on a trail on top of Root Village to get to Marvelous Marvel. The trail had numerous signs with the same words, "Stay Behind Fence and Save the Trees." Park service people had cut a road to Sequoia Grove and put thick asphalt over one large section of Root Village so that buses and cars could park on top of it. The road and parking lot have not stayed behind a fence. Carbon dioxide from our vehicles did not keep behind a fence.

Sequoia Grove is a plant zoo within a whole-world zoo, as illustrated by a story set in north woods country near where I am writing on Spirit Island. Consider a woman talking with a ranger at a campsite. He instructs her and other campers to seal their food supplies because black bears are about. She exclaims, "You don't just let them run loose, do you?"

Finally, I stood in front of Marvelous Marvel. Meditating upon my own violation of the integrity of Sequoia Grove and Root Village, I sniffled. I was trampling, along with other human voyeurs before me, upon the tendrils of the Tree of Life. With eyes welling, I did not know where to begin to make amends. Should I have walked on my knees from Illinois here in a twelve-month pilgrimage, rather than snorting up to this place one day in my belching machine and snorting down the next?

To make partial amends, I have helped start a project called Children & Elders Forest in my community. A stimulus for this project came during summer 2000 from an event in Germany I experienced with my eight-year-old granddaughter, Chesran.

I visited Chesran in her home village of Hundstadt, Germany, north of Frankfurt. She announced after breakfast that she wanted to show me a surprise. I said, "Good."

My daughter Shamelle, Chesran, and I got on bikes, rode through the village past the school and about a mile up a hill overlooking the village. Finally, Chesran said, "Let's park our bikes." She grabbed my hand and said, "Come. The surprise is over here." After walking very fast into a grove of newly planted trees, she stopped and said, "Look, here's my tree. An ash tree. See, here's my name and birth date on a tag on the tree."

I said, "Good heavens. How did this happen?"

"A man in the village said he'd organize a Children's Forest project. The parents would pay for the trees. So, I came with other children and our parents on the day for planting, and we had a bonfire and food. It was fun."

Chesran said, "Come, see the tree of my friend, Nina."

"Does your brother Nathaniel have a tree?"

"Yes. Come and see. Here it is. And right over here is the tree of Nathaniel's best friend, Tim."

I was amazed. "This is a wonderful idea."

This idea from Hundstadt, Germany evolved into the Children & Elders Forest program in Bloomington/Normal, Illinois. In partnership with various local groups, Children & Elders Forest is planting groves of indigenous trees here.

A team of at least one child and one elder sponsors and pays $150 for each tree. One team, formed by a Woman's Club spokeswoman, involves over three hundred Club members and hundreds of their children and grandchildren. So far, we have planted Turtle Grove with 95 trees and 20 species and Winter Hill (Sledding Hill) Grove, with 123 trees and 17 species. We have completed two additional groves—Eagle and Windrow— and are starting two others: Golden and Prairie groves. All told, we have planted 345 trees of 33 species. We want our community, which currently has around 200,000 trees and 6 percent tree cover to eventually have two million trees and 60 percent tree cover.

One of our heroes is Martin Luther, the Protestant reformer, who said, "If I knew that tomorrow the world would end, I would still plant my apple tree today." Another hero is Wangari Maathai of the Green Belt Movement in East Africa (www.greenbeltmmovement.org). The Green Belt Movement has planted over thirty million trees in recent years. Maathai, working not only on ecological but social justice issues, received the Nobel Peace Prize in 2004. Her current aim is for the Green Belt Movement to plant one billion trees.

A Children & Elders Forest anecdote of hope involves James, 4, and Kate, 3. Their grandparents, in 2005, sponsored a tree in Turtle Grove. Grandchildren James and Kate told anyone who would listen, "Someday, we're going to bring *our* grandchildren to see this tree we planted with Pop and Nana when we were little."

Hope comes from statistics about the benefits of trees for sustainability, as reported in such articles as "Some Cities Are Finding Money Does Grow on Trees," by Haya El Nasser in *USA Today*, "Shade in the City" by Amy Brittain, in the *Christian Science Monitor*; "Green Gold," in *The Economist*; and "Seeing the Forest for the Trees," in *Nature Conservancy*.

Hope is that a sugar maple along a roadway will absorb significant amounts of particulates, sulfur dioxide, carbon monoxide, carbon dioxide, cadmium, chromium, nickel, and lead. One large tree in Modesto, California annually takes out of the air 330 pounds of CO_2.

Hope is that asphalt streets with tree canopies will last ten years longer than asphalt streets without canopies.

Hope is that shaded streets will produce 80 percent more relaxation and stress reduction and 25 percent less asthma for its residents than for people on nonshaded streets.

Hope is that streets lined with mature trees will slow down traffic and cause fewer pedestrian and auto accidents.

Hope is that a mature tree will supply ten pounds of the 400 pounds of oxygen I breathe per year.

Hope is that one large tree canopy will intercept about 700 gallons of water during a storm and reduce run off costs and erosion. Leaves and twigs on the ground and roots absorb hundreds of gallons of water. Significant tree cover in an urban area saves millions of dollars annually in storm water run off costs.

Hope is that trees, depending on their size and closeness to buildings, will reduce heating and cooling costs 10 percent.

Hope is that trees will absorb 50 percent of urban noise.

Hope is that trees beside commercial stores will increase sales 15 percent.

Hope is that trees will decrease health costs by as much as 20 percent.

These expected results cumulatively produce $5 in benefits for every $1 invested in trees. The thousands of members of Children & Elders Forest teams have contributed $50,000 for the trees with an anticipated long-term payoff in savings of $250,000.

Trees planted in temperate and tropical zones contribute to 15 percent absorption of CO_2. Trees in high latitudes contribute to a lower percentage of carbon absorption because they grow leaves slower and because decaying trees release CO_2 at a sufficient rate to offset the leaf absorption.

With profound attitudes of heart appreciation for trees as our living friends, we celebrate that trees attract an endless hodge-podge of biological organisms. Trees are significant for redoubling eco-diversity.

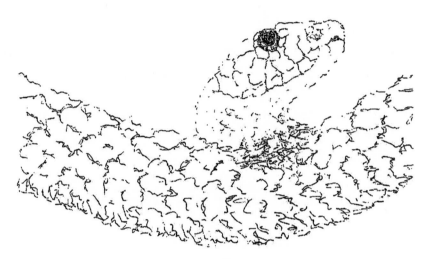

Jesus said, " Be as sly as snakes" (Thomas 39:1-3).

8

ANIMAL TEACHERS

WOULD JESUS ORGANIZE ECOLOGICAL POTLUCKS?

Earth Community web of life,
our network whom we love.
We walk within her, and are grounded by her,
on our way, sly as snake, clear as dove.
Within our mountain snows,
within our prairie winds,
within our oceans, alive with foam.
Rich, deep green Earth web of life,
our common home.
Rich, deep green Earth web of life,
our renewed Commons,
our livable, sustainable home.
— *My lyrics to the tune of "God Bless America"*

During the winter solstice last night, I had bounteous vigor. I wrote without fatigue until four in the morning. Today, I drove to Great Waters Beach and walked for several hundred yards along its ice shelves to the southern point of Spirit Island. The west wind was brisk and steady, signaling the arrival of a storm. As I walked, I recalled my dozen or so encounters with black bears on the island. One encounter was near our

Eagle Moon house, where a cub climbed a tree less than fifteen feet away.

Tonight, I drove on Spirit Lane to attend a potluck at adjoining properties called Black Bear and Birchwood, the latter being the name for the seventeen-sided residence of my friends Deborah and Ron. The potluck included, among other foods, fresh-baked pumpkin bread and pie, free-range turkey, green beans, and baked potatoes. One person present, Diane, was the first to put in a compost toilet on Spirit Island. Birchwood's twenty acres are in the center of the island and include birch, poplar, maple, white spruce, and oak. Bears are hibernating on the north shore not far away.

WE'VE LOOKED, IN chapters six and seven, at soil, mustard, dandelion, and sequoia and what they have to teach us. In this chapter, we look at animal teachers and how they can help us cope with Global Weirding. Here, we recognize that Jesus regarded snakes and doves as sly and clear-minded. We learn from crows that everyone in human society should get a fair share to eat through community potlucks. In a story in the Hebrew Bible, Job got inspiration from the ostrich, hippopotamus, and whale for overcoming self-righteousness. Best-selling author Daniel Quinn uses a gorilla as a professor to teach sustainability.

PRINCIPLE—Eco-diversity decides which foods species eat.

Jesus' most unusual reference to learning from animals had to do with snakes and doves. He said to a general audience, "Pharisees and scholars have taken the keys of knowledge and have hidden them. They have not entered, nor have they allowed those who want to enter to do so. As for you, be as sly as snakes and as simple [clear-minded] as doves" (Thomas 39:1–3, SV).

Today, some of our leaders and scholars have taken the keys

to understanding our current environmental predicament and have hidden them. John and Teresa Heinz Kerry, in *This Moment on Earth*, state that until January 2007 the head of the Senate committee entrusted with protection of the environment, Senator James Inhofe from Oklahoma, called the threat of climate change "the greatest hoax ever perpetrated on the American people." Inhofe compared this deception to Nazi propaganda before the Second World War.

In the first century, Jesus was pointed about the instruction one could take from snakes and doves. He said to his associates before sending them throughout Galilee as itinerants, "Look, I'm sending you out like sheep to a pack of wolves. Therefore you must [*hewa hakil hakim aik Heuya tamima aik Yauna*] be sly as a snake and as simple [clear-minded] as a dove" (Matt. 10:16, SV). *Heuya* means both discerning life and snake. *Yauna* means dove.

Jesus was drawing upon an ancient Semitic custom of viewing snakes as clever beings that annually discern how to shed and renew their skin, dying and rising to life again. There was a town about fifteen miles southeast from Nazareth called Bethshean, which means House of Snake [*Sahan*, possibly an Egyptian word]. In Bethshean, the capital of the ten-town Decapolis region east and south of the Sea of Galilee whose population was mostly Greek but included Jews, there was a stone engraving of Snake and Dove on the portal of a prominent public building. People had open access to this Bethshean building. This free access differed from the Holy of Holies in the temple in Jerusalem, which was open only to male priests.

Snakes hibernate in the winter and return to life in the spring. Freshwater springs, like Snake's Stone Spring in Jerusalem, were favorite places to hibernate (First Kings 1:9). Snakes curl around and see things from many angles, hot and cold, up and down, Earth and water. They're camouflaged, seeing others before they are seen.

In a Hebrew story, Moses intertwined brass snakes on a pole as a shrine for healing, a tradition lasting at least six centuries until the time of Hezekiah (Numbers 21:9; Second Kings 18:4). Many health professions today employ the symbol of two snakes twined around a pole, a symbol called the caduceus.

Snakes, with over thirty species in Palestine, appear over eighty times in the Hebrew Bible, most notably in the Garden of Eden story where *Heuya* (Snake) talks to Adam and Eve. I will present this story under the section on attitudes below.

Jesus referred to snakes in different ways, including a parable I'm putting in contemporary English. He said, "Two kids are hungry and ask their mom and dad for bread. When the kids come to the supper table, they see on the table stones and snakes."

"What gives?" the kids say.

Jesus said to his listeners, "Of course the kids don't see snakes and stones on the table. Mom and dad supply bread and fish" (Matt. 7:9–10).

Stones and snakes occur in the parable because the experience of Jesus with fishermen showed him that dragnets often pulled in stones and snakes mixed with fish. Jesus was teaching in the parable that sufficiency of bread and fish, not scarcity represented by snake and stone, is possible in society.

The Rabbi used the snake image indirectly in another parable to teach sufficiency. In this parable Jesus featured a wealthy, elite man, perhaps a lawyer. This man prepared a great banquet and sent out invitations to three of his wealthy friends. These friends made excuses about why they couldn't come that were so far-fetched that the listeners to the parable knew the excuses were things that no one would think or say in an honor society. "I've married a wife," says one. "I've bought land," says the second. "I've bought a cow," says the third. The listeners of the parable couldn't believe their ears. To refuse a friend's invitation to sit down at table in a honor society was a great insult to both inviter and invited.

In the parable, the host became angry. The listeners, expecting that anger, could not have imagined what came next. The host sent his servants out into the streets and lanes to invite the "scum" of the Earth, reeking with odors, to the banquet. In the byways, the servants encountered ritually impure peasants and beggars and invited them to the banquet. The servants approached male and female poor people, folks maimed, blind, and lame, and invited them to come to their master's feast. "You are welcome." Stupefied out of their wits but excited, the impure streamed into the rich man's house in as glaring a violation of purity rules as one could cook up. These scummy folk kept coming until the house was full (Luke 14:15–24).

What in the name of the Kingdom of God, The Presence of The One, was the point? Jesus was opening awareness to the possibility that both pious, elite folk and unclean men and women could shed their old skin and open a locked door to fair access to food and to social integration. Radical changes like these, Jesus was teaching, could fill the house of society and bring health and adequate food for all.

Jesus used other images to get people to think about an equitable distribution of food. He said, "Think about the crows [*Beqa na'ba*]. They don't plant or harvest, they don't have storerooms or barns. Yet God feeds them" (Luke 12:24, SV).

Beqa na'ba. Consider crows. *Beqa* means to ponder and examine carefully. Rethink. Consider.

The way the Rabbi held up crows as examples, and my discovery that my surname has the word crow in it, has led me to examine crows as teachers. My surname, Grabill, is an English transliteration of the Swiss-German *Krahen-buhl*, literally, Mother Crow Hill. What does Mother Crow have to teach me? Communal crows — male, female, and child crows — are entirely black, including beak and feet, with purple highlights. Crows love to play and pretend to be asleep. When a cat stalks a crow and is ready to pounce, the crow may swoop into the air, cackling. Parents and nonparental singles cooperatively feed broods of five to seven chicks and each other. Extended families communicate with an unusual range of calls and help each other gather insects, fruit, and carrion that Earth Community provides.

Extensive tests show that crows know how to think, as reported in an article in *National Geographic*. A crow named Betty, in varied situations, enters a room with a tiny basket holding a bit of meat hanging inside a glass tube. She finds a wire, pushes it with her beak into a crack, and bends the wire into a hook, with which she lifts the basket with meat in it out of the tube. In another trial, she bends a piece of flat aluminum for the same purpose. The researcher, Alex Kacelnik of Oxford University, says that Betty has a mental picture of what she wants to create. Her cognitive sophistication humbles him and clearly indicates that humans are not alone in the ability to invent and plan. Kacelnik has the theory that both humans and other species learn to develop strategies and make decisions through innovative interactions among the full range of members within the overall Creating Process.

In my trips to the Sea of Galilee and the Jordan River, I have spent hours and days watching birds. Over these bodies of water fly a wider diversity of migrating European, Asian, and African birds that any place in the Middle East.

Jesus could just as well have said, "*Beqa* cormorants." Consider cormorants.

During the rainy season, I watched one evening at sunset as a thousand or more web-footed cormorants departed from the Sea of Galilee and headed twelve miles up the Jordan River gorge to the wetlands of Lake Huleh where they assembled on trees for the night. The Jordan River seeps through the Lake Huleh wetlands, which are above the level of the Mediterranean, and cascades down a gorge to the Sea of Galilee seven hundred feet below sea level.

Before the sun surged up over mountains east of the Sea of Galilee the next day, these black cormorants with their white heads and red and yellow beaks left their Luke Huleh overnight perches and sped south in synchronicity at forty miles an hour down the Jordan River gorge.

From a cave along the western shore of the Sea of Galilee called The Eye of The One (which tradition holds that Jesus used for shelter and meditation; see visual, Chapter Ten), I watched at sunrise as waves of cormorants in V-formation swept high or skimmed low over the water. Wave after wave swooshed in, with around a hundred birds in each formation. All the cormorants in a wave acted as one, fluttering and settling on the water communally.

Cormorants then dove for tilapia fish using a special lens for underwater vision that allows them to see clearly for several feet below the surface. After eating, the cormorants rested on rocks near volcanic springs called Waters of Good Fortune just below my cave lookout and sunned themselves. Jesus, over years of seeing cormorant, crow, and other bird behavior, understood why birds did not suffer from chronic anxiety. God — *Allah(t)a*, The Feminine One — provided.

Here's an absurd, far-fetched parable I wrote about crows to help illustrate that these birds don't suffer anxiety. A chief crow supervises agricultural tasks for a flock of three hundred crows. He and others oversee gangs of ten males each. In late autumn and early spring, the gangs use fallen willow branches that they stack in a square pattern, dovetailing the ends of branches at each right angle, and make a flat roof over the squared walls with more willow branches. The crows pick up river mud with their beaks to plaster the walls and roof. It takes a whole gang to carry one willow branch and many gangs to build and plaster a crow barn.

Some inhale too much mud, get pneumonia, and die.

In the late spring, crow bosses give orders for worker males to dig up last year's corn stalks, carry them to the edge of a field, find ashes from a lightning fire, and carry a burning ember to set the stalks on fire.

Hot embers ignite feathers on some workers and they crash.

Worker crows next scratch up a field to prepare it for planting. Male bosses fly from one edge of the field to the other as a crow flies, dropping twigs in a straight line to mark rows. Female crows fly to storerooms, pick off one kernel of seed corn from an ear, and fly to the field. The females use their beaks to dig hole by hole in row after row and plant kernel by kernel.

At dawn during the summer months, bosses rouse male, female, and young worker crows from sleep and send them to the fields to scratch out weeds between the rows. Gang leaders punish young crows who goof off or who don't get out all of the roots of the weeds by pecking them at the base of their tails.

In the autumn, bosses tell worker crows to bite on stalks of corn just below the ears. Some male crows fracture their beaks, biting over and over until they finally sever the ear from the stalk. Some broken-beaked crows find it hard to pick up their food, their immune system breaks down, and they die of West Nile virus.

Females and the younger crows pick and claw at cornhusks and fly ears to storerooms. They tighten their claws over and over around the ears of corn and develop carpel tunnel syndrome.

Most of the flock takes sick leave while the bosses organize a private harvest festival for themselves and eat the sweetest kernels.

It's not a stretch to imagine that Jesus embellished his sayings and parables, like the above caricatured crow tale. Exactly what the stories and dialogues were we will never know. What we do know is that he engaged in shrewd and jocular interaction with people. What gospel writers and editors record are core sayings, embedded within extended conversations.

A new human food strategy of Jesus and Mary Magdalene was like the communal eating strategy of cormorants and crows. The records do not explicitly mention Mary Magdalene, but her prominence among the associates of Jesus implies that she had a role in this fundamental scheme.

One day, there was a large crowd around Jesus on the grassland alluvial plain south of Bethsaida where the Jordan enters the Sea of Galilee. Bethsaida was the home of Peter, Andrew, and Philip, and possibly James and John. Jesus asked the crowd to sit down on the "green grass" (Mark 6:39). The only place on the shores of the Sea of Galilee not strewn with basalt rocks and thistles and not cultivated was this Bethsaida plain on the northern shore. Here were aromatic camel, lemon, and ginger grasses, green even in the dry season.

The six versions of the feeding of 4,000 and 5,000 people in the gospels are formula parables created by the early Jesus communities to distill symbolically the essence of a fresh ritual initiated by Jesus and Mary Magdalene. The setting was wilderness in each version, not agricultural. Two versions have women and children present. Their presence violated the purity law that required women, unless prostitutes or wealthy widows, to eat privately in the presence of family males. In every story, people ate bread and fish.

Numbers in the six versions vary, but all represent wholeness. Five loaves and two fish equal seven, the number of fullness. One story has seven loaves and an undefined number of fish. Afterward, people gathered either seven or twelve baskets of leftovers. The number twelve stands for the full number of Jacob's sons and the full number of Hebrew tribes. The number 4,000 is a multiple of forty, which in Hebrew tradition means an indeterminate but significant amount. The number 5,000, important in the decimal system of the Romans, signifies the entire community. Matthew shows that these numbers are symbolic by saying in one place there were 4,000 plus women and children, and in another, 5,000 plus women and children (Matt. 14:20; 15:38).

Let's consider the choreography of this novel ceremony. In the parable, there was exaggerated talk of scarcity. The Rabbi said to Philip, with a monstrous projection about what Jesus already knew would not be Philip's responsibility, "Where are we going to get enough bread to feed this mob?" Philip replied, "Two hundred silver coins [six month's wages] worth of bread wouldn't be enough for everyone to have a bite" (John 6:5–7, SV).

The crowd is about to eat fish and barley loaves, which suggests a time after the festival of Shavuot and the barley harvest. During Shavuot, people traditionally told the story of Ruth and her mother-in-law, Naomi. Following reapers, Ruth and Naomi barely picked up enough barley grains to eat. Only when Ruth slept with the landowner, Boaz, did she and Naomi receive ample food.

Jesus and Mary Magdalene dramatize that the elite's standard of religious purity operated according to the scarcity principle. Peasants, who were over 90 percent of the population, could never escape the scarcity system. To get inside the abundance system, they had to be able to afford dove or lamb sacrifices, to observe holy days, to eat clean foods with clean hands only within one's social class, to take ritual baths, not to touch a corpse or a leper or a menstruating woman, not to have intercourse during menstruation, not to travel too far or to work on the Sabbath, ad infinitum. After defilement, only elaborate rites could restore purity. Peasants could not escape the vicious cycle of scarcity, and thus they lived in perpetual, unjust defilement.

Jesus and his associates deliberately violated the purity code and taught that abundance was twofold: a self-directed inner habit and face-to-face cooperation within the whole community.

The parables about bread and fish feedings, repeated so many times in the gospels, suggest that this new irreverent, flagrant, anti-purity ceremony was repeated in various ways, times, and places. Jesus said, "It's not what goes into the mouth [unclean food] that defiles a person. Rather, it's what comes out of the mouth [unclean rules] that defiles a person" (Matt. 15:11, SV). Jesus was a migraine headache for purity fundamentalists!

The choreographed ceremony proceeded with a lad offering food. This beginning with a lad, not a dad, tipped off the listener that the ceremony was not going to follow religious rules. Unless one becomes like a child, one cannot experience *Malkuta Allah(t)a*. Next, in unfolding horror to the purity fundamentalists, but unfolding wonder to the masses, Jesus had people sit randomly on the green Earth so they could not escape sitting next to someone who was ritually impure. People with expensive ointments sat next to folk with putrid, unwashed garments. Today, this would be like National Presbyterian Church having homeless beggars with lice and festering sores sit shoulder to shoulder with former Secretary of State Condoleezza Rice, who has regularly attended this church, and former President George W. Bush. Then Jesus, acting with the same kind of authority as priests in the temple, liturgically broke bread and fish from the lad and gave thanks for provision.

The masses collectively and revolutionarily broke the purity law. They opened their knapsacks, divided their own bread and fish in pieces, and handed food to unclean neighbors. Mary Magdalene gave her dried sardines in abundance. Peter, Andrew, Philip, James, and John gave their tilapia. Rich, poor, beggars, lepers, women, and children openly touched each other, flouting custom. The ceremony was a bashing of tradition and a celebratory, egalitarian potluck. The parable concluded with an abundance benediction. Everyone had more than enough to eat.

In another situation, Jesus said, in essence, "The hungry pig out." The precise quote is "You hungry! You will have a feast" (Luke 6:21; SV).

In the beginning of the Christian era, followers of Jesus observed a common meal of bread and fish, not of bread and wine. Early catacomb and sarcophagus art show bread and fish at the meal. A fish, not a cross, was a sign of the Jesus way. The ritual was an actual dinner, not a rite performed in the front of a hall. Bread and fish did not stand for anything other than the whole community taking care of each other, like communal crows take care of each other.

In utter irony, urban Christian clergy eventually behaved like the Jewish priests whom Jesus and Mary Magdalene undermined. Christian elite, operating in a milieu shut off from wilderness, replaced fish with wine, ended the common outdoor meal, and theorized that bread and wine stood for the substitutionary atonement of Jesus' body and blood on a cross. Christian Pharisees, in the name of Jesus, trivialized and emasculated the ceremony acted out long ago in the first century in the dry season of Shavuot on the grassy green plain of Bethsaida beside the Sea of Galilee.

An extension of the principle of crows modeling an equal distribution of food in human society is found in the Hebrew story of Job. In the story, Job had dreadful afflictions and learned little or nothing from endless discussions with his friends about his suffering. But he remembered during the interminable blabbering, "Ask the animals, and they will teach you, the birds of the air, and they will tell you, or the plants of the Earth, and they will teach you. The fish of the sea will declare to you" (Job 12:7–8, RSV).

After torturous days of pain, Yahweh appeared in a whirling vision to Job and showed him the extravagant creativity and interdependence among members of the universe. Yahweh asked the following kind of questions:

Where were you when star constellations began?
Where were you when bear, clouds, and mud began?
Did you fashion lion, raven, and goat?
Where were you when wild ass, horse, and ostrich began?
Did you create hawk, lotus plants, and hippopotamus?
Where were you when whale and crocodile began?

At the end of this cosmic drama, Job was dumbstruck. He repented of his human-centric philosophizing and justifying himself as righteous leader of proper rituals and ethics. He understood that he was one among other members of the Community of Life, made of dust and returning to dust. Job learned from animals that he was a member of, not separate from, the Circle of Life. His afflictions ended.

If we choose to continue our long war against such large carnivores as lions and tigers, we will not only throw the balance of nature out of whack, we will create a world of incomprehensible loneliness where wild beings will never be again. We have hunted, trapped, and poisoned wolves, resulting in a plague of deer and elk who kill vegetation. If we destroy sea otters and sharks, the Ocean ecology collapses. A world devoid of animal predators beside ourselves (tragically, we are the chief predators) would be catastrophic, as William Stolzenburg writes in *Where the Wild Things Were*.

Today, an eminent instructor of our species, like the animals in the Job story, is the gorilla professor, Ishmael, in Daniel Quinn's novel of the same name. Ishmael teaches a human pupil wanting to save the world that there are two stories within the human community, introduced at the beginning of this book. The gorilla Ishmael says that the Taker story, an Agricultural Revolution tale, assumes that Earth Community exists for herders and farmers. The Leaver story, a preagricultural tale, assumes that humans, just like salmon, sparrows, and gorillas, exist for Earth

Community. Takers assume they have the right to decide which species will eat and live and which will not eat and die, according to the needs and wants of protecting herds and clearing land for farming. Leavers, who are the heroes in Ishmael's pedagogy, leave it to the networks of animals, plants, and humans within Earth Community to decide synergistically and sustainably who gets to eat and who gets to die.

Animals, thus, teach interwoven principles. Crows model for humans that everyone in the community has an equal right to eat. Ishmael the gorilla says that the Leaver story teaches that animals, plants, and humans collectively and cooperatively decide, according to the optimal opportunity for all, who among them gets to eat and live or not eat and die.

If we choose to continue our long war against such large carnivores as lions and tigers, we will not only throw the balance of nature out of whack, we will create a world of incomprehensible loneliness where wild beings will never be again. We have hunted, trapped, and poisoned wolves, resulting in a plague of deer and elk who kill vegetation. If we remove sea otters and sharks, then the Ocean ecology collapses. A world devoid of animal predators beside ourselves (tragically, we are the chief predators) would be catastrophic, as William Stolzenburg writes in *Where the Wild Things Were*.

The animals in the Job story illustrate that humans are co-members of Earth Community. In the *Frank and Ernest* comic strip Ernie tells a story about a flower and a rock.

Flower: "Hi! I'm new here. Have you been around here long?"

Rock: "A few eons or so."

"Do you have a family?"

"Dad was fire and mom was a volcano. I started out as a little blob of lava."

"That's so cool! How did you get here?"

"Mom was always shooting her mouth off."

Ernie concludes: "If a rock and a flower can do it, anybody can be a friendly neighbor!"

PRACTICE—We institute community potlucks and learn sustainability from animals.

I grew up experiencing frequent church potlucks. So did author Bill Bryson when he visited his grandparents during summers in the little town of Winfield in southeast Iowa, as described in *The Life and Times of the Thunderbolt Kid*. During his childhood in the 1950s, Bill loved everything about Winfield, "its imperturbable tranquility, its lapping cornfields, the healthful smell of farming all around." Many summer evenings, Bill would walk uptown to a shady Methodist church lawn and take part in a vast potluck presided over by an army of women, "all named Mabel." The Mabels chuckled, never complained, shooed flies with spatulas that set their sagging arms wobbling, blew wisps of sweating hair from their faces, and made sure that each person had a helping of meatloaf the size of a V-8 engine. No type meatloaf was too strange or too upside down, even Peanut Brittle 'n' Cheez Whiz Upside-Down Spam Loaf. Foods were superior when upended.

Here is a paraphrase of Bryson's telling about the potluck dialogue:

"Hey, Sam, try some Spiced Liver 'n' Candy Corn Upside-Down Casserole. Mabel made it. Delicious."

"Upside down? What happened—she drop it?"

Mabel butted in. "Maybe I did drop it. You want chocolate gravy, biscuit gravy, or cow tongue 'n' niblets gravy?"

"How about all three?"

"You got it."

By the time Mabel loaded the paper plate, it weighed twelve pounds. People came from miles around for the potluck. Nearly everyone was Methodist anyway, even the Catholics. These weren't religious events. It was about shared food. Desserts were the best, essentially the same as the other dishes but with the meat removed.

Today, Green Jesus asks us to revive the ancient, outdoor communal model of a festive potluck among the peoples of Earth. Potluck Jesus invites gays and straights, criminals and noncriminals, and homeless and suburban people to mix together and share food at a community event.

Jesus also invites us to redouble biodiversity by eating in a bio-diverse way. There are 30,000 edible plants, and we only eat twenty in any quantity. Wheat, corn, and rice account for about half the plants the people of the temperate world eat.

A miracle moringa oleifera plant exists, whose leaves and pods contain more beta carotene than carrots, more calcium than milk, more iron than spinach, more Vitamin C than oranges, more potassium than bananas, and protein comparable to milk and eggs. This moringa bush, very hard to kill by drought or heat, is a nutrition superstar, and most people in the tropical world of Asia and Africa where it grow indigenously and in the temperate world have not heard of moringa.

Of the more than 3,000 fruits, we eat about twenty. Before the rise of agriculture and husbandry, indigenous people knew by name and ate on average 1,000 different species. Let's increase vastly the variety of vegetables and fruits we eat from yards and from farmers' market, and decrease vastly the 30 percent of land set aside for cows and other animals to graze. We could convert most of this grazing land to wildness so that many species could eat. Let's have humans and More-than-Humans both eating potlucks derived from a wide variety of animals and plants.

What does Black Bear on Spirit Island teach me about food? What can any member of Wild Commons, from tadpole to cactus, teach us? It depends on how strategically we place ourselves in the habitat of the More-than-Human teacher and how teachable we are. Bacteria, bats, and black alder trees can teach us encyclopedias if we are willing to absorb.

Michael Furtman writes in *Black Bear Country* that winter is the miracle of miracles season for Black Bear. This remarkable mammal is in the middle of the several month period of hibernation. During hibernation, Black Bear gets all its nutritional needs from stored fat, converting fat to water, which it circulates, and fat to carbon dioxide, which it exhales. Black Bear internally turns its small amount of urine into water, carbon dioxide, and ammonia. The ammonia metamorphoses into protein to prevent its muscles from atrophying. In a process researchers have not yet understood, Black Bear recycles calcium to protect bone mass.

If these things are not stupendous enough, Mama Black Bear gives birth during hibernation, the only animal to do so during a time when it is not eating, urinating, or defecating. Prior to dormancy, she carries her fertilized eggs from spring until fall outside the uterus in the fallopian tubes so as not to divert food to the embryos during the heavy eating months. Implantation in the womb occurs in the fall, and births occur early in winter. Tiny babies weigh less than a pound each and less proportionately in weight than any other omnivore. Mama licks the babies after delivering them and eats their afterbirth. She nurses them with milk that has 25 percent fat content (human milk is 4 percent), and she occasionally awakens to lick and stimulate them to defecate. She then eats the feces to keep the den clean. When Mama emerges from her den in early spring, the cubs weigh about eight pounds — the mass of a newborn human.

For those of us who consider ourselves superior to animals and plants even though we are not, consider this: there is not a single human on the globe who can perform any of the miracles that Mama Bear does in the winter. Vice-versa, there is no animal or plant that is superior to humans. Earth Community, according to the Leaver principle, does not work that way. Each member of a species or a rock or a chemical family acts in the various stages of its life cycle like no one else, not even itself in another stage. The actors within Earth Community have many differences of behavior and of power, but not a fixed hierarchy of superior and inferior behaviors.

What do I learn from Black Bear? I learn to seek to be in sync with the rhythm of the seasons and not to help drive other species to extinction. This requires that I engross myself within the habitats of life and not engross myself too much in the technological habitats of clothes, houses, cars, and electronic tools, like the computer before me. I learn during the winter solstice season to explore my creative potential more deeply than any other season, just like Mama Bear. On Spirit Island where I have met her, sometimes face-to-face, she flabbergasts me with her singular Creating Process.

Bald Eagle charges my circuits. I once saw this magnificent bird, a female with a wingspan of eight feet (longer than a male's), flying over our house. This sighting on Spirit Island gave me goose bumps, goose bumps I feel rising on my skin right now as I type. The presence of Bald Eagle, combined with my mother's name of Arveda, meaning Female Eagle in Swiss-German, and the round, full moon shape of our house, influenced us to name our retreat home Eagle Moon.

At Many Cedars Beach, I have watched bald eagle youths and adults dive for fish. The courtship ritual of bald eagles has stimulated intense amazement in me. A male and female ascend a thousand feet or more into the sky. Then the two plummet at one hundred miles per hour, wings folded, cavorting, briefly touching talons, and diving until they swoop just before plunging into Lake Superior. Sometimes, the female grips the male's talons firmly, and the pair cartwheel down, wings outstretched, tumbling over one another, for the sheer joy of it. They may repeat an ascent and a cartwheeling descent several times.

We can appreciate the fascination of Ojibway and other Native Americans with Bald Eagle. They sometimes name themselves for this glorious raptor. I have very personal reasons for admiration. My mother, Female Eagle, in her last days at the age of ninety-seven but still very cogent and sharp like her namesake, repeated a favorite Bible verse: "But they who wait for the Lord shall renew their strength. They shall mount up with wings like eagles. They shall run and not be weary. They shall walk and not faint" (Isaiah 40:31, RSV).

What do I learn from bald eagles? They do not overeat and drive other species to extinction. Their lifelong pairings inspire me to renew my lifelong commitment to my wife, Donella Hess-Grabill. Donella and I do not go to bed mad, but stay up and fight. In our early years, we fought because we didn't understand each other. Now we fight because we do understand each other. We have cultivated the friendship of a long conversation. Both of us, having experienced divorce, understand that any marriage more than a week old has grounds for divorce. We find grounds for marriage. What counts is not how compatible we are, but how lovingly we deal with incompatibility. We plan to keep on committing like eagles, until death do us join.

No species, except ours, has taken so much from Earth Community under the spell of the Taker story as to drive others to extinction. Other species, all of them our kindred, are Leavers, not Takers. They leave a large enough portion of the Earth's sustenance so as to allow other species to be Leavers.

The earthworm is a master Leaver. Earthworms improve the growth of roots and plants, hold moisture, bind nutrients to the soil, and fertilize. If we want to increase the Leaver effect, we can make an earthworm bin. We add to the bin shredded newspapers as bedding, earthworms, and garbage. We harvest humus, and add this living soil to our gardens and yards. Composting with earthworms does release some carbon dioxide, but not methane, which is twenty-three times worse for the atmosphere. We can enjoy this composting cycle of life right under our noses, as described in *The Live Earth Global Warming Survival Handbook*.

Some years back, fishermen in the New England states accepted a ten-year moratorium on taking cod whose numbers were declining close to extinction. By being Leavers for a decade, the fishermen allowed the cod to rebound in numbers throughout coastal areas, bays, and rivers.

One of the most effective ways for us to become Leavers is to leave meat behind (see the *Survival Handbook)* and to eat fruits and vegetables. One pound of beef requires eight times more energy than one pound of soy. Writer Nathan Fiala in *Scientific American* symbolizes meat by the phrase "greenhouse hamburger." Meat causes around 7 billion of the 36 billion tons of greenhouse gases annually. The production of one hamburger patty releases as much greenhouse emission as driving a 3,000-pound car 10 miles. We devote, as noted, about 30 percent of our land for grazing livestock. We devote 0.5 percent (sixty times less) for growing fruits and vegetables. Americans produce 660 pounds per second of excrement and livestock 86,000 pounds (over 100 times more) per second. Livestock flatulence and excrement produce more greenhouse gases than motorized transportation. Increased eco-diversity is vast if we greatly curtail meat consumption. We also reduce risk of heart attacks.

ATTITUDE—We develop open hearts and expectant spirits about being Leavers.

A Leaver change of spirit requires core love for the species of the world. Currently many of us fear other species. Snakes? Yuk. Spiders. Double yuk. Mosquitoes. Triple yuk. And on it goes. These fears are not natural but are culturally conditioned attitudes based on the technological distance from immersion within eco-diversity and on the Taker mentality. Any living being inconvenient or annoying deserves contempt and a swat. Or pesticide. Or shooting.

Some stories from the Bible teach us to fear animals, like the story of Daniel and the lion's den. Recently, I came across an anecdote about an Anglican vicar whose sermons were boring but became much better if he drank gin before a service. One Sunday, he was dramatic in his telling of Daniel in the lion's den. The vicar paced, acted out parts, laughed, cried, shouted, and whispered. Afterward, a bishop shook the vicar's hand and said, "Very good sermon. One small point. God sent an angel to shut the mouths of the lions. Daniel didn't zap them between the eyes and strew their brains across the wall like spaghetti."

Here are words for all of us to sing to a Sunday school tune, "Jesus Loves the Little Children," from my childhood, and separately, words by Ray Stevens to his song from the 1970s:

Yes, we love the varied species,
every species of the world.
Lion, insect, bear who's brown,
all are valued with renown.
Yes, we love the varied species of the world.

Everything is beautiful in its own way,
like a starry summer night
or a snow covered winter's day.
Everybody's beautiful in their own way.
Under God's heaven,
the world's gonna find a way.

To help us love all species, we need to review the story of beginnings from the Bible set in and outside the Garden of Eden (called Garden of Yahweh in Gen. 13:10). Using Hebrew and Aramaic, we find many words in the story compatible with a Leaver perspective: *Eden* (Lush Oasis), *Adamah* (Adam, Red Earth), *Hawah* (Eve, Life Mother), *Havel* (Abel, Breath), *Qayin* (Cain, Acquisition), *Heuya* (Discerning Life, Snake), and Tree of *Haya*

(Life). In a play on words, *Hawah* and *Heuya* grow linguistically as branches on the Tree of *Haya*.

Please excuse a diversion. You may know the anecdote.

Someone says to Adam, "You must have been lonely after God created you all by yourself."

Adam says, "Yes, God eventually came to help me out."

God says, "Adam, I want to make you happy. I am going to give you a companion, someone who will be loving."

"That sounds incredible."

"Well, it is," says God, "but it doesn't come free. In fact, this is someone so special that it's going to cost you an arm and a leg."

"That's a pretty high price to pay." Adam thinks for a moment. "What can I get for a rib?"

In the Garden of Eden, a lush, wild oasis, Adam and Eve were vegetarian Leavers. They ate wild fruits and plants and left it to the Community of Life to decide who ate and who didn't. The Tree of the Knowledge of Good and Evil symbolizes a dramatic switch from Adam and Eve being Leavers. Now humans consider with narrow self-interest which species are good and which are evil. Good species are domesticated ones under human rule, and evil species are those that threaten the good species. Abel (Breath) is a herder, caring for domesticated sheep. Abel's herding style is the first step away from humans being Leavers. Herders make their priority to keep one or more species (sheep, goats, or cows) breathing and assume the right to kill any species that threatens or can feed on the sheep, goats, and cows. Cain (Acquisition) is an agricultural tiller of the ground, a Taker. He assumes that he has the right to acquire agricultural land and take away the breath of anyone or anything that threatens his cultivated fields. Abel's sheep and goats possibly eat Cain's plants on Cain's land. Out in a field, probably an agricultural one, Cain murders his brother. This murder is a prototype for the genocidal, twentieth-century obsession to control and conquer land and for the ultimate obsession, ecocidal nuclear weapons.

Interestingly, the tones of the Genesis story are ambivalent, and the reason is that two sets of editors shape the version of the Bible we have today. Yahweh editors are the oral storytellers who lived close to oases and wilderness, which provided food to everyone year around, and who were herders like Abraham, Isaac, and Jacob. Priestly editors are the literate storytellers who lived in the urban areas of Jerusalem and, in exile, of Babylon.

Yahweh editors have male and female created equal (Gen. 1:27) and do not demonize animals and plants. They probably initiated the idea of a talking Snake. The Yahweh editors herald Adam and Eve as Leavers in the oasis, like Jericho, of the Garden of Eden. After the story about the Tree of the Knowledge of Good and Evil, Yahweh editors favor Abel, whose animal husbandry is less abusive of the wilderness than Cain's agricultural style. These Yahweh editors treat the expulsion from the Garden and the ending of humans being Leavers as the Fall. Yahweh editors recognize the toll in sweat of the brow, the work involved in tilling the ground, and the pain of women who are manipulated to breed agricultural workers the way seeds are manipulated by humans to breed plants in a field.

The Priest editors demonize the snake who deceives Eve. These editors treat heroically a patriarchy entitled to manage who will live and die. The priest editors describe Eve as a derivative of Adam's rib and as a deceiver of Adam (2:21–22). The priest editors also have animals and plants subordinate to humans who can take seeds from plants and trees and eat and subdue any species they want (1:28–30).

One aim these members of the literate priestly and scribal elite have throughout their editing of the Hebrew story-telling tradition, from the eighth to the first century, was to slander Asherah, the mother of Canaanite divinities, denounce green tree shrines, and concentrate their own patriarchal power and authority in the temple in Jerusalem. Archeological evidence indicates that many common folk and officials venerated Asherah, trees, and snakes, and regarded Asherah as the wife of Yahweh. These people practiced this green veneration up to the time of Jesus, despite the aim of a segment of the male elite to suppress and to eradicate Asherah culturally.

To save the world for sustainability, we must have a conversion to a point of view more like the Yahweh editors and more like Asherah. We need to revise the right to decide who to kill and which domesticated species to let live. Embracing that arbitrary right, we inevitably practice ecocide, killing our brother Abel, killing our sisters, killing our cousin primates, and killing without discrimination. We are down to less than one hundred species that we favor to cultivate and keep alive. The end product of the Taker story, if we keep practicing it, is that we will take our own lives as a species. Evangelical Brian McLaren calls the current practice of exploiting Earth Community the suicide machine. Pope Benedict XVI, the "green pope," calls it "insatiable consumption."

Now is the time to disavow the habit of being a Taker and to develop hearty and expectant spirits about practicing Leaver traits.

Can we do it? Yes, we can. It's in our genes, and it is the original way of behavior for our species. The end product of the Leaver story is sustainability for us and other species. We have the wherewithal to draw upon our deep, conservation-of-diversity Leaver tradition and to moderate our fixation with herding and with farming. This revived Leaver agenda would bring the people labeled today as liberals and conservatives together in a common cause.

PART THREE

Kind Community

The "American Wilds" CD blends pitches and sonorities from various habitats and times. Now I am listening to cicadas, crickets, and frogs. On Spirit Island, frogs are unusually enthusiastic during the mating season in June. Enthusiasm literally means filled with God. Carpenter frogs in chorus sound like seeds rattling in several gourds. Crickets chirp by rubbing their wing edges as often as four and as many as two hundred times per second. These chirps vibrate like ocean surf. Cicada males quiver abdomen membranes to click, buzz, and hum. Amphibian and insect riffs both sooth and excite.

In this third part of *Green Kingdom Come!* we look at humans caring and showing concern for each other in ways that flow with the process of washed toes and of other physical therapies. We build "sane asylums." We remember that we were born bare and broke. What are the pouring, dripping sounds of someone washing toes and heels of a neighbor? Of people hammering a building into place and living in spaces that are sane with greenness? Of folks who consider themselves essentially bare and broke and thus have a proportion of goods to give to others with expressions of joy?

These sound waves, and those of frogs, cicadas, crickets, and other members of Earth Community, synchronize within, what I hope for us, is the New Earth Symphony.

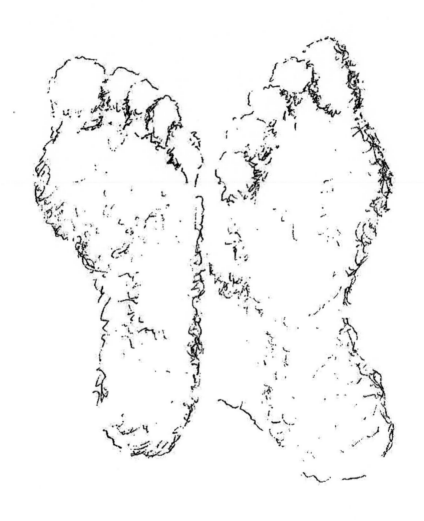

Jesus said, "Wash each other's feet" (John 13:12-15).

9

WASHED TOES

WOULD JESUS MASSAGE PEOPLE WITH AIDS?

A Sunday school class was studying the Ten Commandments.
The teacher asked if anyone could tell her the last one.
Susie raised her hand, stood tall, and recited,
"Thou shalt not take the covers off thy neighbor's wife."
— *Anonymous*

Tonight is the full moon, which calls me to walk to Many Cedars Beach to view the Long Nights Moon cycle at its most dazzling. Today, December 23, Long Nights Moon is a bright complete circle. This full moon event is sandwiched between the winter solstice, two days ago, and Christmas, two days hence. I wish I could get my green kayak, Dragonfly (covered with ice and snow nearby under an ash tree), and go out in the channel between Spirit Island and Long Island. I want to point my binoculars at the lilting water three feet away around Dragonfly and bring the full orb of the Long Nights Moon's mirror expressions big and flashy inside. I want gleaming silver flares from the wavelets to dance through my pupils, up so close that I, Long Nights Moon, and Lake Superior seem as one. Being on Lake Superior is therapeutic to me.

TO BUILD A sustainable world, we need people who are therapeutic with each other in tangible ways. In this chapter, we see Jesus as a master therapist who helped restore health with hugs, massages, anointings with oil, and washings of feet. Today, we need to listen to each other (instead of interrupting each other as we see so often on TV), make warm direct eye contact, shake hands with both hands, and give friendship hugs. In certain situations, we learn to massage and wash each other's feet. I suggest we attach a Laughing Circle agenda to Green Corps and Ecoholics Anonymous groups. We empower each other to use holistic aerobic, cardiovascular, and magnetic energy to connect and empower each other.

PRINCIPLE—Healthy humans practice reciprocal therapy.

The therapies of Jesus connected feet to head, heart to skin, and spirit to action. The first healings included therapeutic touch and occurred at Capernaum. The Rabbi stretched out his hand and touched a person with a skin disease. He next took the hand of Peter's mother-in-law, who had a fever, and raised her up. Many people pressed around Jesus to *qereb* (touch) him.

The word *qereb* occurs over one hundred times in the gospels and signifies more intimacy than in American culture. In Galilee, *qereb* included what Chinese physicians have done for thousands of years, putting fingertips on the pulse to sense the health of the internal organs of the body. The essence of *qereb*—to draw near, touch, and come close—is to align one's energy with another's so that the physician can let the Web of Energy (*Shemaya*) flow freely within and around the patient.

Jesus instructed his friends to anoint people with oil and to rub it on their bodies, healing them (Mark 6:13). Today, massage, physical, and aroma therapists continue this tradition. I've experienced many forms of physical therapy, and my grandson, Calvin, is a massage therapist. The more therapeutic touch we experience, the higher the possibility that we act green in a healthier way.

Jesus took kids in his arms and hugged them (Mark 10:13–15). Children have not built up barriers against being hugged and hugging. The physical and social barriers that adults build between classes of people, genders, nations, and religions are not natural in children. Without extensive and therapeutic touching and hugging, youths become neurotic. As a college student, my son, Jeffrey, liked to put his feet in my lap and ask me to rub them. Hugs are both preventive and restorative to health.

My grandson, Erik, when aged two and three, came running toward me for a unique body-to-body squeeze. Unprompted by me, he wedged himself between my left side and the left arm of my Lazy Boy chair. We did *qereb* up close and snug. He always chose my left side, closest to my heart.

Children and pet dogs and cats lead the way, in terms of warm hugging and snuggling, within the Presence of The One. Temple religion in first century Palestine kept pet dogs and cats, women, and children out of the Holy of Holies. But Jesus, by contrast, I picture growing up and experiencing youngsters having free range and endless hugs in the open air meeting on *Sabbat* in Nazareth's plaza.

One day, people brought a man, possibly Greek, to Jesus near the city of Bethshean. The man could hardly speak and hear, and people pleaded with Jesus to lay his hands on him. Jesus took this person into a private place behind some reeds where the crowd couldn't see. He placed his fingers into the man's ears and focused upon *Shemaya*. Jesus withdrew his fingers, bent over, and spit on the ground. He picked up a mixture of spittle and mud and rubbed his hands together until the mixture covered his fingers. Mouth enzymes in saliva have restorative power. Jesus put his fingers coated with mud and spit into the man's mouth and massaged his tongue. The man tasted the living Earth and swallowed his own saliva with the saliva of Jesus. The constricted mouth and throat opened to new senses. Jesus breathed close to the man's face in rhythm with the man's breaths.

The fingers of Jesus went into the man's ears. As the Rabbi pulled them out, he said forcefully, "*Ephphatha!*" Be opened. Clear the way. Receive energy from the soil and saliva. The man's heart and lips said yes. His ears opened, and he started speaking clearly. People were amazed. The Aramaic word *ephphatha* appears untranslated in English bibles (Mark 7:31–37).

Jesus used physical therapy practices that were common in the first century and also introduced practices that were culturally out-of-bounds. He and his friend Mary of Bethany, the sister of Martha and Lazarus, showed up at the home of Simon the Pharisee. Mary had a jar of myrrh and stood weeping behind the reclined Jesus. Myrrh, a pungent oil from an east African bush, is perhaps the most grounding of essential oils. Mary's tears wet his feet, and she wiped them dry with her hair. She kissed his feet and anointed them with myrrh. The oil's fragrance filled the house (Luke 7:37–38; John 12:3). Simon supposed that Mary was a prostitute. This aromatic scene was so extraordinary that four gospels include it in one fashion or another. Two gospels state that Mary's action would be praised to the ends of the Earth.

It is likely that Mary of Bethany and Jesus staged the unforgettable event at Simon's house. She was doing what Jesus instructed, *Sag regla*. Wash feet. Jesus asked his associates to wash each other's feet in reciprocal fashion. This practice at the time, especially between the genders, was extraordinarily scandalous, and was as shocking as it would be today to feature a gay couple French kissing at a presidential inauguration.

Jesus also broke the taboo that male hosts should not act like slaves and women. After a meal with his closest associates, he took off his outer garment, wrapped a towel around his waist, and got a basin of water. He knelt in front of Peter, Mary Magdalene, John, and Mary of Bethany. (There are implicit hints in the records that women were present; for example, a large number of women gathered around Jesus at the time of the crucifixion.) One by one, he washed and toweled the feet of his male and female friends. Then he put his outer garment back on and reclined at the table. He said, "Do you realize what I've done? You call me [Rabbi]... and you're right: that's who I am. So if I am your [Rabbi]...and have washed your feet, you ought to wash each other's feet. [*Ant hayaba sag regla had.*] In other words, I've set you an example. You are to do as I've done to you" (John 13:12–15, SV).

PRACTICE—We reduce participation in the money economy and renew energy by reciprocal, friendship therapy.

Today the third Jesus, described by writer Deepak Chopra at the beginning of the book, is here, and as Rumi reminds us, is in the streets and byways of our world. Jesus wants, through our following his examples of therapeutic touch, to "resurrect" us by inspiring us to heal ourselves and others.

We need to develop deep bonds with our friends and neighbors through preventive therapy. Each of us today has mercury in our body tissues, one of the most dangerous toxins. We also have dozens of synthetic chemicals in our bodies that break down our immune systems. Thus, we need to take a proactive, preventive stance toward health, not a passive stance waiting until cancer or other symptoms arise. We can practice physical therapies as friendship exchanges, and thus expend less energy in the money economy.

Friendship therapy starts with ordinary, daily behavior. We greet each other cheerfully, clasping a hand with both of our hands. We smile into our friends' eyes and inquire about their welfare. We listen with our whole being, not with shallow attention. We pat their hands, touch their shoulders, hug them, if appropriate, and wish them well. We give and hope to receive in kind.

Evidence is clear that friendly touch and hugs heal, based on research at the Touch Research Institute at the University of

Miami School of Medicine and at other institutions in the United States, Sweden, and Scotland. Friendly touch and hugging can reliably communicate the emotions of love, gratitude, and sympathy. Unfriendly touching can signal anger, fear, and disgust. Kind physical contact releases such hormones as oxytocin, melatonin, and serotonin. These hormones reduce pain, lower blood pressure, and relieve depression and stress. Other therapeutic effects include strengthening social bonding, boosting the immune system, and halting or slowing such symptoms as diabetes, migraine headaches, cancer, and autoimmune disorder.

Mennonites, Pentecostals, Catholics, Orthodox, and other groups practice foot washing. I have helped organize foot-washing ceremonies in two Presbyterian churches. The First Baptist Church of North Augusta, North Carolina, in December 2007 organized a project of giving free shoes to needy children. Volunteers sat before the children, washed their feet, and put on clean socks and shoes.

If washing feet seems awkward, we can offer to massage a friend's feet. Foot reflexology deals with nerve endings in the feet, which connect to other parts of the body, including internal organs. Evidence indicates that foot massage brings benefits like other forms of touch.

We also can massage our own feet daily in a ten-part ritual that the Japanese use regularly, which I learned from my friend Midori (her name means green) whose home is in Nagoya, Japan. This ten-part foot treatment picks me up and centers me.

1. Clasp the fingers of your right hand between the toes of your left foot and vice versa in a hand/foot shake.
2. With your fingers clasped between the toes, rotate the foot clockwise and counter-clockwise.
3. Bend your toes front and back.
4. Pull your fingers up the valleys between the toes and foot ligaments.

5. Do the same with the ankle tendons.
6. Dig your fingers into the bottoms of your feet, from the toes to the heels.
7. Rub and rotate each toe.
8. Slap the insteps.
9. Clasp your ankle with both hands, and shake each foot.
10. Press sharply with your fingernails on the cuticles of each toenail.

The most sensible way for us to make use of the only part of our body that regularly touches the Earth is, as the dictionary describes it, "to advance the feet alternately, always keeping one foot on the ground in bipedal locomotion." Let's invite a friend to join us in walking, creating a socially bonding experience. A prime command for green living is to walk. Thou shalt get up off thy posterior and take a walk outside daily.

According to a psychological study reported in *USA Today* (August 13, 2008), walking outside for just fifteen minutes will make you feel happier, more energetic, and more protective of the environment.

A friend started walking five miles a day when she was sixty years of age. Now, at ninety-three years, *I have no idea where she is.*

The average American takes nine hundred steps a day. Can we imagine living under a law that confines us to walking no more than the length of three football fields a day? We'd yell about tyranny. But we tyrannize ourselves. About 35 percent of Americans are sedentary sitters and riders who think feet essentially are for dangling. When we go outside the front door, 93 percent of the time it is to get in the car. The federal budget devotes only 1 percent of billions of dollars in the highway budget on facilities for pedestrians. A witty book on the health of walking (including eccentric walking, walking songs, and spiritual walking) is *The Lost Art of Walking* by Geoff Nicholson.

Walking is a perfect prescription for the 30 percent of Americans who are obese—big enough to think twice about getting on an elevator with them, says the writer Bill Bryson, who I have cited several times. Bill writes that people close to him call him Mr. Blimpy and ask what he thinks he is doing opening a cupboard by accident and removing Cheez Doodles. At a restaurant, his trim wife and kids order themselves the Deluxe Supreme Goo Skillet Feast with extra sour cream and a side order of nachos with hot fudge sauce.

"And for Mr. Blimpy here?" asks the waiter.

"Just bring him some bran cutlets."

ATTITUDE—We use wholehearted, whole-brained, and whole-bodied laughter exercise in Green Corps, Ecoholics Anonymous, and other groups to empower sustainability processes in the whole world.

Jesus used satire to get people around him to laugh, which involves the whole brain and the whole body.

Let's recall that laughing is about exercise for people of all ages that requires no jokes or humor but can overlap with them. Laughing exercise is inclusive of people who often don't get jokes, feel mocked or insulted by jokes, or feel they don't have a sense of humor. Research shows that laughter strengthens the immune system, reduces stress, increases relaxation, lowers pain, and provides cardiovascular aerobic exercise. My granddaughter, Lindsey Lee, and I have often laughed together, simply because one of us starts and the other joins in. My internist and geriatric specialist friend, Uday Deoskar, says, "Drink laughter in large doses! You do not need jokes to laugh in groups. Laugh, and more laughter ensues."

Laughter is contagious and is causing an epidemic. In the 1980s, a social movement called Laughing Circles developed independently in India with Madan Kataria and in America with

Steve Wilson. These two laugh leaders and their networks met each other in the 1990s and have been cooperating since. Laughing Circles now exist throughout the world and meet a deep need for Vitamin T, the "tribal" and neighborhood connection that we all long for that gives us a sense of belonging.

Laughing Circles exist in Seattle at the Harborview Medical Center and at the Seattle Cancer Treatment and Wellness Center. In Harborview, a clinical psychiatric nurse wearing a striped hat starts a "Ho, ho, ha, ha, ha," and others stretch, pick imaginary grapes, clap, tickle, hoot, and howl. During the thirty-minute session, the roar sometimes rises to an ear-splitting level.

A laughing circle in Duluth, Minnesota meets weekly in a city square for fifteen minutes. People report euphoric benefits that last for hours, days, and in some cases, all week.

A prime reason to combine green groups with laughing exercise is that they both have a holistic perspective. Laughing groups welcome people of every tongue and ethnic group, because laughter is a universal language. No one has an accent or a lisp when laughing. Think globally, laugh locally. Unlike specific emotions that activate a particular part of the brain, laughing groups activate the whole brain, stimulating images in the right hemisphere, names of people in the left hemisphere, social bonding in the frontal lobe, diaphragm and facial movements in the motor sections, and sensory processing in the rear lobe. Laughing Circles integrate the whole person and the whole social group. Their universal appeal makes them ideal for sustainability groups whose agenda involves the whole world.

Don't get mad, get funny. When feeling pain, laugh until it heals. In a car, replace road rage with an opportunity for being on a laughter stage. I do some of my best laughing while driving in a car. Rumi asked, "What is hidden in our chests? Laughter." A benediction for a group laughing is, "May the farce be with you."

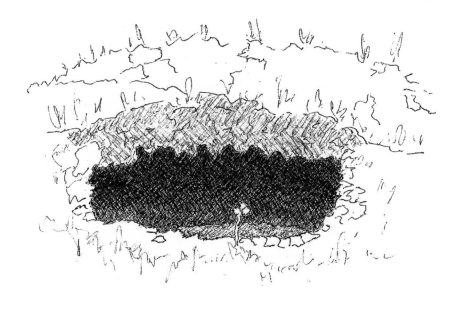

Jesus took shelter, meditated, and slept in this limstone cave called
The Eye of The One
(The Eye of God).
The cave is about twenty feet long, with a stone seat along the back
and sand floor. The Eye of The One, three miles south of Jesus' head-
quarters in Capernaum, is 300 feet from the Sea of Galilee on a slope
above hot springs called Waters of Good Fortune.
The cave gives a panoramic view of the entire Sea of Galilee.
A mustard plant is growing between rocks in the
middle foreground entrance.

10

SANE ASYLUMS

WOULD JESUS HAVE A LOW CARBON FOOTPRINT?

You can't have everything. Where would you put it?
— *Steven Wright*

*I*T was morning of the day before Christmas, and all through my Eagle Moon house occupied only by me, not a moderately bright human was stirring, not even a mouse.

I awoke to twelve inches of fresh snow plastered on the north side of trees in such a way that when I was looking south from the sun room, the trees looked like one-hundred-foot-tall icicles standing straight up. On the eaves, icicles two inches thick at their base tapered straight down. In every direction, there was a glittering paradise of evergreens so heavy with snowflakes that I could barely see the branches. I dreamed of a white Christmas, and the weather elves said, "Let's do it."

With anticipation of a cup of steaming chai tea prepared by Marie at Mission Hill Coffee House, I brushed a foot of snow off my Windstar, nicknamed Zeroing In on Zeroing In, or Zero for short. I shoveled snow from around Zero. Three years ago on a day with nine inches of snow, I was able to get to the coffee house with my front-wheel drive. "So today," I said to myself, "I can make it."

I put Zero in its lowest gear and moved slowly through the thick blanket of snowflakes. For the first few moments, I was elated. I was moving right along. But then, Zero began slowing down. More gas didn't help. Zero was pushing a wave of snow that was getting higher, and eventually, we made zero progress. I put the gear in reverse, and happily, Zero went backward. I tried again. I went forward, strained, and came to another stop. I repeated the back and forward process.

What's that at the end of the driveway? It's a large bank of snow deposited by the snowplow. That wasn't there when we had nine inches three years ago. I backed up a little further this time to get enough momentum to barge through and knock over the snow wall. Instead of shoveling away the snow wall before making this attempt, I ended up in a car stranded like a beached whale. For an hour, I chiseled ice around the tires with the only cutting tool available, a claw hammer. Sweat, shovel, chisel, sweat. On my hands and knees, I reached for snow that was packed under the car.

I got in Zero and spun deeper into the ice under the snow. Zero's movement, forward or backward, was precisely zero. There would be no coffee house this morning. Plus, I earned an award for being "not a moderately bright human stirring" on the day before Christmas. "Machine can triumph over nature," I had told myself, and the machine lost. I had to desert the car and walk back to Eagle Moon. Later, a person on the island named Zach called our house where I was writing about Zero's plight. Zack offered to help. He happened to be driving by, a rare occurrence since I live on a dead-end lane. The helpfulness of people on Spirit Island is part of our code. "Got a problem? Give me a sec, and I'll be there."

Tonight, the wonder of Christmas Eve on Spirit Island is that we do not need electric displays to celebrate. I walked outside, and there was no light pollution here. Down at Many Cedars Beach, I saw the faint glow of the towns of Ashland and Wash-

burn shimmering miles away across the Chequamegon Bay of
Lake Superior. Spirit Island is a cosmic Christmas. Who of us
wants to put lighted icicles on the eaves when we have Red Pine
Forest on the north shore with its ice crystal ornaments?

FROM THE FIRST visit to the island in the summer of 2000 until
now, I haven't felt so much that these six acres of Eagle Moon belong to me, but that I belong to an abode as large as all ten thousand island acres of Spirit Island. I belong to a residence that
includes the miles of open Lake Superior around me. (Some visitors to our island, so socialized to being land-bound, ask when
they get off the ferry, "Does water go all the way around?") I
belong to the domicile of the hundred miles of Lake Superior
that stretch to Duluth, Minnesota, the hundred miles that extend
to Canada, and the hundreds of miles that go as far east as the
Mackinac Bridge in Michigan. I inhabit the manor of the Great
Lakes basin.

I belong to the address of my home planet resonating with
the hourly gong of the iron and nickel core of Mother Earth, lower than the Tibetan contrabass monks can chant. The thunder
of this gong, coming up through the nerves and fibers in my
feet, is, as I write even now, reverberating several octaves lower
than human ears can hear. That gonging, going on for billions of
years, is what vibrates here where I sit, or sometimes kneel on
my knee pads, at my computer. I feel its foundational joy to the
world.

PRINCIPLE—Earth Community shelters
species.

Jesus did not own a house. He was an itinerant who traveled
with only one robe and one undergarment, and thus, he had
no change of clothes. He carried no staff, even though people
typically carried a staff to protect themselves from robbers. He

usually traveled with no knapsack. His feet became calloused. He frequently slept on the ground. Jesus instructed his associates to act in the same manner. In exchange for wisdom teaching and therapy by Jesus and his associates, such friends as Mary Magdalene, Peter's mother-in-law in Capernaum, Philip, Andrew, and others opened their houses and offered food and temporary shelter.

Jesus did not accumulate possessions, and he didn't have to waste time figuring out where to put them. Everything was fine where it was. He knew that he already had full access to the Presence of The One and full access to Earth Community, and thus he was free to partner with everything without the burden of protecting his stuff or lugging it around. Own nothing and partner with everything.

On one occasion, a scholar came up to Jesus and his associates while they were walking down a road. The scholar said dramatically to the Rabbi, "I'll follow you wherever you go."

Jesus toyed with the scholar's mind and said, "Foxes have dens, and birds of the sky have nests." Gesturing I imagine all around the horizon, he added that he had not one spot on Earth, anywhere, to rest his head (Matt. 8:19–20, SV).

Mr. Scholar muffled a snicker, catching the hyperbole of Jesus. Sensing that Jesus loved play, he laughed, I suppose, and said, "Sure enough, Rabbi. You don't own one den or nest. You don't own one house. But you, unlike me, own thousands of choices for places to sleep on the ground. You own dozens of choices for homes that provide temporary shelter and food. You are wealthy. Earth is your sane asylum."

Itinerant Jesus probably joined the repartee, responding, "You're smarter than a scholar. You understand our plan to show everyone how to break the stranglehold of rich landlords over resources. We're teaching folk to share nature's abundance and not accumulate excessive goods. You're most welcome to join our itinerant mission. Become homeless and have access to numerous homes."

The carbon footprint of Jesus, in terms of his investment in his own privately owned shelter, was zero. In this regard, I do not personally know anyone today who claims to be a follower of Jesus who follows Jesus.

Earlier, we saw the houses and caves in Nazareth when Jesus was growing up. Now, we are going to revisit Nazareth, this time for the birth of Jesus, to get a more vivid idea of the sustainable style of his earliest days and his earliest dwelling. Many scholars think that the evidence is strong that Jesus was born in Nazareth and that the birth stories of Matthew and Luke, written last among portions of gospel narratives, were parables by early Christians to support the claim that the Rabbi was the messiah. There is no clear evidence about the season of the birth of Jesus, so I am placing it at the end of the rainy season, unlike the decision in the fourth century to place it at the time of the winter solstice and the Roman Saturnalia festival.

A child was born to Mary and Joseph during the Festival of Purim in February. Villagers were singing and circle dancing about gazelles (Song of Songs 2:17). These elegant animals grazed within the watershed of the Tabor stream, whose headwaters began at Nazareth. In this rainy season time, gazelles partook of grasses and wildflowers on the lower parts of the Mount Tabor watershed slopes in the morning and moved toward the upper parts by sunset. Wolves and foxes culled and ate gazelles, keeping the population numbers down so that gazelles did not take more than their share of grasses and shrubs. Give us this day our proportionate daily grass.

The story that follows comes from anthropology and archeology about birthing and housing practices in the first century.

Mary's time came in a fieldstone house with a dirt floor covered by straw. A midwife assisted Mary in her breathing, and other women attended. Olive oil lamps dimly lit the one room. Shadows rippled on the walls. Mary pushed and hunkered. Then the child slipped out. The midwife put this ruddy one in Mary's arms. Mary fed and held the child. After the baby's first squeal, the midwife severed the umbilical cord and wrapped it and the afterbirth in straw.

The midwife got up with her bloody, strong smelling straw bundle and went to a nearby cave. She told Joseph and the other men that Mary had delivered a son. The midwife took a hoe and walked until she found a female fig tree. Here she dug a hole near the roots and placed the umbilical cord and afterbirth in the hole.

Eight days after the birth of Mary's child, family and friends gathered for the circumcision of the boy. Guests brought dates, fig cakes, and wine and assembled in and around the field stone house. Mary and Joseph announced his name, Eshua. Joseph offered a dove to *Allaha* as a symbol of thankfulness for the gift of Eshua. Joseph had bartered for a dove from a clan member who bred these birds.

Some days after the circumcision festival, Joseph and some clan members walked six miles to Mount Tabor to dig up a young oak sapling. Mount Tabor is unusual because no other height in the Jordan Valley watershed stands alone. An unforgettable limestone prominence, Tabor rises several hundred feet above the wide plain of Jezreel. No other mountain in Galilee is prominently symmetrical and round. From the east, west, north, and south, its shape is like a woman's breast. One of the ancient Hebrew divine names is *El Shaddai*, literally The Breast, typically translated Almighty. Mount Tabor has been where people have venerated oaks, which are compact, strong, deciduous living beings, with black-green acorns. The Hebrew patriarch Jacob revered oaks, putting figurines under them and burying people under oaks. Israelites made the son of Gideon their ruler under an oak tree. During the time of Mary and Joseph, people observed rituals amid oak groves on Mount Tabor. Today, people take green cloths as gifts of thanks to oaks and as expressions of hopes for healing.

Joseph and his companions took their oak sapling back to Nazareth and planted it in honor of Eshua's birth, a long-standing social custom upon the birth of a son. As Eshua would grow up, he would go to his Tabor oak, and the two would mature together. Joseph planted the young oak sapling amid purple irises and other wildflowers and such herbs as fragrant rosemary and jasmine near his fieldstone house and artisan cave. If Mary's baby had been a girl, social custom determined that Joseph would have dug up and replanted an acacia tree sapling. Putting the oak sapling in the Earth spoke of the day when Eshua, a young betrothed man, would marry. For the marriage, people would take a branch from his betrothed's acacia tree and a branch from his oak tree and weave them together as a canopy. Jewish weddings to this day weave branches in a canopy.

The first days of the infant Eshua's life occurred in a fieldstone house in one of the most off-the-main-road Jewish villages in the Middle Eastern world. What are the odds that this child, a peasant nobody, a noncitizen in the Roman Empire, a child of nonelite, illiterate parents, would become the favorite person and friend of millions?

What are the odds that the dung and mud-roofed shelter with an earthen floor in which Eshua grew up and his later itinerant, homeless lifestyle could become a model for people in our day for making our Earth shelters green? When we ask "What would Jesus do?" about sustainable housing practices, we don't have to guess about his choices.

PRACTICE—We green our structures, seeking to have zero net energy use and zero carbon impact.

According to an article in the Summer 2007 issue of *Nature Con-*

servancy, a member of the Intergovernmental Panel on Climate Change, Patrick Gonzalez, practices a lifestyle with his wife that makes them carbon neutral. This lifestyle began two decades ago when, as a Peace Corps volunteer in Senegal, Patrick helped villagers with reforestation. Fifteen years ago, he sold the only car he ever owned, a red Toyota Corolla Sport. His wife got rid of her car before they met. They buy and preserve local food by canning and take public transportation everywhere. He uses a spreadsheet to track his energy use and then purchases carbon offsets from a company that builds windmills and methane recovery plants. He says, "Going climate neutral is both a personal and professional issue for me. Melting glaciers, burning forests, flooded coasts — climate change threatens ecosystems and human well-being."

Compare the lifestyle of Patrick and the homelessness of Rabbi Jesus with the house that basketball star Michael Jordan built in Highland Park, Illinois. Some who have seen photos of Jordan's house think it's a shopping mall. One person said it is about the size of the country of Liechtenstein. Michael has house-sized bathrooms, closets, and bedrooms. His "McMansion" includes thirty thousand square feet of brick, mortar, and steel and encompasses over twenty times more space than my Illinois house.

According to an analysis of my carbon footprint, as mentioned earlier, my own energy consumption is such that, if every human consumed as much as I do, humanity would require six Earths. Jordan's consumption pace proportionately requires 120 Earths. He gets the means to live this way by putting a ball through a steel hoop and wearing Hanes shorts!

Our houses can be energy and water smart, in contrast. A model home of 2,500 square feet at Chicago's Museum of Science and Industry, with solar-paneled roof, uses half the energy and a third of the water of traditional homes. Bathroom tiles are recycled wine bottles. Hardwood floors are sustainable bamboo.

Water from the bathroom sink flows to the toilet. A bicycle in the children's bedroom charges a video battery. The house's architect, Michelle Kaufmann, says, "Green should be for everyone."

Green can be tiny. The Tumbleweed Tiny House Company in Sebastopol, California sells small, transportable homes. This company inspired a Yale, environmental studies major, Elizabeth Turnbull, to estimate she would spend $14,000 in housing costs for grad school. So with recycled materials she built her own tiny, transportable house, 8 feet by 18 feet, on a flatbed trailer. It has a sleeping and storage loft, a study nook, a kitchen, living area, and a composting toilet. Solar panels will provide electricity, and she'll cook and heat with propane. Estimated total cost will be around $11,000, including propane and furniture.

We don't need to overconsume in our buildings in general. A certification system was developed in 1998 by the United States Green Building Council called Leadership in Energy and Environmental Design (LEED). This system now involves over 14,000 projects in 50 states and 30 countries. Standards for certification include the categories of sustainable sites, water efficiency, energy and atmosphere, material and resources, indoor environmental quality, and innovative design process.

One community giving leadership to green building, as presented in the website www.rapidgrowthmedia.com, is Grand Rapids, Michigan. A key player is Peter Wege, who makes grants to building programs that meet green criteria. A prime example of a LEED-certified building, among many in the downtown area, is the new Grand Rapids Art Museum. Another building, the East Hills Center where Peter has his office space, has water saving dual-flush toilets and lighting that senses the ambient daylight. A remarkable feature is the roof garden and a rain garden next to the parking lot that treats all the rain falling on the site. Peter has a dollars and sense explanation for what he's doing. His office space costs about 50 percent of what his peers spend for light and heat in non-LEED commercial space.

I am pleased that my community of Bloomington/Normal has several LEED-certified buildings, including the first one to use state money, the Workforce Development Center at Heartland Community College. The extra 2 percent in construction costs of the Development Center compares with at least 20 percent savings in energy for maintenance during the life of the building. One feature is a geothermal heating and cooling system.

High aims for buildings are to produce zero net energy consumption in a year, and zero carbon impact. Abu Dhabi on the Persian Gulf has just announced (www.breitbart.com/article, Jan. 21, 2008) that it is beginning to construct the world's first zero-carbon city, Masdar City, to house 50,000 people in a car-free environment. The six-square-mile Masdar City will have solar panels on each roof and will have no carbon footprint. Residents will move around in a light railway line and automated transport pods. Travelers in the pods, like riders in an elevator, will simply indicate where they want to go and the pod will take them there.

ATTITUDE—We have the audacity to hope for sane, sustainable buildings.

Today, Americans own bigger houses and more things than any humans in history. What has our extensive ownership of things done? We have automatic doors, fast foods, electric can openers, and, as Bill Bryson satirizes, "disposable toothbrushes that comes with the toothpaste already loaded." We buy lighted, revolving tie racks. The more convenience gizmos we own, the more we worry about work and money so that we can buy bigger dwellings and more "whatchamacallits." We assume that the more conveniences we have, the happier we will be. But the first syllable of convenience is "con."

Our hope needs to be green, not to have convenience, for no

other hope will put us in sync with our truest selves and with our More-than-Human neighbors in Earth Community.

What can we hope to do? The average American house emits about twenty thousand pounds of CO_2 a year, twice as much as a car and more than all the emissions — house, car, and air travel — by an average Swedish household. A super-green home can cut bills by 66 percent as outlined in *The Live Earth Global Warming Survival Handbook*.

Can we hope to move down the thermostat two degrees and save 4 percent in bills? Can we insulate, the higher "R-value" the better, with blown-in cellulose, recycled denim, or foams like Icynene? Can we plant trees and save as much as 15 percent in heating and air conditioning costs?

Can we hope to install double-pane windows with a "low-e" coating that can reduce energy use by 30 percent? Can we put weather seal around windows and doors? Can we look for the Energy Star label on electronics, refrigerators, washers, and air-conditioners? Can we air-dry clothes?

Can we wrap the water heater in a cozy blanket? Can we install a composting toilet? Can we get natural linoleum, cork, or bamboo floors?

Some folks today are doing packed-dirt floors, like the birth home of Jesus in the first century, not because they are poor, but because they are hoping for a saner world for themselves, their children, and their grandchildren.

If we fulfilled these hopes, we would live in a relatively sane asylum.

Wild purple lily

11

Bare and Broke Folks

Would Jesus shop till he drops?

I must have been incredibly insane to sneak into my own house
and steal money.
— Rumi

Today is Christmas. Jesus was born broke with a birthday suit. Christmas can remind us to celebrate the bare essentials. We don't bring stuff with us at birth and can't take stuff with us.

In this chapter, we hear the music of sustainability in regard to raiment and to the bottom line. One of the greatest gifts of Green Jesus is teaching us how to deal with anxiety about clothes and finances. Even though we have access to the biggest buffet line of pills and counseling modalities in the history of the human species, over twenty million Americans have acute worries, such as panic anxiety disorder, obsessive-compulsive disorder, and social phobia. It is possible to pick up our fretting mind, like a running child, and calm its running, hyperactive emotional feet until they slow down. It is possible to set our mind down again and go at a calmer, easier pace. It is possible to do breathing exercises — short nasal out breaths and intakes — to divert our attention from distress.

PRINCIPLE—The ecology, not money, creates value.

Jesus said, "Why worry about clothes? Notice how the wild lilies grow. They don't slave and they never spin...Solomon at the height of his glory was never decked out like one of them. If God dresses up the grass in the field...won't God [The One] care for you?" (Matt. 6:25–30, SV).

In the Sermon on the Mount, Jesus spoke to audience members who wore two garments: a robe and an undergarment. I am putting the scene in contemporary English. Jesus said, "If someone comes and takes away your robe..." Audience members mused, "Well, at least I will have my undergarment left." But Jesus didn't stop there. He said, "Don't prevent that person from taking your undergarment also" (Luke 6:29).

Jesus said another loony thing. "If you have money, don't lend it at interest. Rather, give it to someone from whom you won't get it back" (Thomas 95:1–2, SV). Rumi wrote about the same nonpossessiveness as Jesus in a more absurd statement. "I must have been incredibly insane to sneak into my own house and steal money."

PRACTICE—In the areas of clothing and finance, we reduce products and renew energy.

Let's look at the statement by Jesus about wild lilies not slaving and spinning in the form of a parody.

One spring, the bulb of a lily plant heard an observer criticize the purplish shade of its bloom. While her bloom faded, Bulb worried about looking better next spring, envied world-famous fashion models, and developed a plan.

That summer, Bulb slaved in the hot sun picking cotton. In

the autumn, she spun the cotton into fibers and collected wild plants to dye the fibers blue. During the winter, she wove the fibers into cloth. She stitched a dress. Fretful about having it ready and looking perfect, she made several mistakes. She ripped out seams and started over again. In the early spring, Bulb took anti-anxiety pills so her hands wouldn't shake while restitching. Then, the blue didn't look right. So, she bleached the cloth and re-dyed the material.

Now frantic, Bulb stayed up every night, including the night before the bloom opened, to get the dress ready. Exhausted on bloom day, she barely had the strength to slip on her dress. She then fell into bed for extended rest and recuperation.

Visitors to Bulb heard her say that making the dress took four hundred hours. One visitor said, "At $10 an hour, this streaked, rumpled blue dress cost you $4,000. What you worked so hard to make, I'm sorry to say, my dear, doesn't come close to the beauty of your purplish bloom that cost you nothing." Another visitor said, "Your fantastic bloom has more glamour than fashionable Hollywood stars. Forget the dress. You look stunning without it."

Rabbi Jesus says today that the answer to anxiety about whether or not we have enough clothes or the right style of clothes is not to have any. His lampoon helps us to let go of possessiveness of clothes and to make us aware of our acquisitive habits. Do we want to accumulate clothes? Are we preoccupied with the latest brands? If we don't truly own any clothes since we weren't born with them, then one or two sets of clothes can seem like abundance and luxury.

There are things we can do to renew energy related to clothing, especially if we give clothes we are not using or seldom wearing to Goodwill or the Salvation Army. Likewise, if we need clothes, we can go to these same places or to garage sales.

Here are other things to reduce and renew.

We keep the thermostat down in the winter. Since 90 percent

of our body heat escapes from the top of our head, we wear a hat.

We wear a sweater and save 4 percent on our energy bill. Right now, I am wearing lightweight, thermal underwear and a thermal vest.

We acquire clothes with vegetable coloring and without chemical dyes, which seep into the water supply.

We avoid dry cleaners that use the chemical PERC (85 percent of dry cleaners do), which causes cancer and reproductive damage.

We buy vegetable-tanned leather and avoid leather prepared with such toxics as tannic acid and formaldehyde.

We wear bamboo fabrics, which do not involve pesticides and are biodegradable.

We use hemp belts, which are also biodegradable.

We get organic cotton jeans. Regular cotton is the most pesticide-driven crop there is.

As for money, the statement by Jesus that we give it away, like his paradoxical statement about letting people take our clothes, is not literal. His words about clothing and money are primarily about anxiety and proportionality. If we go penniless in our minds, then we reduce our worry about money and possessions.

There are two people who come close to carrying out the statement of Jesus about giving away money and not lending it at interest. Hal and Norma Taussig live in a small home and run a low-interest organization called Untours Foundation (www.untoursfoundation.org). Hal rides a bike to the office. Loans granted by the Untours Foundation range from $6,000 to $250,000 and support fair trade groups. Employees of Untours Foundation receive equal wages. Hal and Norma pay themselves nothing and live on Social Security and her small savings. Basic profits from the foundation go back into the general fund. In 1999, Untours

Foundation received an award as the most generous business in the United States.

Bill Bryson helps us to reflect on the American government not acting responsibly with money, spending profligately, and stealing from coming generations. The United States national debt is trillions of dollars. To put that amount in perspective, Bill suggests that we initial and keep a dollar bill every second. At the end of three years of nonstop effort, we would have $100 million. After a thousand years, we would be as wealthy as Bill Gates. After 31,709.8 years, we could bank one trillion dollars.

We need also to reflect on how environmentally useless is the standard national index of monetary value, the GDP (Gross Domestic Product). The GDP counts anything, ecologically constructive or destructive. For example, tally up the profits for a zinc plant in Pennsylvania with its many emissions that denuded a mountain of every biological plant, the millions the government spent to clean up the mountain, and the medical bills of people made chronically ill by the contaminants. From a GDP perspective, each of these money transactions has value. Overfishing and deforestation make the GDP go up. The more reckless we are with nature, the more the GDP grows. Our current accounting system treats the Earth as a business in liquidation.

The Rabbi's wacky saying about giving away money helps motivate us to calculate using a new measure that I am labeling GEV (Gross Ecological Value). Some calculations are moving in this direction, such as those in Canada that use figures based on ecological value in relation to the Mackenzie River watershed. As discussed earlier, the watershed has a GEV ten times higher than GDP. We need to use Gross Ecological Value to calculate all public and private accounting.

Germany is a world leader in moving toward ecological accounting. This move is a necessity since the assumption that increased economic growth is a good has become counterproductive without adding in environmental and social costs.

A pioneering German law requires utilities to buy solar, wind, or other renewable energy-powered electricity from anyone at premium rates. This puts green accounting in the hands of the people and of local communities. One man, Rolf Disch, has put a rotating solar panel on top of his house. Rolf's system generates 5 times more electricity than he needs and makes him $3,000 a month in income in sales to the utilities. About a dozen German communities in 2008 produced all of their own energy needs. California in 2006 began a variation on this German system. Over 30 nations are applying some aspects of the German model.

As individuals, let's invest in green mutual funds and give at least ten percent of our income to green organizations.

In rich societies let's give a minimum of 2 percent of our income for micro-loans to third world people. Let's institute debt relief or debt cancellation to third world people. Our governments throughout the world need to agree to the same international minimum wage. Our corporations should pay none of their employees more than ten times the lowest salary.

ATTITUDE—In our hearts, we feel content with adequate raiment and money.

Contentment and happiness have an inverse relation to owning such things as clothes and money, as described in an article by Moises Velasquez-Manoff, "'Happy' Helps the Planet: Research Equates Well-Being with a Smaller Eco-Footprint," in the *Christian Science Monitor*. The World Values Survey finds that today Americans, who own twice as much as in 1950, are no happier now than then. Over-consumption does not make people happy. The first bite of flavorful French vanilla ice cream tastes yummy. The fiftieth tastes like cardboard.

Engagement with and service to others makes people happy. Which nations do you think are the happiest according to the World Values Survey? You might correctly pick Denmark, perhaps the greenest nation on Earth, as number one. But Puerto Rico and Columbia, numbers two and three? These Latin societies are less Taker oriented than first-world nations. Where societies with Leaver traits still exist today, they are the happiest, with stress on relatedness and curiosity.

The New Economics Foundation in London has established its own happiness survey instrument, Happy Planet Index. You will never guess the number one nation. It's an archipelago nation of 83 islands north of New Zealand, called Vanatu, which has tribal Leaver culture relatively intact. The United States ranks 150 on the Happy Planet Index.

One of the least-developed nations in the world, the Buddhist nation of Bhutan in the Himalayas, is the only country in the world to use a measure called Gross National Happiness as a way to value social success.

If attitudinally we own nothing, then we take heart by downsizing and not spending a lot of our energy taking care of things. If all we have basically is breath and spirit, then we don't focus upon clothes, but adornment in the form of health—health of body, mind, and spirit. Since we don't bring money into this world or take it with us, then we can laugh—if our laughing exercise has been going hilariously well—about the incongruity of striving so hard to own something that cannot last for us. As noted earlier, the one who laughs lasts!

POSTSCRIPT

After the Ending

Yahweh said,
"Proclaim liberty throughout the land to all the inhabitants."
— *Leviticus 25:17*

Unity is peace and silence. You are not God's mouthpiece. Try to
be an ear.
— *Rumi*

I walked this Christmas afternoon thinking of you, the reader. In my mind, I said, "Thanks for reading *Green Kingdom Come!* and for reflecting on it with me." Then you joined me on this Christmas walk, like you have observed me on my walks on Spirit Island throughout the various chapters of this book.

In our imaginary walk this Christmas afternoon we moved step by step through the snow as we made our way to Many Cedars Beach. We greeted over thirty cedars at the bluff overlooking Lake Superior, enjoying their woody, sweet-smelling presence. On the beach, we pulled up one foot, then the other, out of a boot-shaped hole in the snow. The low-lying sun, sinking in the west, scattered millions of flecks of light on the frisky water. Through our binoculars, these flecks sometimes appeared iridescent purple and sometimes golden green. We stood on the ice shelf, looking down at Lake Superior through our binoculars. The ripples, sprays, and tumbles, with their ever-skittering baubles, each a flitting mini-sun, appeared to leap against us. The sky above was in some places azure, other places aqua, and still others violet. Long, willowy shadows backlit snow white lace on shrubs as we returned to Eagle Moon from Many Cedars Beach. Around sunset, Long Nights Moon rose up full minus one day, at first a big orange blob and then a mix of tints. The moon phase on the cover of this book is nearing full moon. As I write now, our lunar friend is overhead, filling the forest with white luminescence.

I HAVE A dream, mentioned in the conversation with Jesus back at the beginning of this book, of the biblical idea, never enacted, of having a Jubilee period. At least 2,500 years ago, Yahweh, the Lord, asked the Hebrews to observe a Jubilee Year every fifty years. During this fiftieth year, Yahweh instructed people to give agricultural soil a rest and to open it up to poor people and to wild plants and animals. The Jubilee Year plan in those ancient times was a memory of what Leaver culture was like before the herding and farming Taker culture took over. It is amazing that this biblical command has gotten little attention. I have not found a book that applies the Jubilee Year to our current situation.

Yahweh said about the Jubilee Year, "Proclaim liberty throughout the land to all its inhabitants. You shall neither sow nor reap" (Lev. 25:10-11). Yahweh continued, "The land will yield its fruit, and you will eat your fill, and dwell in it securely" (Lev. 25:19). The Hebrews never did carry out these instructions of Yahweh.

During the last 2,500 years, humans have missed fifty Jubilee Years. But what has not been lost during more than two millennia is the essence of Leaver culture that the Bible clearly describes here in Leviticus. Let's begin to get in place common sense strategies for our species to unfold a never-before gala, a Grand Jubilee Half Century from 2010 to 2060, which would gradually reverse the unsustainable era in human history. President Obama and officials across the spectrum around the world need to give dynamic leadership.

One strategy, already discussed, is to "eat the view" beside our houses. (See EatTheView.Org) In the summer of 2008 edible landscaping was one of the fastest growing movements in our country. Food costs have grown. The nation's largest seed company, W. Atlee Burpee & Co., sold twice as many seeds in 2008 as 2007. A dime spent on seeds yields one dollar in produce. In 2008 I had tomatoes, peppers, celery, and cabbage in the front yard, and corn, onions, eggplant, cucumbers, watermelon, beans, and muskmelon in the back.

The first president in the White House, John Adams, had a White House garden, as did Woodrow Wilson (Liberty Garden) and FDR (Victory Garden). On spring equinox, March 21, 2009, First Lady Michelle Obama and 26 elementary school students planted a 1,100 square foot garden for vegetables, herbs, and berries on the south lawn of the White House. There will also be a beehive.

Another strategy, also discussed earlier, is deep listening to the species and habitats of Earth Community with all of our hearts, minds, and strength and embracing them within. We humans have been speaking over the top of the voices of departed species and over the top of chimpanzees, bonobos, and black bears, none of whom are our inferiors. Let's lower the volume on hyper-speaking and on the noise contamination of our machines.

An acoustical ecologist, Gordon Hempton, recorded places around the world ten years ago free of human-created sounds. Today he says, "Quiet is going extinct." Land places entirely free for 24 hours a day and seven days a week of human-created sound are disappearing. Research shows that quiet times alone in nature reduce stress, expand insight, and promote well-being. We need to reduce mechanical clamor and electronic beeps and to restore the balm of stillness that provides a think tank for the soul. See Richard Mahler. (February 27, 2009) "Defender of Quiet Places," *Christian Science Monitor*.

Let Stillness reign. Let's not miss a good chance to shut up! A closed mouth gathers no foot!

Let's open our hearts wider than ever and quiet our mind chatter as we envision a projected Grand Jubilee experience. Let's use the sayings and lifestyle of Jesus; the principles, practices, and attitudes in this book; and green wisdom wherever we find it. A sign of hope is that the United Nation reports a "green energy gold rush," with 60 percent more spent on wind, solar and other alternative energy assets in 2007 than in 2006. Future generations would remember a Grand Jubilee as the transition to a sustainable Earth Community. Our great-great-grandchildren, hopefully, would look back with gratitude upon this Grand Jubilee and call us the Greenest Generations since before the Taker mentality began. They would, we trust, celebrate us as the first generations to revive the conserving Leaver tradition.

We develop a new maxim for the Leaver age: "We leave enough; therefore, we are." We exhale "we" and inhale "are," a rhythm that does not emphasize our mental jabber but our diaphragmatic breathing. With the maxim, "We leave enough, therefore, we are," resonating within we don't react, as Eckhart Tolle writes, against More-than-Humans but synchronize with them.

We voice the Green Dream proposed by Jesus at the end of the dialogue with him in the "Tea for Three" section at the beginning of the book. We who dwell within Earth Community move together as a team, with all of us getting the glory.

Sayings of Jesus

This is a list of the sayings of the Rabbi cited in this book, with summaries of the sayings, not necessarily quotes, following the reference. For the meaning of these sayings, consult the book and Aramaic appendices.

Matthew

5:8	Blessed are the pure in heart.
5:39	If someone slaps you on the right cheek, turn the left cheek.
5:43–47	Love enemies. God sends rain on just and unjust. Bless those who curse you.
6:10	Thy Kingdom come.
6:11	Give us our daily bread.
6:25–30	Don't worry about clothes. Have trust like a lily.
6:34	Don't fret about tomorrow.
7:9–10	A parent doesn't feed kids stones and snakes.
7:21	Not every one who says, Lord, Lord, enters.
8:19–20	Foxes have dens, but I don't have a place to lay my head.
10:16	Be sly as a snake.
10:31	Don't fear.
10:37	Set aside mother and father.
10:39	Those who hate possessive life gain essential life.
11:25	Babies have more wisdom than scholars.
12:28	The Kingdom of God has arrived.

12:48–49	Who is my mother and brother?
13:33	The Kingdom of Heaven is like a woman putting yeast in bread.
15:11	Unclean rules from inside defile, not unclean foods.
16:25–26	Those who hate possessive life gain essential life.
17:20	Trust like a mustard seed can uproot a mountain.
18:1–4	Children are the greatest in the Kingdom of Heaven.
19:13–15	Children are the greatest in the Kingdom of Heaven.
21:16	Babies have more wisdom than scholars.
22:15–22	Give to Caesar what is Caesar's.

Mark

3:33	Who is my mother and brother?
4:21	People don't put a lamp under a bed.
4:26–29	Virgin Earth produces on her own.
4:30–32	The Kingdom of Heaven is like a mustard seed.
6:13	Rub oil on bodies to heal them.
7:31–34	Be opened. *Ephphatha.*
8:35	What is the profit in gaining the whole world and losing one's life?
9:43–47	If your hand gives you trouble, cut if off.
10:13–15	The Kingdom of God is like a child.
11:23	Trust like a mustard seed can uproot a mountain.

Luke

6:21	Blessed are weepers, who will laugh. The hungry will pig out.
6:27–38	Love your enemies. Bless those who curse you.
6:29	Let a person take your clothes.
6:32–35	Love your enemies.

8:19–21	Whoever does the Father's will is my mother and brother.
9:24	What is the profit in gaining the whole world and losing one's life?
9:59–60	Let the dead bury their dead.
11:29–36	People don't put a lamp under a bed.
11:52	Lawyers take away the key and don't use it themselves.
12:15	You can't add one hour to life by fretting.
12:17–20	A rich fool imagines bigger barns and then dies.
12:24	Consider crows. Don't fret about clothes and food.
12:25	Don't fret about time.
13:18–19	The Kingdom of God is like a mustard seed.
14:15–24	A great banquet brings into a rich man's house impure people off the street.
14:26	Set aside your mother and brother.
17:6	Trust like a mustard seed uproots a tree.
17:20–21	The Kingdom of God is within you.
17:33	Those who possessively cling to life will lose it, and those who don't will gain unending life.
18:15–17	The Kingdom of God is like a child.

John

3:1–9	Be born again of water and spirit.
6:5–7	Where is bread to feed this mob?
12:24	The kernel of wheat dies and lives.
12:25	Those who hate possessive life gain essential life.
13:12–15	Wash each other's feet.

Thomas

3:1–3	The Kingdom of God is here.
20:1–3	The Kingdom of Heaven is like a mustard seed.
22:1–3	The Father's domain is like a nursing baby.

39:1–3	Be sly as a snake.
51:1–2	The new world has come.
55:1–2	Set aside family.
95:1–2	Give money away.
99:3	Whoever does the Father's will is my mother and brother.
101:1–3	Set aside family.
113:1–4	The Kingdom of God is spread out on Earth.

Mary Magdalene

| 4:2–5 | The seed of humanity [the Kingdom of God] is within. |

Judas

| Scenes | I am not laughing at you, Judas. |

GREEN PRINCIPLES

The sayings and deeds of Jesus are compatible with the following green principles.

We meet the needs of the present without compromising the ability of future members of Earth Community to meet their needs. We stop using the Earth's resources faster than the Earth can replenish them. We are made for Earth Community. Earth Community is not made for us.

Until ten thousand years ago, our tradition was to be Leavers who let Earth Community (a synergy among ourselves, water, soil, plants, and animals) choose who lived and who died. Only after herding and farming began have we become Takers, dominating ecologies by taking plants and animals for life or death. Today, we need to revive the Leaver tradition, eating a wide diversity of species close to home and promoting fair access to wilderness and food for all species. We leave enough for everyone; therefore, we are.

Each chapter has a green principle based on sayings of Jesus in the gospels. With a green heart, we can apply these principles in daily living.

One: Dead and Reborn — Would Jesus drive a Hummer?
The death of over-consumption produces greenness.

Two: Here Now — Would Jesus forecast an ecological disaster?
Earth Community is here now, within and without.

Three: Inside Water, Out — Would Jesus honor a chimpanzee baby?
Life flows from inside water out.

Four: Downside Up — Would Jesus laugh 400 times a day?
Children are the greatest humans.

Five: Dropping Rain — Would Jesus picket against warfare?
Rain drops have no enemies.

Six: Soiled Goods — Would Jesus grow vegetables in the front yard?
Eco-diversity decides which foods species eat.

Seven: Mustard and Dandelion — Would Jesus spray weeds?
Wildness manifests itself everywhere.

Eight: Animal Teachers — Would Jesus organize ecological picnics?
Eco-diversity decides which foods species eat.

Nine: Washed Toes — Would Jesus massage people with AIDS?
Healthy humans practice reciprocal therapy.

Ten: Sane Asylums — Would Jesus have a low carbon footprint?
Earth Community shelters species.

Eleven: Bare and Broke Folks — Would Jesus shop till he drops?
The ecology, not money, creates value.

Green Practices

What follows is a selected list of green practices mentioned in the book. Review the text to get the complete inventory.

OnEarth: An Introduction

We "blast" to kingdom "departing" our Taker addictions and welcome a united kingdom of one Earth, under God, with liberty, justice, and equal green opportunity for all.

We pledge ourselves to relate with neighborliness to members of the human and the More-than-Human mineral, plant, and animal kingdoms.

We don't wait for but act to create the fullness of green kingdom come.

Tea for Three: A Conversation

We voice the following Green Dream.

We dream of the sun smiling upon our sustainable Earth home.

We dream of the rain falling upon a revival of species.

We dream of valuing an equal right to life and liberty for all species.

We dream of being one mind with Mother Earth.

We dream of renewable energy from east to west.

We dream of singing, "Green at last. We're green at last."

One—Dead and Reborn

We sing the song, "Enough for Everyone."
We reduce extractions in mining and in fossil fuel. We

1. Increase car fuel economy to 70 mpg by 2050.
2. Reduce car travel from 10,000 miles a year to 5,000 by increased mass transit, telecommuting, and urban design conducive to walking and biking.
3. Develop zero emission vehicles.
4. Develop bio-fuel from waste materials as a short-term replacement for fossil fuels until carbon-free technologies are invented.
5. Increase the efficiency of current coal plants from 32 percent to 60 percent and permit no new coal plants.
6. Increase building and appliance efficiency to achieve zero emissions by 2050.
7. Sequester CO_2 underground.

We renew Energy. We

8. Increase natural gas use fourfold as a short-term move until renewable technologies can replace natural gas.
9. Expand wind power to 75 times the current capacity.
10. Expand solar power to 1000 times the current capacity.

We redouble eco-diversity. We

11. Decrease deforestation to zero and double the rate of new tree plantings.
12. Stop soil erosion by conservative tillage at ten times the current usage, and expand local, organic agriculture.

We put charcoal biomass in the soil to store carbon for thousands of years.

We practice green internment with biodegradable containers.

We breathe with intentionality through our noses for five minutes daily to reduce fear and anxiety.

Two—Here Now

GE makes locomotives with clean energy.

GreenOrder teaches companies how to put green DNA into their whole business.

We learn from the book, *Low Carbon Diet* twenty-four ways to reduce CO_2 emissions in our households here and now.

Three—Inside Water, Out

We honor the mental ability of all species.

We recommend giving the Nobel Peace Prize to a fresh-from-the-womb chimpanzee nursing baby as a way to reduce human condescension toward eco-diversity.

We set high prices for water in the areas of highest use, so as to give incentives for saving water. We reduce irrigation water by drip and other methods. We adopt low-water sanitation as, for example, Stockholm does by separating excrement from urine and using both for fertilizer. We exploit such new, more economical desalinization technologies as reverse-osmosis and carbon nanotubes, as Singapore and Tampa Bay are doing.

We downsize our carbon footprint and reduce the drying of water sources and melting of glaciers by such methods as selling a second home.

We limit our use of water. We collect rain in barrels. We plant a rain garden and use leaf and other mulch. We install low-flow shower heads and shorten showers. We use buckets rather than hoses or car washes. We put in a low-flush or compost toilet. We reduce the number of times we use a dishwasher or a washing machine. We install a permeable driveway.

We drink tap water, 800 times more energy efficient than bottled water.

We learn to mother ourselves and take responsibility for our own role in global warming.

With our children, we tell stories that honor Mother Water and the Ocean as sources of life.

We experience the world from our hearts.

Four—Downside Up

We build the green movement downside up, with children foremost, more than top down.

We make experiential education fundamental, including outdoor green education, and we start a Green Corps for young people similar to the Peace Corps.

We support youth-focused experiential learning processes like Journey for the Planet, Eco Kids, *Conservationist for Kids*, Wilderness 101 in New York's Central Park, the U. S. Department of Energy's Solar Decathlon, Bill McKibben's Step It Up campaign, and Campus Climate Challenge.

We participate in Laughing Clubs, imitating children who laugh, on average, four hundred times a day.

Five—Dropping Rain

We imitate our cousins, the peacemaking, antiwar bonobo primates. We abolish institutional warfare, as we have abolished legal slavery, to protect eco-diversity and conserve energy. We establish international police, special forces, and peacekeeping forces. We train children and adults in cooperative, conflict-resolution skills. We train ourselves in global, person-to-person, person-to-species diplomacy and hospitality.

We create the Eco-Effective Revolution, recycling and composting environmentally safe products, using renewable energy and using water efficiently.

We carry out a global atonement ritual in the area of Kilimanjaro in East Africa, the birthplace area of the human species, and set up an Ecoholics Anonymous movement modeled after Alcoholics Anonymous. We make the five pledges of the Ecoholics Anonymous movement:

1. I admit that I often act to enlarge product consumption, to waste energy, and to reduce eco-diversity.
2. I make a list of the attitudes and actions that make me insensitive to More-than-Humans and seek to remove these attitudes and actions from my character.
3. I pledge allegiance to The One, by any name, and I ask for the will to reduce products, to renew energy, and to redouble eco-diversity.
4. I make amends to More-than-Humans by being in awe of and pray for threatened species and habitats and doing Green Corps projects in my community and around the world.
5. I volunteer to help form and mentor Green Corps groups.

Six—Soiled Goods

We grow food in our yards and buy food from farmers' markets.

We create greener music, including the use of lyrics from the earthiest book in the Bible, Song of Songs.

Seven—Mustard and Dandelion

We protect existing forests and plant billions of trees.

We participate in projects like Children & Elders Forest and the Green Belt Movement.

Eight—Animal Teachers

We institute community potlucks. We imitate crows, cormorants, black bears, eagles, and other animals and our own ancient tradition and promote measures that leave Earth Community more, rather than less, eco-diverse. We become Leavers. We eat an extraordinarily diverse diet of plants and fruits. We reduce eating meat as much as possible.

We compost earthworms.

We follow the Yahweh, Leaver version of the Genesis story of beginnings.

Nine—Washed Toes

We offer reciprocal physical and emotional therapies. We massage our own feet. We walk daily. We practice laughter exercise in Green Corps and Ecoholics Anonymous groups.

Ten—Sane Asylums

We seek to make our households carbon neutral. We turn down the thermostat, insulate, install double-pane windows, put weather seal around windows and doors, buy Energy Star label appliances, air-dry our clothes, and wrap the water heater with a blanket.

We build solar-powered houses.

We construct buildings that follow the certification criteria of LEED (Leadership in Energy and Environmental Design).

We seek to build zero-net energy consumption and zero-carbon cities, like Abu Dhabi is doing.

Eleven—Bare and Broke Folks

We reduce dependence on money, like Hal and Norma Tausig do.

We buy fewer clothes, get secondhand clothes, and give away unused clothes. We buy clothes that use all-vegetable coloring and fabrics that do not involve pesticides and are biodegradable. We buy vegetable-tanned leather. We avoid dry cleaners that use the chemical PERC (85 percent of dry cleaners do) that causes cancer.

We invest in green funds, give to green organizations, and support micro-lending to third-world people.

We in rich societies give a minimum of 2 percent of our income for micro-loans to third world people. We institute debt relief or debt cancellation to third world people. Our governments throughout the world agree to the same international minimum wage. Our corporations pay none of their employees more than ten times the lowest salary.

In our money measurement, we use Gross Ecological Value standards rather than Gross Domestic Product standards which reward ecological destruction.

Postscript: After the Ending

We start unfolding a fifty-year Jubilee, based on the Bible instruction about Leaver culture in Leviticus 25, returning as much as possible grazing and agricultural land to wilderness.

We "eat the view" beside our houses.

We say, "We leave enough; therefore, we are."

GREEN LYRICS

These green lyrics for nine songs (I have written 1, 4–5, 7–8) are quoted earlier in the order below. My new words to well-known patriotic and religious songs infer no criticism of the traditional words, which deserve respect. My point is to offer green words to tunes already part of our collective memory.

A green reformation offers the possibility of fresh lyrics to familiar tunes. In the Protestant Reformation, Martin Luther used a drinking tune for the words of "A Mighty Fortress is Our God." Those who have more poetic ability than I, have an incredible opportunity to stir and to motivate our species with new green songs.

1

We wave our pom-pom.
Mother Earth is our mom,
from deep green forests,
to snow-white ice caps,
from black sea trenches,
to fat orange full moon rises.
We wave our pom-pom
for our mom.
— To the tune by Woody Guthrie, "This Land is Your Land"

2

If a man can dream of a better land,
where all his brothers walk hand in hand,
Lord, tell me why, oh why, oh why, oh why can't their dream
come true?
— W. E. Brown, "If I Can Dream"

3

There's enough, there's enough, enough for everyone.
More than enough, enough for us, enough for everyone.
— Bryan Field McFarland

4

Outer world is not my hub.
I am right now passing through.
Within is my center,
and Spirit fills what I do.
Heart currents guide me,
'round inside's ocean core.
And I here make my axis,
in my core ever more.
— To the tune by Albert E. Brumley,
"This World Is Not My Home"

5

Earth's here for everyone,
and feeds upon our sun,
of trees we sing.
Globe where many species died,
globe of blue Ocean's pride,
under each mountain side,
let Earth's gong ring.
— To the tune of "My Country, 'Tis of Thee"

6

Standing like a tree, with my roots dug down,
my branches wide and open.
Come down rain, come down sun, come down fruit to my
heart
that is open to be standing like a tree.
— Traditional folk song

7

Earth Community web of life,
our network whom we love.
We walk within her, and are grounded by her,
on our way, sly as snake, clear as dove.
Within our mountain snows,
within our prairie winds,
within our oceans, alive with foam.
Rich, deep green Earth web of life,
our common home.
Rich, deep green Earth web of life,
our renewed Commons,
our livable, sustainable home.
—To the tune of "God Bless America"

8

Yes, we love the varied species,
every species of the world.
Lion, insect, bear who's brown,
all are valued with renown.
Yes, we love the varied species of the world.
—To the tune of "Jesus Loves the Little Children"

9

Everything is beautiful in its own way,
like a starry summer night
or a snow covered winter's day.
Everybody's beautiful in their own way.
Under God's heaven,
the world's gonna find a way.
—Ray Stevens

Whole Systems Terms

As you've noticed, I have used throughout the book a mix of secular and religious terms to symbolize the full Energy system of Earth Community and of the universe at large. This mix models our need to heal the split between science and religion. We need to see the complementary more than the adversarial aspects of diverse images representing whole systems. Here are around sixty terms that collectively form a collage to reflect the full Energy system that ultimately cannot be precisely equated with words. This list does not include all the whole system terms in the book.

Perhaps a word which comes close to representing the full Energy system is Stillness. Jews do not voice the name of Yahweh. The word Stillness suggests that the more we listen and the less we stereotype "correct" words, the more we learn. Yahweh said, "Be still and know that I am God [The One]" (Psalms 46:10, RSV). The prophet Elijah did not sense the essence of Yahweh in a great strong wind that broke rocks in pieces, in an earthquake, or in a fire, but in a "still small voice" (I Kings 19:11-12, RSV).

The terms on the next page, listed alphabetically in two columns, reveal by their juxtaposition the incredible variety of word labels for whole systems.

Allah [The One]
Allaha [The One, Male]
Allahta [The One, Fem.]
Alma [Whole World]
Ar'ah [Mother Earth]
Asherah *[Mother of Earth*
    Divinities]
Being
Biodiversity
Christ
Circle of Life
Commons
Community of Life
Creating Process
Dependent Co-Arising
Earth
Earth Community
Eco-diversity
El [The]
El Shaddai [The Breast]
Energy
God
Green Jesus
Green Kingdom
Here Now
I Am
I Am Here Now
I Am Who I Am
Global Village
Good Earth

Kingdom of God
Kingdom of Heaven
Leaver Culture
Living Earth
Lord
Madbra [Wildness]
Malkuta Allaha [Presence of The
    One]
Malkuta Shemaya [Presence of
    the Web of Energy]
Mother Earth
New Earth
Ocean
Presence
Reality
Ru'ha [Spirit, Wind, Breath]
Shemaya [Web of Energy]
Spirit, Wind, Breath
Stillness
Sustainability
The One
The Presence of The One
The Presence of the Web of
    Energy
Third Jesus
Tree of Life
Universe
Web of Energy
Wilderness
Yahweh [I Am Who I Am]

ARAMAIC JESUS

The love religion has no code or doctrine.
There are no rules for worship.

— *Rumi*

L et's look at words for Jesus in languages of the Indo-European
tradition. Greek: *Iesus*. Latin: *Yesu*. Jesus, of course, is also Indo-European.

In Semitic tradition, we have Aramaic *Eshua*. Hebrew: *Yeshua*.
Arabic: *Issa*.

A shroud veils Aramaic *Eshua* from people around the world
today like a liturgical Jesus hid a biblical Jesus from ordinary people before the Protestant Reformation. The printing of Bible translations in spoken languages, like Luther's German Bible and the
King James English Bible, opened up Bible reading to the masses
for the first time.

King James, Revised Standard, Good News, Scholars and dozens of other translations of the gospels from Greek into English
have made Jesus vibrantly visible. In comparison, Aramaic *Eshua*
remains nearly invisible.

The Hebrew and Aramaic Dead Sea Scrolls from the first century, the Aramaic *Peshitta* manuscript of the gospels from the fifth
century, and other sources help us reconstruct an approximation
of what Eshua spoke. Contemporary Aramaic-speaking groups
are keeping alive varied dialects in scattered communities with
various names like the Assyrians, Syrians, and Nestorians in the
Middle East and other parts of the world. A church community in

Chicago, St. John's, formed by émigrés from the Middle East, uses Aramaic in its services.

Scholars representing the various Christianities agree, as summarized by L. Michael White in *From Jesus to Christianity* (2004), that not only did Jesus speak Aramaic, but the early experiences of his followers after his death occurred within Aramaic-speaking communities.

The leading linguistic expert on the Aramaic underlying Greek gospel texts, Professor Maurice Casey of the University of Nottingham, employs a scientific methodology in *Aramaic Sources of Mark's Gospel* (1998) and in *An Aramaic Approach to Q: Sources for the Gospels of Matthew and Luke* (2002). He takes selected passages and identifies the Aramaic sentence structure and grammar in the Dead Sea scrolls with both word-for-word and interpretive translations from Aramaic to Greek. He says we will have the eye-opener of our cultural lives when the Aramaic Jesus more fully manifests himself to us.

Professor Casey demonstrates that Aramaic literary fragments, perhaps written as early as 40 Common Era, form the basis for the essence of the Greek texts of the gospels of Matthew, Mark, and Luke. Professor Casey states that to understand the words of Jesus, "we shall have to reconstruct them in Aramaic." Learning Aramaic is "essential."

Understanding Aramaic Jesus will increase the power of the love religion that Rumi describes.

I am not an expert on Aramaic and Greek and cannot do what Casey and others have begun doing in unraveling the Aramaic hidden underneath and within Greek translations of Aramaic. Original Aramaic texts of the gospels—in wax, animal skins, or papyrus—have apparently disappeared. No physical evidence remains until one gets to the Aramaic *Peshitta* text of the gospels from the fifth century Common Era. We have Greek texts from the fourth and earlier centuries.

No conspiracy has hidden the Aramaic Jesus. Rather, the

evangelist Paul and other Greek-speaking Jews in the first century wrote from their own conversion experiences with Eshua. These Jews imitated Eshua's openhearted egalitarianism and introduced a Greek *Iesus* and a Latin *Yesu* who challenged hierarchical Roman society. Divine Iesus undermined divine Augustus Caesar's top-down social polarities and promoted equality among Jews and Greeks, slaves and free, and male and female.

Over time, male bishop authority — modeled after the privilege of Roman nobility — and theological formulas muted the revolutionary, spiritual democracy of Eshua. Eventually, the Roman Emperor Constantine and top bishops standardized church formulas in the Greek language and sought to destroy gospels other than Matthew, Mark, Luke, and John. If they had not gotten rid of evidence with which they did not agree, we would have more evidence for Eshua's iconoclastic unconventionality and perhaps more Aramaic records.

Greek, Latin, and English translations of Eshua's Aramaic words, composed for literate people, have blurred the oral culture of a Semitic person who engaged people in dialogue with both verbal and body language. People in first century Palestine used their ears and bodies for communication more than literate people do today. We rely on our eyes for gathering consciousness. Less than one per cent of the people in Galilee wrote or read.

We will never know the precise pronunciation of Eshua's words, his accented and unaccented syllables, or his word sequence. We have no surviving Aramaic ear-witness writing or transcript, like a press conference report, of any saying by Eshua.

Eshua spoke Aramaic in a Palestine colonized by Indo-European Greeks and Romans. Prominent Jewish leaders — like the ruler of Galilee, Herod Antipas — communicated with the occupiers by learning their Indo-European literary languages. As a youth, Antipas did most of his education in Rome, not in an Aramaic school in Palestine. Aramaic had second-class status in Palestine then and still has second-class status in western culture today.

Thus, the English language has no translation of Eshua's fifteen hundred variations of five hundred sayings in Aramaic not coated with European Greek culture. Very few Aramaic words survive untranslated in the Greek manuscripts, a practice continued in English translations. Look in your English Bible, for examples: *Talitha koum!* (Little girl, get up!) in Mark 5:41; *Ephphatha!* (Be Opened!) in Mark 7:34; and *Abba* (Papa) in Mark 14:36.

A most inspiring translator of selected Aramaic sayings of Eshua is intercultural pioneer Neil Douglas-Klotz. He gathers many of the Semitic nuances, allusions, homonyms, and culturally rich meanings in Aramaic. He has done more than anyone to put Eshua of Nazareth within his Aramaic context for the general public. See *Prayers of the Cosmos: Meditations on the Aramaic Words of Jesus* (1990), *The Hidden Gospel: Decoding the Spiritual Message of the Aramaic Jesus* (1999), and *Blessings of the Cosmos: Benedictions from the Aramaic Words of Jesus* (2006).

Rocco Errico has written books that help recreate some of the sayings of the Aramaic Jesus, particularly *And There Was Light* and *Setting a Trap for God: The Aramaic Prayer of Jesus.*

A useful website about the history and study of the Aramaic language, the Peshitta Bible, and leading writers about the Aramaic New Testament is www.aramaicbiblecenter.com.

Look at examples of poetic plays on words in the Aramaic gospels on linguist Christopher Lancaster's website, www.aramaicpeshitta.com and in chapter three of his free, online book, *Was the New Testament Really Written in Greek?*

Important resources I used for Aramaic transliterations and meanings are the following three publications by The Way International: *Aramaic-English Interlinear New Testament, The Concordance to the Peshitta Version of the Aramaic New Testament,* and *English Dictionary Supplement to the Concordance to the Peshitta Version.*

Aramaic Glossary

Below are mostly Aramaic words. A few words are Hebrew and Canaanite. Scholars don't agree on the basic root meaning of some of these words, so you'll find alternatives to what I've listed. Transliterations and spellings of Aramaic words into English vary considerably among authors. For example, some authors prefer *Yeshua* to *Eshua*. No consensus exists about spelling many words. You can find in print *alaha*, as compared with my spelling and capitalization, *Allaha*.

Abba	Papa.
Adamah	Red Earth. Earth Man. Adam.
Allaha	The One. Masculine. God.
Allahta	The One. Feminine. Goddess.
Alma	Agelessness. Whole world.
Ar'ah	Mother Earth. Soil.
Asherah	Canaanite Mother of Earth and Ocean divinities. Wife of Yahweh.
B'eld'baba	Enemy. Arbitrary, patriarchal ruler of clan.
Beqa	Rethink. Consider. Examine. Understand fundamental reality.
Dechel	Fear.
Eden	Lush oasis or wilderness.
El	The. The One. God.
El Shaddai	The Breast. Almighty.

Eshua	Restoring I Am Who I Am (I Am Here Now). Yeshua. Jesus.
Ephphatha	Be opened.
Gehech	Laugh.
Hab	Contagious compassion reaching out from inner recesses to envelope everyone. Love.
Hanukah	December Festival of Lights.
Hardeta	Mustard.
Havel	Breath or vapor. Abel.
Hawah	Life Mother. Eve.
Haya	Life.
Heuya	Discerning Life. Snake.
Lebah	Center from which life radiates. Heart.
Legau	Guts. Intestines. Fully common. Within. Among. Around.
Madbra	Wildness. Not cultivated area.
Malkuta	The Feminine Presence. Queendom. Kingdom. Imperial rule.
Maryam	Mary, mother of Jesus. Mary Magdalene. Mary of Bethany.
Mayah	Water flowing like rain to a gathering place.
Menorah	Candlestick holder for eight candles.
Naphsha	Breath of Life. Self or soul.
Na'ba	Crow.
Natsrat	Nazareth.
Niqodimaw	Nicodemus.
Pakah	Cheek.

Pesach	Passover and Barley Harvest Festival. End of March, beginning of April.
Peshitta	Aramaic manuscript of the Bible.
Purim	Festival celebrating Esther as deliverer. End of February, beginning of March.
Qayin	Acquisition. Cain.
Qereb	Align one's energy with another. Draw near. Touch. Come close.
Rabbi	Teacher.
Rabboni	My teacher.
Regla	Feet.
Ruha	Spirit, Wind, Breath simultaneously.
Sahan	Snake divinity. Possibly an Egyptian word like "shean" in the the city Beth-shean.
Shabbat	Sabbath.
Shavuot	Festival of Wheat Harvest. End of May, beginning of June.
Shema	Let meaning vibrate within one's behavior. Hear with all senses and experience.
Shemaya	The Web of Energy. The Web of Sight and Sound. Heaven.
Slotha	Open heart to receive wild and unexpected voices. Meditate. Pray.
Sukkot	Festival of Booths and Sowing Barley and Wheat. End of September, beginning of October.
Tamima	Clear-minded.
Tubva	Contented. Lucky. Blessed.

Yahweh	I Am Who I Am. I Am Here Now. Lord.
Yam Kinneret	*Yam* is the Canaanite water deity. *Kinneret* refers to harplike water sounds. Sea of Galilee.
Yaminah	Right, as compared with left.
Yauna	Dove.
Yeshua	See *Eshua*.
Yousef	Joseph.

Aramaic Phrases

T he translations below are bare bones. Consult the book for a fuller sense of the meaning of these phrases.

Aik peredta hu hardeta.	Consider the mustard seed.
Ameyn, ameyn, amar ana lakh	Grounded, grounded is my saying.
Ar'ah geir eta pira.	Earth produces fruit on her own.
Beqa na'ba.	Think about the crows.
'Elah nepal mat ar'ah.	The kernel of wheat falls to earth and dies.
Ephphatha.	Be opened.
Hab b'eld'baba.	Love your enemies.
He geir Malkuta Allah(t)a men legau hu.	The Feminine Presence of the One (Kingdom of God) is within.
Hewa hakil hakima aik Heuya tamina aik Yauna.	Be sly as a snake and clear-minded as a dove.
La dechel.	Don't fear.
Malkuta Allaha.	The Feminine Presence of the One. Kingdom of God.

Malkuta Shemaya.	The Feminine Presence of the Web of Energy. Kingdom of Heaven.
Man saba haya naphsha 'ebad, man ebad naphsha haya.	Whoever seeks to possess life will lose it. Whoever breathes non-possessively will gain life.
Sag regla.	Wash feet.
Sibaq talya eta liwat.	Let the children come up to me.
Taba ar'ah.	Good Earth
Tubva becha hasha, gehech.	Lucky and blessed are you who bawl, for you will laugh.
Yiled men Mayah Ruha.	Be born again of Water and Spirit, Wind, Breath.
Yaminah pakah.	Right cheek.

GENERAL BIBLE REFERENCES

Genesis

1–3	Leaver and Taker stories.
1:2	Spirit creates.
1:27	Male and female created equal.
1:28–30	Humans can subdue any species they want.
2:9	Tree of Life.
2:21–22	Eve taken from Adam's rib.
13:10	Garden of Yahweh.
27:41	Esau hates Jacob.
34:1–31	Simeon and Levi lie, steal, and murder.
35:4–8	Jacob buries images and people under an oak tree.

Exodus

3:2–14	Yahweh in Burning Bush is I Am Who I Am (I Am Here Now).

Leviticus

25:8-55	Year of Jubilee. Restore land to wilderness and to Leaver tradition.

Numbers

21:9	Moses sets up snake symbols.

Deuteronomy

12:2	People venerate trees.

First Kings

1:9	Snake's Stone Spring is in Jerusalem.
19:11-12	Essence of Yahweh is in a still, small voice.

Second Kings

| 18:4 | Snakes are set up as focus for healing. |

Job

| 1–42 | Job recovers health within Earth Community. |
| 12:7–8 | Ask the animals and they will teach. |

Psalms

46:10	Yahweh said, "Be still and know that I am God."
65:12–13	Wilderness is lush.
139:19–22	King David hates those who hate Yahweh.

Song of Songs

1–8	Songs celebrating Earth Community.
2:1–3	I, a wild flower, grow.
2:8–14	My beloved comes leaping upon the mountains. O my dove.
4:6–14	I enjoy myrrh and all the chief spices.
4:15–16	Living Water, you are a fountain. Come winds, breathe.

Isaiah

| 40:31 | People shall mount up as eagles. |

Ezekiel

| 17:22–23 | Israel is like a cedar tree. |
| 31:2–9 | Egypt is like a cedar tree. |

Daniel

| 4:10–11 | King Nebuchadnezzar dreams of a tree like the cedar. |

Matthew

14:13	Jesus meditates in wildness.
14:16–21	Community potluck folk eat bread and fish.
15:32–39	Community potluck folk eat bread and fish.

Mark

| 1–8 | Jesus provides therapy for individuals in Sea of Galilee area. |

1:12–13	Spirit drives Jesus into wildness and wild animals.
1:35	Jesus prays in wildness.
3:21	Friends of Jesus think he is out of his mind.
6:35–44	Community potluck folk eat bread and fish.
8:23–25	Jesus heals blind man.

Luke

7:37–50	Mary of Bethany washes the feet of Jesus.
8:1–3	Women support Jesus group, especially Mary Magdalene.
24:1-53	Mary Magdalene and others experience Jesus in a series of visions.

John

6:5–14	Community potluck folk eat bread and fish.
9:6	Jesus uses spit in blind man's eyes.
12:1–8	Mary of Bethany washes the feet of Jesus.

Mary Magdalene

6:1–2	Peter says Jesus loved Mary more than any associate.
7:1–2	Mary sees risen Jesus in a vision.
10:9–10	Levi (Matthew) implies Mary closer to Jesus than anyone.
10:11–13	Mary says to follow inner life, not outer rules.

Acts

| 9:1–9 | Paul sees Jesus in a vision. |
| 19:27, 37 | *Allah(t)a* [feminine form of God] mentioned three times. |

Ephesians

| 5:20 | Always and for everything giving thanks. |

Revelation

| 22:2 | Tree of Life. |

SOURCES

The sources that have influenced me are larger in number than the sources listed.

ARAMAIC SOURCES

Black, Matthew, third ed. (1967) *An Aramaic Approach to the Gospels and Acts*. London: Oxford University Press.

Casey, Maurice. (1998) *Aramaic Sources of Mark's Gospel*. Cambridge: Cambridge University Press. Argues that the quest for the essential Jesus largely has ignored the Aramaic language. Casey uses the latest theories of bilingualism and translation studies to show that Aramaic literary texts are sources for literal or symbolic translation into the Greek text of Mark.

— — —. (2002) *An Aramaic Approach to Q: Sources for the Gospels of Matthew and Luke*. Cambridge: Cambridge University Press. Proposes an eightfold method to come up with the Aramaic substratum for the Greek texts of Matthew, Mark, and Luke.

Douglas-Klotz, Neil. (1990) *Prayers of the Cosmos: Meditations on the Aramaic Words of Jesus*. San Francisco: HarperSanFrancisco. Focuses on the Lord's Prayer and the Beatitudes.

— — —. (1999) *The Hidden Gospels: Decoding the Spiritual Message of the Aramaic Jesus*. Wheaton, Illinois: Quest Books. These two books by Neil Douglas-Klotz helped influence and inspire me to put the sayings of Eshua in a deep intercultural and dialogic frame of reference.

— — —. (2006) *Blessings of the Cosmos: Benedictions from the Aramaic Words of Jesus.* Boulder, Colorado: Sounds True.

Errico, Rocco A. (1998) *And There Was Light.* Santa Fe, New Mexico: Noohra Foundation. The first half is an excellent introduction to the ministry and Aramaic sayings of Jesus. The appendices offer brief and clear histories of the English Bible and of the Aramaic language.

— — —. (1997) *Setting a Trap for God: The Aramaic Prayer of Jesus.* Unity Village, Missouri: Unity Books.

Kutscher, E. Y. (1976) *Studies in Galilean Aramaic.* Jerusalem: Bar-Ilan University.

Lamsa, George M. (1933) *Holy Bible from the Ancient Eastern Text.* San Francisco: HarperSanFrancisco.

— — —. (1931) *Idioms in the Bible Explained and a Key to the Original Gospels.* San Francisco: HarperSanFrancisco.

Lancaster, Christopher. Skilled in Aramaic and Greek, Lancaster presents the argument that the Aramaic Peshitta manuscript is the source for the Greek manuscripts of the New Testament. You can read for free online his book, *Was the New Testament Really Written in Greek?* Chapter Three gives examples of poetic plays on words in the Aramaic gospels. www.aramaicpeshitta.com.

San Antonio Vocal Arts Ensemble. (2002) *Ancient Echoes: Music from the Time of Jesus and Jerusalem's Second Temple.* World Library Publications. www.wlpmusic.com. This CD comes close to the sounds of sung Aramaic in the first century, accompanied by first-century instruments. We can hear the Lord's Prayer as well as three beatitudes in Aramaic.

The Way International Research Team, eds. (1992) *Aramaic-English Interlinear New Testament: Volume I, Matthew-John.* New Knoxville, Ohio: American Christian Press.

— — —. (1985) *English Dictionary Supplement to the Concordance to the Peshitta Version of the Aramaic New Testament.* New Knoxville, Ohio: American Christian Press.

— — —. (1985) *The Concordance to the Peshitta Version of the Aramaic New Testament.* New Knoxville, Ohio: American Christian Press. I used these three resources by the The Way Team as the main source for transliteration of Aramaic into English.

www.aramaicbiblecenter.com Website for history and study of the Aramaic language, for the Peshitta gospels, and for leading writers on the Aramaic New Testament.

www.noohra.com Source for books and tapes of Rocco Errico.

GREEN SOURCES

"Abu Dhabi to Build World's First Zero-Carbon City." (Jan. 21, 2008) www.breitbart.com/article

Arbel, Tali. (July 7, 2008) Associated Press article, "Back to the Tap," *Pantagraph.*

Bell, Robin E. (February 2008) "The Unquiet Ice," *Scientific American.*

Blake, Mariah. (August 20, 2008) "Germany's Key to Green Energy," *Christian Science Monitor.*

Block, Susan. "The Bonobo Way: Peace through Pleasure." www.blockbonobofoundation.org

Brittain, Amy. (Aug. 1, 2007) "Shade in the City," *Christian Science Monitor.*

Brock, Rita Nakashima and Rebecca Ann Parker. (2008) *Saving Paradise: How Christianity Traded Love of This World for Crucifixion and Empire.* Boston: Beacon Press.

Bruinius, Harry. (February 24, 2006) "The Joy Laugh Club." *Christian Science Monitor.*

Childre, Doc. (1998) *Freeze Frame: A Scientifically Proven Technique for Clear Decision Making and Improved Health.* Boulder Creek, California: Planetary Publications. An introduction to heart math and emotional health.

Clayton, Mark. (December 10, 2008) "Environmentalists Send Their Wish List to Obama," *Christian Science Monitor.*

Conselice, Christopher J. (February 2007) "The Universe's Invisible Hand," *Scientific American,* 34-41. The latest theories on black energy.

Coulter, Phyllis. (February 8, 2008). "Get 'em While They're Green," *Pantagraph.*

Cousin, Norman. (1979) *Anatomy of an Illness.* New York: W. W. Norton. Story of the healing power of laughter.

Darom, David. (N.D.) *Beautiful Plants of the Bible: From the Hyssop to the Mighty Cedar Trees.* Herzlia, Israel: Palphot Ltd.

David, Laurie. (2006) *The Solution Is You! An Activist's Guide.* Golden, Colorado: Fulcrum Publishing.

Diamond, Jared. (2005) *Collapse: How Societies Choose to Fail or to Succeed.* New York: Viking.

De Rothschild, David. (2007) *The Live Earth Global Warming Survival Handbook: 77 Essential Skills to Stop Climate Change – or Live Through It.* New York: Live Earth. Up-to-date source for practical steps to take.

De Waal, Frans B. M. (March 1995) "Bonobo Sex and Society," *Scientific American,* 82–88.

Dobson, Roger. (October 10, 2006) "How the Power of Touch Reduces Pain and Even Fights Disease," *The Independent* (London).

Duke, James A. (1983) *Medicinal Plants of the Bible.* New York: Trado-Medic Books.

EatTheView.Com

Eden, Donna. (1998) *Energy Medicine.* New York: Jeremy P. Tarcher/Putnam.

El Nasser, Haya. (July 28, 2005) "Some Cities Are Finding Money Does Grow on Trees," *USA Today.*

Fiala, Nathan. (February 2009) "The Greenhouse Hamburger," *Scientific American.*

Foggi, Bruno. (1999) *Flowers of Israel.* N.P.: Bonechi & Steimatzky.

Fosdick, Dean. (February 13, 2008) "How to Restore Dark Skies at Night," *Christian Science Monitor.*

— — —. (June 29, 2008) "What Would Jesus Plant? *Pantagraph.*

Friedman, Thomas L. (April 15, 2007) "The Power of Green," *New York Times.*

— — —. (December 2, 2007) "The People We Have Been Waiting For," *New York Times.* Discussion of Hunter Lovins and the concept of Global Weirding.

— — —. (2005) *The World Is Flat: A Brief History of the Twenty-first Century.* New York: Farrar, Straus, and Giroux.

— — —. (2008) *Hot, Flat and Crowded: Why We Need a Green Revolution and How It Can Renew America.* New York: Farrar, Straus, and Giroux. Strong complement to *Green Kingdom Come!*

Furtman, Michael. (1998) *Black Bear Country.* Minnetonka, Minnesota: Northword Press.

Gershon, David. (2006) *Low Carbon Diet: A 30 Day Program to Lose 5,000 Pounds.* Woodstock, New York: Empowerment Institute.

Goodman, Ellen. (Dec. 28, 2007) "War and Peace with the Environment," *The Boston Globe.*

— — —. (July 5, 2008) "Locavores Say, Let's Return to 'Victory Garden,'" *Pantagraph.*

Grambo, Rebecca L. (1999) *Eagles.* Osceola, Wisconsin: Voyageurs Press.

Grant, Steve. (August 28, 2008) "Yale Student Skips Dorm and Builds an Eco-friendly House Instead," *Christian Science Monitor.*

Gravitz, Alisa. (Winter 2007) "12-Step Program to Stop Climate Change," *Yes!* Climate Mitigation Initiative.

Gray, Elizabeth Dodson. (1981) *Green Paradise Lost.* Wellesley, Mass.: Roundtable Press.

"'Green Energy' Draws Investors, U.N. Says." (July 2, 2008),

Pantagraph. Sixty percent more spent on alternative energy in 2007 than in 2006.

"Green Gold." (July 7, 2007), *The Economist*. About the financial value of trees.

Hagerty, Barbara Bradley. (February 8, 2006) "Evangelical Leaders Urge Action on Climate Change." National Public Radio report.

Haeg, Fritz. (2008) *Edible Estates: Attack on the Front Lawn*. Los Angeles: Metropolis Books.

Hamashige, Hope. (June 27, 2005) "Surprise Finds Top List of Best National Parks," *National Geographic News*.

Hayden, Tom. (1996) *The Lost Gospel of the Earth: A Call for Renewing Nature, Spirit, and Politics*. San Francisco: Sierra Club Books.

"How to Get Picky Kids to Eat Veggies? (July 3, 2008), *Christian Science Monitor*.

http://stepitup2007.org/

Jarvis, Brooke. (Spring 2008) "Terra Preta, a Solution Buried in the Dirt," *Yes!*, 48. Excellent description of agrichar, and its ability to store carbon in the soils for thousands of years.

Jeffrey, Yvonne, Liz Barclay, and Michael Grosvenor. (2008) *Green Living for Dummies*. Hoboken, N.J.: Wiley Publishing.

Kates, William. (February 8, 2008) "New York Touts New Conservation Magazine to Connect Kids to Nature," *Pantagraph*.

Kerry, John and Teresa Heinz Kerry. (2007) *This Moment on Earth: Today's New Environmentalists and Their Vision for the Future*. New York: Public Affairs.

Kingsolver, Barbara. (2007) *Animal, Vegetable, Miracle: A Year of Food Life*. New York: HarperCollins.

Knickerbocker, Brad. (March 1, 2007) "'Green' Governors, A Warmer Lake, and Al," *Christian Science Monitor*.

Korten, David C. (2006) *The Great Turning: From Empire to Earth Community*. San Francisco: Berrett-Koehler Publishers.

Krupp, Fred and Miriam Horn. (2008) *Earth: The Sequel, The Race to Reinvent Energy and Stop Global Warming.* New York: Norton. A guide to the latest solar, biomass, geothermal, ocean, and wind renewable energy technology.

Kunstler, James Howard. (2005) *The Long Emergency: Surviving the Converging Catastrophes of the Twenty-First Century.* New York: Atlantic Monthly Press.

Lampman, Jane. (March 12, 2008) "Southern Baptists Urged to Take Climate Stance," *Christian Science Monitor.*

Leatherman, Courtney. (Summer 2007) "Patrick Gonzalez," *Nature Conservancy.*

Libbrecht, Kenneth. (2003) *Winter's Secret Beauty.* Stillwater, Minnesota: Voyageur Press.

Lienitz, Tony. (2005) *The Year I Ate My Yard.* Palo Alto, California: Vegetare.

Macrae, Fiona. (January 25, 2008) "I'm the Champion! Ape Trounces the Best of the Human World in Memory Competition." *London Daily Mail.*

McDonough, William and Michael Braungart. (2002) *Cradle to Cradle: Remaking the Way We Make Things.* New York: North Point Press. A source on Eco-Effective Revolution.

McFarland, Bryan Field. The song, "Enough for Everyone." www.songvault.fm/

Mirsky, Steve. (September 2002) "Einstein's Hot Time," *Scientific American,* 102.

Morell, Virginia. (March 2008) "Minds of Their Own: Animals Are Smarter than You Think," *National Geographic,* 36–61.

Najibullah, Farangis. (April 11, 2007) "Central Asia: Aral Sea Shows Signs of Recovery," Radio Free Europe on line.

Newcomb, Amelia. (December 16, 2008) "Japan as Global Ground Zero for No-waste Living," *Christian Science Monitor.*

Nicholson, Geoff. (2008) *The Lost Art of Walking: The History, Science, Philosophy, and Literature of Pedestrianism.* New York: Riverhead Books.

Nun, Mendel. (1989) *The Sea of Galilee and Its Fishermen in the New Testament*. Ein Gev, Israel: Kibbutz Ein Gev.

Overbye, Dennis. (December 7, 2004). "String Theory, at 20, Explains It All (or Not)," *New York Times*.

Page, Charles R. (1995) *Jesus & The Land*. Nashville, Tennessee: Abingdon Press. Great source on the social and ecological life of first-century Galilee.

Paz, Uzi. (n.d.) *Birds in the Land of the Bible*. Herzlia, Israel: Palphot Ltd.

Pearce, Fred. (2007) *With Speed and Violence: Why Scientists Fear Tipping Points in Climate Change*. Boston: Beacon Press.

Pert, Candace B. (2003) *Molecules of Emotion: The Science Behind Mind-Body Medicine*. New York: Scribners.

Phinney, Susan. (March 14, 2006) "Humor Has Fans in Medical Circles," *P-I Reporter*. About Laughing Circles, particularly ones in the Seattle area. See seattlepi.nwsource.com

Pullella, Philip. (March 10, 2008) "Vatican Lists 'New Sins,' including Pollution." Reuters story online, www.reuters.com

Robert, Karl-Henrik. (2008) *The Natural Step Story: Seeding a Quiet Revolution*. Gabriola Island, BC, Canada: New Society Publishers.

Robinson, Betsy. (January–February 2008) "Health Benefits in Non-Humor-Dependent Aerobic Laughter," *Spirituality & Health*, 23.

Rogers, Peter. (August 2008) "Facing the Freshwater Crisis," *Scientific American*.

Rogerson, John. (1985) *Atlas of the Bible*. New York: Facts on File.

Schultz, Connie. "John Glenn: Our Similarities — From a Distance." www.creators.com

"Seeing the Forest for the Trees." (Summer 2007) *Nature Conservancy*.

Sethi, Anita. (September 2007) "Your Baby's Sense of Smell," *Babytalk*.

Simpson, Victor L. (July 18, 2008) "Pope: Taking Care of Scarred Planet Crucial," Associated Press story. *Pantagraph.*

Simon, Ellen. (July 5, 2008) "With Prices Up, Home Gardens Grow," *Pantagraph.*

Spotts, Peter N. (January 24, 2008) "Can Ocean's 'Amazon' Be Saved?" *Christian Science Monitor.*

— — —. (February 14, 2008) "Lakes Mead and Powell Could Run Dry by 2021," *Christian Science Monitor.*

— — —. (December 19, 2008) "World's Oceans Turning Acidic Fast," *Christian Science Monitor.*

Steinbacher, Michele. (February 20, 2008) "Climate Expert Gives Students Charge to Take Lead on Finding Energy Solution," *Pantagraph.* Report on the recommendations of James Hansen from a speech at Illinois Wesleyan University.

Stolzenburg, William. (2008) *Where the Wild Things Were: Life, Death, and Ecological Wreakage in a Land of Vanishing Predators.* London: Bloomsbury.

Strindberg, Amanda. (January 16, 2006) "Exercising the Funny Bone," *Pantagraph.* Story from Knight Ridder Newspapers on Jeffrey Briar, who teaches seminars on laughing.

The Green Bible: Understand the Bible's Powerful Message for the Earth. (2008) New York: HarperOne.

Velasquez-Manoff, Moises. (July 23, 2008) "'Happy' Helps the Planet: Research Equates Well-Being with a Smaller Eco-Footprint," *Christian Science Monitor.*

Venkatraman, Vijaysree. (September 17, 2008) "'Drumstick' Tree Tackles Hunger: Underused Moringa May Be Tropics' Nutrition Superstar," *Christian Science Monitor.*

"Voices of Youth: The Global Youth Action Network." (May 2007) *Kosmos: An Integral Approach to Global Awakening.*

Weidensaul, Scott. (Summer 2007) "The Last Stand." *Nature Conservancy,* 20–33. About the Canadian boreal forest.

Well, Jeff, David Wilcove, and Scott Weidensaul. (September 22, 2008) "US Conservation Win — in Canada," *Christian Sci-*

ence Monitor. About Ontario premier setting aside half of the province as wilderness.

Wilson, E. O. (2006) *The Creation: An Appeal to Save Life on Earth*. New York: W. W. Norton.

Wood, Shadia Fayne. (Spring 2008) "Youth Feel the Power," *Yes!*, 46–47.

Zohary, Michael. (1982) *Plants of the Bible*. Cambridge: Cambridge University Press.

www.answers.google.com
    Atom and cell deaths and replacements.

www.bn-green.org
    Imagine Green Bloomington/Normal.

www.ceforest.org
    Website of Children & Elders Forest.

www.capitolclimateaction.com

www.dream-catchers.org
    Ojibway creation story of Turtle Island.

www.ecologicalcalendar.info

www.emofree.com
    Emotional Freedom Technique.

www.empowermentinstitute.net/lcd
    About Journey for the Planet and low carbon curriculum.

www.foot-reflexologist.com
    The website of foot reflexologists Barbara and Kevin Kunz.

www.globalerie.com/blog/category/ge-transportation/
    About John Dineen and General Electric Transportation.

www.greenbeltmmovement.org
    Source on Wangari Maathai and her movement's planting of 30,000,000 trees in Kenya and East Africa.

www.greenfacts.org
    Access to the Millennium Ecosystem Assessment.

www.greenorder.com/

www.heartmath.org

www.monitorweek.com/2007/0726/p13s03-legn.html?page=2

Article on course Wilderness 101 in Central Park.
www.nationalburialcompany.com
www.princeton.edu/~cmi/
Carbon Mitigation Initiative.
www.rapidgrowthmedia.com
About green buildings in Grand Rapids, Michigan.
www.richsoil.com/lawn/god.html
Dialogue between God and St. Francis about lawns.
www.rss2go.net/topic/hunter_lovins
A source for Global Weirding.
www.solardecathlon.org/
www.space.com
Information about Long Nights Moon.
www.time.com/time/magazine/article/0,9171,1689222,00.
html
Brian Williams, 2007 Person of the Year.
www.untoursfoundation.org
www.worldlaughtertour.com
About Steve Wilson and Laughing Clubs.
www.worldwatercouncil.org/

BIBLE, CHRISTIANITY, AND JESUS SOURCES

Adams, Douglas. (1997) *The Prostitute in the Family Tree: Discovering Humor And Irony in the Bible.* Louisville, Kentucky: Westminster John Knox. An inspiring and creative book with several chapters on Jesus.

Bergant, Dianne. (2001) *The Song of Songs.* Collegeville, Minnesota: Liturgical Press.

Borg, Marcus J. (2003) *The Heart of Christianity: Rediscovering a Life of Faith.* San Francisco: HarperSanFrancisco. Thoughtful and gracious book about the differences between exclusive and inclusive Christianity in America.

— — —. (2006) *Jesus: Uncovering the Life, Teachings, and Relevance of a Religious Revolutionary.* San Francisco: HarperSanFrancisco. Clear, pastoral, and wise.

Brown, Dan. (2003) *The DaVinci Code.* New York: Doubleday.

Barnstone, Willis, ed. (1984) *The Other Bible.* San Francisco: Harper & Row. Includes texts that did not make it into the canonical Bible.

Chilton, Bruce. (2006) *Mary Magdalene: A Biography.* New York: Doubleday.

Chopra, Deepak. (2008) *The Third Jesus: The Christ We Cannot Ignore.* New York: Random House.

Claiborne, Shane and Chris Haw. (2008) *Jesus for President: Politics for Ordinary Radicals.* Grand Rapids: Zondervan.

Corley, Kathleen E. (1993) *Private Woman, Public Meals: Social Conflict in the Synoptic Tradition.* Peabody, Massachusetts: Hendrickson Publishers. Helpful interpretations of Mary of Bethany and foot washing.

Crossan, John Dominic. (1994) *Jesus: A Revolutionary Biography.* San Francisco: HarperSanFrancisco.

— — —. (1994) *The Essential Jesus: Original Sayings and Earliest Images.* San Francisco: HarperSanFrancisco.

Crossan, John Dominic and Jonathan L. Reed. (2001) *Excavating Jesus: Beneath the Stones, Behind the Texts.* San Francisco: HarperSanFrancisco.

— — —. (2004) *In Search of Paul.* San Francisco: HarperSanFrancisco.

Deconick, April D. (2005) *Recovering the Original Gospel of Thomas: A History of the Gospel and Its Growth.* London: T & T Clark.

Dever, William G. (2005) *Did God Have a Wife? Archaeology and Folk Religion in Ancient Israel.* Grand Rapids, Michigan: William B. Eerdmans Publishing Co.

Douglas-Klotz, Neil. (2003) *The Genesis Meditations: A Shared Practice of Peace for Christians, Jews, and Muslims.* Wheaton, Illinois: Quest Books.

Ehrman, Bart D. (2003) *Lost Christianities: The Battles for Scripture and The Faiths We Never Knew*. New York: Oxford University Press.

— — —. (2005) *Misquoting Jesus: The Story Behind Who Changed The Bible and Why*. New York: HarperCollins. Clear arguments about the low level of literary competence in the first centuries of the Common Era, demonstrating that the original recordings of Jesus' words contained various levels of accuracy.

— — —. (2006) *Peter, Paul, and Mary Magdalene: The Followers of Jesus in History and Legend*. Oxford University Press.

Falk, Marcia. (1990) *The Song of Songs: A New Translation and Interpretation*. San Francisco: HarperSanFrancisco.

Flynn, Leslie B. (1960) *Serve Him with Mirth: The Place of Humor in the Christian Life*. Grand Rapids, Michigan: Zondervan Publishing.

Fox, Richard Wightman. (2004) *Jesus in America: Personal Savior, Cultural Hero, National Obsession*. San Francisco: HarperSanFrancisco. Examination by an anthropologist of the many faces of Jesus in American culture from the colonial period to the present.

Funk, Robert W. (2002) *A Credible Jesus: Fragments of a Vision*. Santa Rosa, California: Poleridge Press.

Funk, Robert W. and Roy W. Hoover. (1997) *The Five Gospels: The Search for the Authentic Words of Jesus*. San Francisco: HarperSanFrancisco. Scholars Version of Matthew, Mark, Luke, John, and Thomas, which is my main source for quotes.

— — —. (1999) *The Gospel of Jesus*. Santa Rosa, California: Poleridge Press.

Hample, Stuart and Eric Marshall, compilers. (1991) *Children's Letters to God*. New York: Workman Publishing. Some children's quotes at the beginning of chapters are from this source.

Hanegraaff, Hank and Sigmund Brouwer. (2004) *The Last Disciple*. Wheaton, Illinois: Tyndale House Publishers. A novel, based on historical background about first-century life during the reign of Emperor Nero, arguing against the Armageddon and *Left Behind* futurists. Written by evangelicals.

Hennessy, Anne. (1994) *The Galilee of Jesus.* Rome: Editrice Pontifica Universita Gregoriana.

Hiebert, Theodore. (1996) *The Yahwist's Landscape: Nature and Religion in Early Israel.* New York: Oxford University Press. This source helped me with the Garden of Eden story.

Hillel, Daniel. (2006) *The Natural History of the Bible: An Environmental Exploration of the Hebrew Scriptures.* New York. Columbia University Press.

Joines, Karen Randolph. (1974) *Serpent Symbolism in the Old Testament: A Linguistic, Archeological, and Literary Study.* Haddonfield, New Jersey: Haddonfield House.

Kaufman, Gordon D. (2006) *Jesus and Creativity.* Minneapolis: Fortress Press.

Kozak, Ralph. Laughing Jesus painting. www.jesuslaughing. com/

Lerner, Carol. (1982) *A Biblical Garden.* New York: William Morrow.

MacDonald, G. Jeffrey. (April 14, 2006) "Christian Mavericks Find Affirmation in Ancient Heresies," *Christian Science Monitor.*

McLaren, Brian D. (2001) *A New Kind of Christian: A Tale of Two Friends on a Spiritual Journey.* San Francisco: Jossey-Bass. Evangelical pastor who argues for a nonliteralist view of the Bible.

— — —. (2007) *Everything Must Change: Jesus, Global Crises, and a Revolution of Hope.* Nashville: Thomas Nelson.

Malina, Bruce J., (1993) *The New Testament World: Insights from Cultural Anthropology.* Louisville, Kentucky: Westminster/ John Knox Press.

Miller, Robert J., ed. (1994) *The Complete Gospels: Annotated Scholars Version.* San Francisco: HarperSanFrancisco. Texts of twenty-one gospels.

Moore, Christopher. (2002) *Lamb: The Gospel According to Biff,*

Christ's Childhood Friend. New York: William Morrow. Historical novel.

Nagy, Rebecca Martin, et al., eds. (1996) *Sepphoris in Galilee: Crosscurrents of Culture.* North Carolina Museum of Art. Important source for the youth and young manhood of Jesus.

National Geographic. (May 2006) Publication of articles on the Gospel of Judas.

Palmer, Earl F. (2001) *The Humor of Jesus: Sources of Laughter in the Bible.* Vancouver, British Columbia: Regent College Publishing.

Phillips, J. B. (1997) *Your God Is Too Small.* New York: Touchstone.

Reed, Jonathan L. (2000) *Archeology and the Galilean Jesus: A Re-Examination of the Evidence.* Harrisburg, Pennsylvania: Trinity Press International.

Ricci, Carla. (1994) *Mary Magdalene and Many Others: Women Who Followed Jesus.* Minneapolis: Fortress Press.

Sanford, John A. (1987) *The Kingdom Within: The Inner Meaning of Jesus' Sayings.* San Francisco: HarperSanFrancisco.

Sheldon, Charles. (1984) *In His Steps.* Grand Rapids, Michigan: Spire. This novel raised the question, What Would Jesus Do? (WWJD?). Sheldon was an American social activist, spending a week in jail to help bring about prison reform and speaking out in the 1930s against Nazi persecution of Jews. This book was a prod for me to have Jesus talk to us in contemporary English.

Swimme, Brian and Thomas Berry. (1994) *The Universe Story: From the Primorial Flaring Forth to the Ecozoic Era, A Celebration of the Unfolding of the Cosmos.* New York: HarperCollins.

Swindoll, Charles. "The Winsome Witness," www.oneplace. com

Vermes, Geza. (2000) *The Changing Faces of Jesus.* New York: Viking Compass. Helps reclaim a Semitic, Jewish Jesus, the Rabbi.

Wallace, Bob. "The Wit and Humor of Jesus." www.home.att.
net/bob/wallace/jesus1.html

Walsch, Neale Donald. (1999) *Friendship with God: An Uncommon Dialogue*. New York: G. P. Putnam's Sons.

Warren, Rick. (2002) *The Purpose-Driven Life: What on Earth Am I Here For?* Grand Rapids, Michigan: Zondervan.

Watts, Murray. (1987) *Rolling in the Aisles*. York, England: The Children's Society. Humorous stories in the Bible and in church life.

White, L. Michael. (2004) *From Jesus to Christianity*. San Francisco: HarperSanFrancisco.

www.jewsonfirst.org

A description of First Baptist Church in South Carolina giving foot washing and free shoes to needy children and the protest that the project is a violation of church and state separation because the children receive the foot washing and shoes in public schools.

www.onechallenge.org/

Sports Ambassadors program, part of OC International.

www.popularmechanics.com/science/research/1282186.html

Simulated image of a first-century Jewish man based on comparative study of skeletons.

www.religioustolerance.org

Includes the American Religious Identification Survey, showing that the proportion of Christians is declining and people with no formal religious identification is increasing.

GENERAL SOURCES

Appiah, Kwane Anthony. (2006) *Cosmopolitanism: Ethics in a World of Strangers.* New York: W. W. Norton.

Bark, Coleman, trans. (1998) *The Essential Rumi.* New York: Quality Paperback. The Rumi quotes are from this source.

Beck, Martha. (2005) *Leaving the Saints: How I Lost the Mormons, and Found My Faith.* New York: Three Rivers Press.

— — —. (1999) *Expecting Adam: A True Story of Birth, Rebirth, and Everyday Magic.* New York: Berkley Book.

Bryson, Bill. (1999) *I'm a Stranger Here Myself: Notes on Returning to America after Twenty Years Away.* New York: Broadway Books.

— — —. (2006) *The Life and Times of the Thunderbolt Kid: A Memoir.* New York: Broadway Books. These two books display fabulous irony and sensitivity to American culture and have been inspirational to me.

Chopra, Deepak. (2004) *The Book of Secrets: Unlocking the Hidden Dimension of Your Life.* New York: Harmony Books.

Friedan, Betty. (1963) *The Feminine Mystique.* New York. W. W. Norton.

Gladwell, Malcolm. (2002) *The Tipping Point: How Little Things Can Make a Big Difference.* New York: Little, Brown.

Grabill, Joseph L. (1971) *Protestant Diplomacy and the Near East: Missionary Influence on American Policy, 1810–1927.* Minneapolis: University of Minnesota Press.

Guinness, Os. (2008) *The Case for Civility and Why Our Future Depends On It.* New York: HarperOne.

Lammott, Anne. (1993) *Operating Instructions: A Journal of My Son's First Year.* New York: Fawcett Columbine.

— — —. (2005) *Plan B: Further Thoughts on Faith.* New York: Riverhead Books. Anne's wit is contagious.

— — —. (2007) *Grace (Eventually): Thoughts on Faith*. New York: Riverhead Books.

Macy, Joanna. (2007) *Widening Circles: A Memoir*. Gabriola Island, BC, Canada: Net Catalyst Books.

Obama, Barack. (2006) *The Audacity of Hope: Thoughts on Reclaiming the American Dream*. New York: Crown Publishers.

Palmer, Parker J. (2000) *Let Your Life Speak: Listening for the Voice of Vocation*. San Francisco: Jossey-Bass.

Ray, Paul H. and Sherry Ruth Anderson. (2000) *The Cultural Creatives: How 50 Million People Are Changing the World*. New York: Harmony Books.

Remen, Rachel Naomi. (2000) *My Grandfather's Blessings: Stories of Strength, Refuge, and Belonging*. New York: Riverhead Books.

Sochen, June. (1974) *Herstory: A Record of the American Woman's Past*. Van Nuys, Ca.: Alfred Publishing.

Stone, Merlin. (1990) *Ancient Mirrors of Womanhood: A Treasury of Goddess and Heroine Lore from Around the World*. Boston: Beacon Press.

Tolle, Eckhart. (1999) *The Power of Now: A Guide to Spiritual Enlightenment*. Novato, California: New World Library.

— — —. (2006) *A New Earth: Awakening to Your Life's Purpose*. New York: Plume Book.

Weston, Anthony. (2007) *How to Re-Imagine the World: A Pocket Guide for Practical Visionaries*. Gabriola Island, BC, Canada: New Society Publishers.

Discussion Guide for Book Groups

This discussion guide is for book groups and classes in civic, environmental, business, educational, friendship, religious, and other settings. *Green Kingdom Come!* identifies principles, practices and attitudes, each of which is a basis for discussion.

A general question for the chapters is: In what ways do you live out/not live out these principles, practices, and attitudes?

Revisit the general question of the book: What would Jesus do to spur today's Green Revolution? Also, revisit such other questions, listed in chapter titles on the Contents pages, repeated in the chapter headings, and again put in a list on page 178, as: Would Jesus honor a chimpanzee baby? Would Jesus laugh 400 times a day? Would Jesus spray weeds? Would Jesus organize ecological potlucks? Would Jesus have a low carbon footprint? Would Jesus shop till he drops?

Preface, Introduction, and Tea for Three

1. What in your life story has led you to be open to environmental issues? Not to be open?
2. What about the life style and teachings of Jesus in these first three sections for you resonates with a sustainable Earth community? Does not resonate?
3. What is your response to the new three Rs: reduce, renew, and redouble?
4. What is your reaction to the Green Dream?

One—Dead and Reborn

1. Picture that you have let unsustainable behavior die and sustainable come to life. Describe how your lifestyle in this picture differs from your actual lifestyle?
2. Assuming that you want some mention of your green activities in your obituary, what would these words be?

Two—Here Now

1. Give examples of situations in which you lost track of time.
2. What green activities do you carry out (or imagine carrying out) that have you feeling like time is standing still and you are lost in the moment?
3. What condition most has you sensing that green kingdom come is already here now?

Three—Inside Water, Out

1. What are you feeling, saying, and doing when you act whole-heartedly, inside out?
2. What do you need to start doing/stop doing in order to conserve water and treat the Ocean as precious?
3. In what ways do you show/not show that animals, plants, and ecologies have as much value and worth as you have?

Four—Downside Up

1. In what ways do children inspire you?
2. What do you know about the green activities of pre-school, elementary, high school, and college youth in your community? How could you learn more about these activities and involve yourself more with them?
3. What tickles you and has you smiling and laughing?
4. What actions are you willing to take to make a Green Corps, like the Peace Corps, come into being?

Five—Dropping Rain

1. Picture sun and rain favoring people and groups that have mistreated you and your networks as much as sun and rain favor you. How does this picture affect you?
2. How are you like/unlike your bonobo cousins?
3. What are other options you can think of beside the Kilimanjaro atonement ritual?
4. What is necessary for you to forgive yourself for unsustainable behavior?
5. What would benefit/not benefit you about being a member of and making the five pledges of an Ecoholics Anonymous movement?

Six—Soiled Goods

1. Sing some green lyrics, set to familiar tunes, cited in *Green Kingdom Come!*
2. Write your own green lyrics and sing them.
3. Imagine food for your community being grown in your yard and the yards of your neighbors. How can you help this imagination come into being?

Seven—Mustard and Dandelion

1. What species, beside mustard and dandelion, symbolize the omnipresence of Earth Community?
2. Tell about a tree that has been important in your life story.
3. What motive would get you to continue or to begin planting trees?

Eight—Animal Teachers

1. In what ways have/haven't you been teachable by animals?
2. What will you gain/lose by acting out the Leaver story, the

story that all species leave enough for other species to have a fair chance to eat?

3. What obstacles stand in the way of and what fun possibilities await your participation in community potlucks that includes every segment of the human population?

4. What satisfaction/dissatisfaction will you experience by acting so that all species have an opportunity to eat?

Nine—Washed Toes

1. Without the necessity of using humor, laugh as a diaphragm and group exercise. Begin with an inhalation and then hoot, cackle, and guffaw for five minutes. If it helps to close your eyes, do so.

2. Walk around the room for a time (can be combined with the laughing). How can you incorporate walking in your daily routines?

3. Massage your own feet as described in this chapter.

4. Consider practicing foot washing.

Ten—Sane Asylums

1. What is a hard thing you are willing to do to reduce the carbon footprint of your home?

2. What renewable energy resources are available in your community? In what ways do you use/hold back from using these resources?

Eleven—Bare and Broke Folks

1. What do you feel passionate about/indifferent about in relation to lowering accumulation of money and clothes?

2. Imagine a world in which no one's salaried income is more than ten times higher than the lowest person's salaried income. What are you willing/unwilling to do to make that imagination real?

Postscript

1. What are your thoughts about and possible contributions to a special fifty-year period devoted to returning a considerable portion of the land within Earth Community to wilderness?

Appendix—Whole Systems Terms

1. How does the mix of secular and religious terms about whole systems fit in with your values?
2. What are other terms beside the sixty on the list that occur to you?

Appendix—Aramaic Jesus

1. What are the most important differences, for you, between an Aramaic Jesus and an Indo-European Jesus?

Overview

1. Which ideas and images you have read in *Green Kingdom Come!* are most attractive? Least?
2. To what extent do you value Jesus as a figure easily accessible by people from any cultural, secular, or religious tradition, as compared with an exclusively western or Christian figure?
3. To what extent has the book empowered/not empowered you to make a positive difference in moving toward increased sustainability in your lifestyle?

For information about the book,
author, reviews, a blog, images, events,
purchase, and related materials:

www.greenkingdomcome.net

To contact the author:

info@greenkingdomcome.net

Printed in the United States
215313BV00003B/1/P